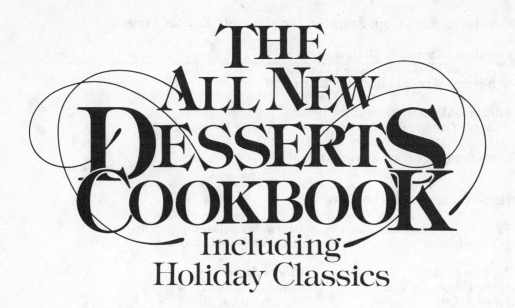

THE ALL NEW DESSERTS COOKBOOK

Including
Holiday Classics

FAVORITE RECIPES®
OF HOME ECONOMICS TEACHERS

Great American Opportunities, Inc./Favorite Recipes Press

President: Thomas F. McDow III
Director of Marketing: Roger Conner
Marketing Services Manager: Karen Bird

Editorial Manager: Mary Jane Blount
Editors: Georgia Brazil, Mary Cummings, Jane Hinshaw,
    Linda Jones, Mary Wilson
Typography: William Maul, Sharon Whitehurst

Photography: Cover by Häagen-Dazs Company, Inc.; Florida Department of Citrus; Hershey Foods Corporation; and Ruth Lundren, Inc.

Copyright© 1988 by
Great American Opportunities, Inc.
  P.O. Box 305142
  Nashville, TN 37230

Library of Congress Catalog Number: 88-5084

ISBN: 0-87197-231-X

Manufactured in the United States of America

First Printing 1988
Second Printing 1988

CONTENTS

JUST DESSERTS

Many of us live by the philosophy that "Life is uncertain; eat dessert first." Nevertheless, dessert is traditionally the final course of a meal. The word is derived from the French verb *desservir*, to clear or take away, and it is as customary today to clear the table before dessert as it was in the 19th century.

We think of desserts as synonymous with "sweets," and it is the very fact that they taste sweet that makes desserts so appealing. All people in all times seem to have shared this innate craving for sweetness. The earliest example may be a cave painting at Valencia, Spain, dating back to 8,000 BC, showing two people raiding a beehive for the sweet honey.

Our present day language even identifies sweetness with love and pleasure. "Honey," "Sugar" and "Sweetheart" are common terms of endearment, and a box of chocolates is the traditional metaphor of love. Apple pie is not only patriotic but also a wholesome example of the traditional values of hearth and home. No one can deny the comfort tendered by the gift of a cake or pie during the crises of our lives, and none of us could begin to celebrate the happy occasions or holidays without the delectable sweets we associate with them.

When planning a menu, choose a dessert to complement the meal it follows. Try a Kiwi Emerald Ice or Gingered Honeydew to finish off a heavy meal such as roast pork with all the trimmings. For a light supper or luncheon, a Maple Coconut Pie or Pineapple-Carrot Cake adds excitement. Austrian Cantaloupe or Picnic Peach Ice Cream would be a very welcome dessert on a hot summer evening, and a Chocolate Meringue Torte or Bûche de Noël is the perfect climax for a special occasion.

The seasonality of various fruits is also a consideration in selecting a dessert. This book is arranged according to flavors to provide a useful guide in selecting recipes to utilize items in season. In addition to fruits and nuts, these flavors include the traditional means of sweetening desserts, such as maple, molasses and honey. And, of course, the all time favorite of everyone—chocolate.

The desserts in *The All New Dessert Cookbook* offer a great variety to choose from and take many delightful forms. They include the cakes, pies, puddings, cookies and candies everyone recognizes as well as their European versions which may have more exotic names. A list of definitions of the less well-known desserts is found in *Desserts Glossary* on pages 7 and 8.

DESSERTS GLOSSARY

Ambrosia: A dessert of fruit or mixed fruits topped with grated coconut.

Baked Alaska: A dessert with molded ice cream placed on a base of cake, covered with meringue, then baked just until meringue is golden brown.

Baklava: A dessert of very thin sheets of pastry layered with a filling of nuts and honey or sugar syrup, baked and cut into diamond shapes.

Bavarian: A dessert made of gelatin, eggs, cream and flavoring, which has been chilled and molded.

Bombe: A dessert made of different flavors of ice cream, sherbet or ices in a chilled decorative mold, then frozen.

Bonbon: A confection made of fondant or one which has been dipped in melted fondant or chocolate.

Brittle: A hard candy containing nuts which is poured in a thin layer over a hard surface, then broken into pieces when cool.

Charlotte: A dessert made by lining a serving dish with strips of cake or ladyfingers, then filled with a whipped cream or custard and fruit.

Cheesecake: A dessert made with cream cheese or cottage cheese, eggs and sugar, then baked in a mold lined with sweet crumbs.

Cobbler: A deep-dish fruit dessert made with a rich pastry or biscuit dough on top.

Compote: A dessert made of fruits, frequently cooked in such a way as to retain their shapes, and served in a stemmed dish.

Cream Puff: A dessert made of a hollow pastry shell or puff pastry and filled with whipped cream or custard. May be glazed or iced.

Crêpe: A small thin pancake filled with fruit and whipped cream and rolled. It may also be folded and heated in a sauce and flambéed.

Crisp: A baked fruit dessert with a crunchy topping.

Divinity: A fluffy candy made by beating hot cooked sugar syrup into stiffly beaten egg whites and dropped by spoonfuls onto waxed paper.

Dumpling: A dessert with a fruit center surrounded by pastry dough and baked or steamed. A dumpling may also be a sweet pastry dropped into hot syrup to cook.

Flambé: A fruit dessert which has had a warm alcoholic beverage poured over it and then ignited.

Flan: A baked dessert custard of eggs and cream, frequently glazed with fruit or caramel.

Floating Island: A pudding or dessert sauce baked with dollops of meringue floating on top.

Fondant: A creamy cooked or uncooked sugar mixture used as the basis for candies, confections and icings.

Fritter: A dessert of fruit coated with a batter and deep-fried until crisp and golden brown.

Fudge: A creamy, smooth cooked candy, typically of chocolate flavor. It often includes nuts, marshmallows, peanut butter, candied fruit, etc.

Glacé Fruit: A fruit which has been candied and glazed.

Hard Sauce: A creamed mixture of butter, confectioners' sugar, cream and flavorings served on warm desserts where it melts and forms a glaze.

Lemon Curd: A soft custard which can be used as a filling, sauce or spread.

Macaroon: A small cake-like cookie made of egg whites, sugar and ground nuts, coconut or almond paste.

Marzipan: A confection of almond paste which may be incorporated into other desserts or shaped, tinted and glazed to resemble tiny fruits.

Meringue: A mixture of stiffly beaten egg whites and sugar, shaped into a shell, baked until dry, and filled with ice cream, fruit or flavored whipped cream. May be used as pie topping also.

Mousse: A chilled whipped dessert with fruit and nuts.

Parfait: A dessert of fruit, custard and ice cream or whipped cream layered in stemmed glasses.

Pavlova: A baked meringue shell which has been filled with fruit and whipped cream or ice cream.

Penuche: A candy made like fudge, substituting brown sugar and omitting chocolate. It is poured into a dish and cut into squares when set.

Praline: A poured sugar candy containing nuts.

Pudding: A custard-like dessert which can be baked, steamed, cooked on top of the stove or refrigerated.

Roca: A hard toffee-like candy containing nuts. It is poured into a thin layer, coated with chocolate and broken into pieces when set.

Sherbet: A dessert made with fruit or fruit juice, egg white and milk blended until smooth, then frozen.

Shortbread: A thick cookie made of flour, a small amount of sugar and a proportionally large amount of shortening. It usually contains finely chopped or ground nuts.

Shortcake: A dessert made of a sweetened or unsweetened biscuit, cookie, teacake or cake which has been baked, split and layered with fruit, ice cream or whipped cream.

Slump: A fruit dessert with a biscuit topping.

Sorbet: A sherbet made without milk. May include liqueurs.

Soufflé: A light airy dessert made with beaten egg whites or whipped cream. It may be baked or chilled.

Tart: A shallow open-faced pastry shell filled with fruits, jam or custard.

Tartlet: An individual tart.

Tassie: A miniature tart.

Torte: A cake or pastry made with sugar and eggs, frequently with ground nuts or bread crumbs in place of flour, and layered with filling, fruit and whipped cream or frosting.

Trifle: A layered dessert of sponge cake spread with jam or sprinkled with wine, fruit and custard.

Truffle: A very rich chocolate confection.

Turnover: A small pie made by folding pastry to enclose a filling, then baking until golden brown.

Zabaglione: A mixture of eggs, sugar, wine or fruit juice beaten over hot water until thick and light and served in a stemmed glass with fruit.

DESSERTS A to Z

ALMOND

ALMOND-CHOCOLATE BOMBE

2 pt. chocolate ice cream,
  softened
1 pt. vanilla ice cream,
  softened
½ c. sugar
2 egg whites
½ c. whipping cream
1 c. chopped almonds
1 tsp. rum flavoring

Spread bottom and sides of 2-quart mold with half the chocolate ice cream. Freeze until firm. Spread vanilla ice cream over chocolate layer. Freeze until firm. Spread remaining chocolate ice cream over vanilla layer. Freeze until firm. Bring sugar and 2 tablespoons water to a boil in saucepan. Boil for 2 minutes. Beat egg whites until stiff peaks form. Add hot syrup gradually, beating constantly until glossy. Whip cream in bowl until soft peaks form. Fold whipped cream, almonds and rum flavoring into egg white mixture. Spoon into center of ice cream-lined mold. Freeze until firm. Unmold onto serving plate. Garnish with additional whipped cream and almonds. Yield: 12 servings.

Renee Pinkston, Alabama

ALMOND SUPREME CAKE

¾ c. butter or margarine,
  softened
1½ c. sugar
2¾ c. sifted cake flour
4 tsp. baking powder
¾ tsp. salt
1 tsp. vanilla extract
1 tsp. almond extract
1 c. milk
4 egg whites
½ c. sliced almonds

Cream butter in mixer bowl until light and fluffy. Add 1 cup sugar gradually; mix well. Sift flour with baking powder and salt 3 times. Stir flavorings into milk. Add flour mixture to creamed mixture alternately with milk, beginning and ending with dry ingredients, mixing well after each addition. Beat egg whites until fluffy. Add remaining ½ cup sugar gradually, beating until stiff peaks form. Fold gently into batter. Pour into 3 greased 9-inch cake pans. Tap pans on hard surface to remove air bubbles. Bake at 350 degrees for 20 minutes or until cake tests done. Cool in pans for 10 minutes before removing to wire racks to cool completely. Spread Almond Frosting between layers and over top and side of cake. Smooth frosting with spatula dipped in hot water. Garnish with sliced almonds.
Yield: 12 servings.

Almond Frosting

⅔ c. butter or margarine,
  softened
6 c. confectioners' sugar
6 tbsp. light cream
2½ tsp. vanilla extract
½ tsp. almond extract

Cream butter in mixer bowl. Add confectioners' sugar gradually, beating until fluffy. Beat in cream and flavorings as frosting thickens.

Tammy Ann Gasho, Oregon

ALMOND-CHOCOLATE CAKE

½ c. baking cocoa
½ c. shortening
1 c. sugar
2 eggs
½ c. sour cream
½ c. milk
½ tsp. vanilla extract
2 c. cake flour
1 tsp. soda
¼ tsp. salt
1 c. finely chopped almonds
4 oz. German's sweet chocolate

Dissolve cocoa in enough hot water to make a smooth paste. Cool. Cream shortening and sugar in mixer bowl until light and fluffy. Add eggs 1 at a time, mixing well after each addition. Combine sour cream, milk and vanilla in bowl; mix well. Add to creamed mixture alternately with sifted dry ingredients, mixing well after each addition. Add cocoa mixture. Beat for 2 minutes. Stir in almonds. Pour into 2 greased and floured 9-inch cake pans. Bake at 350 degrees for 20 to 25 minutes or until cake tests done. Remove to wire rack to cool.

Spread favorite white frosting between layers and over top and side of cake. Melt chocolate in double boiler. Drizzle over top of cake. Garnish with additional almonds. Yield: 16 servings.

Dot Pettey, Florida

AMARETTO CUSTARD CAKE

1   2-layer pkg. golden deluxe
    cake mix
1   3-oz. package French
    vanilla instant pudding mix
2 eggs
1¼ c. milk
¼ c. Amaretto
¼ tsp. nutmeg
1½ c. confectioners' sugar
5 tbsp. cream
1 tsp. almond extract
Nutmeg to taste

Mix cake mix, pudding mix, eggs, milk, Amaretto and ¼ teaspoon nutmeg in mixer bowl. Mix at low speed for 1 minute, scraping bowl constantly. Beat at medium speed for 2 minutes, scraping bowl occasionally. Pour into well-greased and floured 12-inch bundt pan. Bake at 350 degrees for 40 minutes or until cake tests done. Cool in pan for 15 minutes. Remove to cake plate. Combine remaining ingredients in small mixer bowl; beat until smooth. Pierce cake with toothpick. Drizzle confectioners' sugar mixture very gradually over cake. Let stand for 2 days before serving. Yield: 20 servings.

Sue Warren, Kentucky

ALMOND SILK PIE

⅓ c. butter, softened
½ c. sugar
1 tsp. vanilla extract
3 tbsp. baking cocoa
2 eggs
⅔ c. chopped toasted almonds
1 baked 9-in. pie shell
2 c. whipped cream

Cream butter and sugar in mixer bowl until light and fluffy. Add vanilla and cocoa; mix well. Add eggs 1 at a time, beating for 5 minutes after each

addition. Reserve several almonds for topping. Fold remaining almonds gently into chocolate mixture. Pour into pie shell. Top with whipped cream and reserved almonds. Chill until serving time. Yield: 6 to 8 servings.

Rebecca Olson, Idaho

MARZIPAN BARS

½ c. butter, softened
½ c. packed brown sugar
1 egg yolk
1 tsp. vanilla extract
½ tsp. soda
2 c. flour
¼ tsp. salt
¼ c. milk
1 c. red raspberry jelly
Almond Paste Filling
Chocolate Icing

Cream butter and brown sugar in bowl until light and fluffy. Add egg yolk and vanilla; mix well. Sift in soda, flour and salt; mix well. Stir in milk. Spread in greased 10x15-inch baking pan. Spread jelly over dough. Pour Almond Paste Filling over jelly. Bake at 350 degrees for 35 minutes or until set. Cool. Frost with Chocolate Icing.

Almond Paste Filling

8 oz. almond paste
1 egg white
½ c. sugar
1 tsp. vanilla extract
3 tbsp. butter, softened
3 eggs

Combine first 5 ingredients in bowl; mix well. Beat in eggs 1 at a time. Tint with green food coloring.

Chocolate Icing

2 oz. unsweetened chocolate,
   melted
1 tbsp. butter
1 tsp. vanilla extract
2 c. confectioners' sugar
¼ c. hot milk

Combine all ingredients in bowl; beat until smooth.

Audrey Carroll, Missouri

ALMOND ROCA

1 lb. butter
2⅓ c. sugar
1½ c. almonds
1 c. chocolate chips
¼ c. ground walnuts

Mix butter and sugar in heavy skillet. Cook for 8 minutes on medium-high heat, stirring frequently. Add almonds. Cook for 8 minutes longer, stirring constantly. Pour into 9x13-inch pan lined with buttered foil. Sprinkle chocolate chips over top. Spread evenly when melted. Top with walnuts. Break into pieces when cool. Yield: 3 pounds.

Dawn Moudy, Idaho

APPLE

STREUSEL-FILLED BAKED APPLES

4 tart baking apples
2 tbsp. plus ½ cup brown sugar
2 tbsp. butter, softened
1 tbsp. flour
3 tbsp. raisins
3 tbsp. chopped nuts
1 tbsp. lemon juice
1½ tsp. cinnamon

Core apples, leaving bottoms intact. Remove peel from top ⅓ of apples. Combine 2 tablespoons brown sugar, butter, flour, raisins and nuts in bowl; mix well. Spoon into apples. Place in baking dish. Combine remaining ½ cup brown sugar, lemon juice, cinnamon and ¾ cup water in saucepan. Bring to a boil. Cook for 5 minutes, stirring occasionally. Pour over apples. Bake at 325 degrees for 45 minutes, basting occasionally. Serve warm. Yield: 4 servings.

Betty Veach, Texas

APPLE CRISP

4 c. sliced peeled tart apples
½ c. flour
⅔ c. packed brown sugar
½ c. oats
⅓ c. margarine, softened
1 tsp. cinnamon
¾ tsp. nutmeg

Place apples in buttered 8x8-inch baking dish. Combine remaining ingredients in bowl; mix until crumbly. Sprinkle over apples. Bake at 375 degrees for 30 minutes. Serve warm with cream or ice cream. Yield: 6 servings.

Brianna Barraclough, Pennsylvania

APPLE DUMPLINGS

2 c. flour
1½ tsp. baking powder
½ tsp. salt
½ c. shortening
⅔ c. milk
6 apples, cored
½ c. sugar
6 tbsp. butter
Cinnamon and nutmeg to taste
1¼ c. sugar
5 tbsp. butter
Cinnamon and nutmeg to taste
Red food coloring (opt.)

Mix flour, baking powder and salt in bowl. Cut in shortening until crumbly. Stir in milk. Roll into 6 circles on floured surface. Place 1 apple on each circle. Mix ½ cup sugar, 6 tablespoons butter and spices to taste in bowl. Spoon into centers of apples. Fold dough to enclose apple; seal edges. Place in baking pan. Combine remaining ingredients and 1 cup water in saucepan. Bring to a boil, stirring until sugar dissolves. Pour over dumplings. Bake at 400 degrees for 30 to 45 minutes or until apples are tender. Yield: 6 servings.

Amanda Elgin, Pennsylvania

STEAMED APPLE PUDDING

1½ c. fine dry bread crumbs
½ c. flour
1 tsp. baking powder
½ tsp. soda
½ tsp. salt
1 tsp. cinnamon
½ c. sugar
2 eggs
½ c. molasses
2 tbsp. melted butter
  or margarine
2 c. chopped tart apples
1 c. whole fresh cranberries

Combine dry ingredients in bowl. Stir in mixture of eggs, molasses and butter. Fold in apples and cranberries. Pour into greased and sugared pudding mold. Cover tightly with greased foil; secure with string. Place mold on rack in deep saucepan. Add enough simmering water to cover half the mold. Cover saucepan. Steam for 2 to 2½ hours or until pudding tests done. Cool in mold for 10 minutes. Unmold onto serving plate. Serve with whipped cream or ice cream. Yield: 8 to 12 servings.

Janet Phillips, Missouri

BAKED APPLE TREATS

1½ c. sifted flour
1¾ tsp. baking powder
½ tsp. salt
½ tsp. nutmeg
½ c. plus ⅓ cup sugar
⅓ c. shortening
1 egg, beaten
¼ c. milk
1 c. grated apple
1 tsp. cinnamon
½ c. melted margarine

Sift flour, baking powder, salt, nutmeg and ½ cup sugar into bowl. Cut in shortening until crumbly. Mix egg, milk and apple in bowl. Add to dry ingredients; mix well. Fill greased muffin cups ⅔ full. Bake at 350 degrees for 20 to 30 minutes or until golden brown. Mix cinnamon and remaining ⅓ cup sugar. Roll warm apple treats in melted margarine, then in cinnamon-sugar mixture. Serve warm. Yield: 1 dozen.

DRIED APPLE STACK CAKE

4 c. flour, sifted
1 c. sugar
4 tsp. baking powder
½ tsp. soda
1 tsp. salt
2 eggs, beaten
½ c. butter, softened
1 c. buttermilk
2 tsp. vanilla extract

Combine all ingredients in bowl; mix well. Divide into 6 portions. Pat each portion into greased and floured 9-inch cake pan. Bake at 450 degrees until browned. Spread Dried Apple Filling between layers. Let stand for 2 days before serving. Yield: 16 servings.

Dried Apple Filling

1 lb. dried apples,
    cooked, mashed
1 c. packed brown sugar
½ c. sugar
2 tsp. cinnamon
½ tsp. cloves
½ tsp. allspice
½ tsp. nutmeg

Combine apples, brown sugar, sugar, cinnamon, cloves, allspice and nutmeg in bowl; mix well.

Donna Lynne Brack, Ohio

APPLE HILL CAKE

2 c. sugar
½ c. oil
2 eggs
4 c. chopped peeled apples
2 c. flour
2 tsp. soda
1 tsp. salt
2 tsp. cinnamon
1 tsp. nutmeg
1 c. chopped pecans
½ c. raisins

Mix sugar, oil, eggs and apples in mixer bowl. Beat until well mixed. Add sifted dry ingredients; mix well. Stir in pecans and raisins. Spoon into bundt pan sprayed with nonstick cooking spray. Bake at 350 degrees for 1 hour or until cake tests done. Remove to wire rack to cool. Serve hot Nutmeg Sauce over cake slices. Yield: 16 servings.

Nutmeg Sauce

1 c. sugar
2 tbsp. cornstarch
¼ c. butter
2 tsp. nutmeg

Mix sugar and cornstarch in saucepan. Stir in 2 cups boiling water. Cook for 1 minute, stirring constantly. Stir in butter and nutmeg. Yield: 2 cups.

Edith Alexander, Colorado

FRESH APPLE CAKE

2½ c. chopped apples
2 c. sugar
3 eggs
1 c. oil
3 c. self-rising flour
2 tsp. soda
1 tsp. cloves
1 tsp. cinnamon
1 tsp. nutmeg
1 c. nuts

Combine apples with sugar in bowl; mix well. Let stand for 10 minutes. Add eggs and oil; mix well. Stir in sifted dry ingredients; beat well. Stir in nuts. Pour into greased tube pan. Bake at 350 degrees for 1 hour. Cool in pan for 10 minutes. Remove to wire rack to cool completely. Yield: 12 servings.

SPICY APPLESAUCE CAKE

¾ c. margarine, softened
2 c. sugar
3 eggs
1½ c. applesauce
3 c. flour
1½ tsp. soda
1 tsp. cinnamon
1 tsp. nutmeg
1 tsp. allspice
½ c. chopped pecans

Beat margarine and sugar in bowl until light and fluffy. Add eggs 1 at a time, beating well after each addition. Add applesauce; mix well. Sift in flour, soda and spices. Add pecans; mix well. Pour into greased and floured tube pan. Bake at 350 degrees for 1 hour. Cool on wire rack. Yield: 16 servings.

Kristen E. Suter, Virginia

APPLESAUCE CUSTARD PIE

1 c. sugar
2 eggs
¼ c. butter
1 can applesauce
¼ tsp. vanilla extract
1 unbaked 9-in. pie shell
Cinnamon

Cream sugar, eggs and butter in mixer bowl. Add applesauce and vanilla; mix well. Pour into pie shell. Sprinkle with cinnamon. Bake at 425 degrees for 30 to 40 minutes or until set. Yield: 6 servings.

Fay Shaw, Tennessee

PINEAPPLE-GLAZED APPLE PIE

1½ c. unsweetened pineapple
   juice
¾ c. sugar
7 c. tart apple slices
1 tbsp. cornstarch
1 tsp. butter or margarine
½ tsp. vanilla extract
¼ tsp. salt
1 baked 9-in. pie shell

Mix 1¼ cups pineapple juice and sugar in saucepan. Bring to a boil. Add apples. Simmer, covered, for 3 to 4 minutes or just until apples are tender. Remove apples with slotted spoon; set aside. Blend remaining ¼ cup pineapple juice into cornstarch in small bowl. Stir cornstarch mixture into hot pineapple liquid. Cook until thickened, stirring constantly. Cook for 1 minute longer; remove from heat. Stir in butter, vanilla and salt. Let stand, covered, for 30 minutes; do not stir. Spoon half the pineapple juice mixture into pie shell. Arrange apples on top. Spoon remaining pineapple juice mixture over apples. Chill, covered, for several hours. Garnish with whipped cream and macadamia nuts. Yield: 6 to 8 servings.

Tina Patton, Texas

SWEDISH APPLE PIE

6 c. sliced apples
1 tbsp. plus 1 cup sugar
1 tsp. cinnamon
1 tsp. nutmeg
1 c. flour
1 egg
¾ c. melted butter
1 c. chopped nuts

Fill 9-inch pie plate with sliced apples. Sprinkle with mixture of 1 tablespoon sugar, cinnamon and nutmeg. Combine remaining ingredients and remaining 1 cup sugar in bowl; mix well. Spoon over apples. Bake at 350 degrees for 45 minutes. Yield: 6 to 8 servings.

APPLESAUCE BROWNIES

½ c. shortening
1½ c. sugar
2 c. sweetened applesauce
2 eggs, beaten
2 c. flour
2 tbsp. baking cocoa
½ tsp. soda
½ tsp. cinnamon
½ tsp. salt
½ c. chopped pecans
6 oz. chocolate chips

Combine shortening, sugar, applesauce, eggs, flour, cocoa, soda, cinnamon and salt in mixer bowl; beat until well blended. Pour into greased and floured 10x15-inch baking pan. Sprinkle with additional sugar, pecans and chocolate chips. Bake at 350 degrees for 25 minutes. Cool. Cut into bars. Yield: 3 dozen.

Carolyn A. Brenneis, Nebraska

GLAZED FRESH APPLE COOKIES

1⅓ c. packed brown sugar
½ c. margarine, softened
½ tsp. salt
½ tsp. cloves
½ tsp. nutmeg
1 tsp. cinnamon
1 egg
2 c. flour
1 tsp. soda
1 c. finely chopped apple
1 c. raisins
1 c. chopped walnuts
¼ c. plus 2½ tbsp. milk
1½ c. confectioners' sugar
1 tbsp. melted margarine
¼ tsp. vanilla extract

Beat brown sugar and softened margarine in bowl until light and fluffy. Add ½ teaspoon salt, spices and egg; mix well. Add mixture of flour and soda; mix well. Add apple, raisins, walnuts and ¼ cup milk, mixing well after each addition. Drop by teaspoonfuls onto lightly greased cookie sheet. Bake at 375 degrees on center oven rack for 8 minutes or until golden. Remove to wire rack. Cool slightly. Combine confectioners' sugar, melted margarine, vanilla

and remaining 2½ tablespoons milk in bowl; blend well. Spread on warm cookies. Cool completely. Yield: 5 dozen.

Ryan Meyers, Maryland

APRICOT

FRESH APRICOT ICE CREAM

2 lb. fresh apricots
1¼ c. sugar
2 c. light cream
2 c. whipping cream
1 c. milk
⅛ tsp. salt
1 tsp. vanilla extract

Dip apricots in boiling water for 30 seconds. Plunge into cold water; peel. Cut into halves; remove pits. Purée in blender container. Combine with remaining ingredients in 1-gallon ice cream freezer container. Freeze using manufacturer's instructions. Yield: 8 servings.

Regina Madden, North Dakota

APRICOT CREAM PIE

1 tbsp. unflavored gelatin
3 eggs, separated
1 c. packed brown sugar
½ tsp. salt
1½ c. apricot purée
1 tbsp. lemon juice
2 tbsp. sugar
½ c. whipping cream, whipped
1 baked 9-in. pie shell

Soften gelatin in ¼ cup cold water. Combine beaten egg yolks, brown sugar, salt, apricot purée and lemon juice in saucepan. Cook over low heat until thickened, stirring constantly. Add gelatin; stir until dissolved. Chill until partially set. Beat egg whites until foamy. Add sugar gradually, beating until stiff peaks form. Fold egg whites and whipped cream gently into apricot mixture. Spoon into pie shell. Chill until firm. Garnish with additional whipped cream. Yield: 6 servings.

Catherine Ard, Mississippi

APRICOT BRANDY CAKE

1½ c. butter, softened
3 c. sugar
6 eggs
3 c. flour
¼ tsp. soda
½ tsp. salt
½ c. apricot Brandy
1 c. sour cream
½ tsp. rum flavoring
½ tsp. lemon flavoring
1 tsp. vanilla extract
1 tsp. orange flavoring
¼ tsp. almond flavoring
½ c. apricot preserves

Cream butter and sugar in mixer bowl until light and fluffy. Add eggs; beat well. Sift flour with soda and salt. Combine ½ cup Brandy with sour cream and flavorings in small bowl. Add dry ingredients to creamed mixture alternately with Brandy mixture. Beat just until mixed. Pour into greased and floured bundt pan. Bake at 350 degrees for 1 hour and 10 minutes or until cake tests done. Invert onto serving plate; cool for 15 minutes. Melt preserves in saucepan. Thin with a small amount of Brandy. Pour over cake.
Yield: 16 servings.

Dawn Christianer, Oregon

APRICOT BARS

⅔ c. dried apricots
½ c. butter
¼ c. sugar
1⅓ c. sifted flour
½ tsp. baking powder
¼ tsp. salt
1 c. packed brown sugar
2 eggs, well beaten
½ tsp. vanilla extract
½ c. chopped nuts
Confectioners' sugar

Bring apricots and water to cover to a boil in saucepan. Cook for 10 minutes. Drain; cool and chop. Mix butter, sugar and 1 cup flour in bowl until crumbly. Press into greased 8x8-inch pan. Bake at 350 degrees for 25 minutes. Sift remaining ⅓ cup flour with baking powder and salt. Beat brown sugar gradually into eggs in bowl. Mix in flour mixture, vanilla, nuts and apricots.

Spread over baked layer. Bake for 30 minutes longer. Cool in pan. Cut into bars. Roll in confectioners' sugar.
Yield: 3 dozen.

Susan Cravey, California

APRICOT PINWHEELS

¾ c. chopped dried apricots
1 c. packed brown sugar
¼ c. finely chopped walnuts, toasted
½ c. butter, softened
½ c. sugar
½ tsp. vanilla extract
1¾ c. flour
½ tsp. soda
½ tsp. salt
1 oz. unsweetened chocolate, melted

Bring mixture of apricots and ¾ cup water to a boil in saucepan; reduce heat. Simmer, covered, for 20 minutes or until apricots are tender. Remove from heat; stir in ½ cup brown sugar. Cool. Stir in walnuts. Cream butter, sugar, vanilla and remaining ½ cup brown sugar in bowl until light and fluffy. Add mixture of flour, soda and salt; mix well. Divide into 2 portions. Add chocolate to 1 portion. Wrap each in waxed paper. Chill for several hours. Roll each portion into 8x12-inch rectangle between waxed paper. Spread with apricot mixture; roll as for jelly roll. Chill, wrapped in waxed paper, for several hours. Slice ¼ inch thick; place on well-greased cookie sheet. Bake at 400 degrees for 8 minutes or until light brown. Remove to wire rack immediately; cool. Store, covered, in refrigerator.
Yield: 8 dozen.

APRICOT FUDGE

⅔ c. whipping cream
¼ c. light corn syrup
1 16-oz. package confectioners' sugar
¼ tsp. salt
½ c. marshmallow creme
3 tbsp. butter
½ c. chopped dried apricots
1 tsp. vanilla extract
1 c. chopped walnuts

Mix first 4 ingredients in saucepan. Cook over low heat until sugar is completely dissolved, stirring constantly. Cook, covered, over medium heat for 2 to 3 minutes or until steam washes sugar crystals from side of pan. Cook, uncovered, to 234 to 240 degrees on candy thermometer, soft-ball stage; do not stir. Add marshmallow creme, butter and apricots. Let stand for 15 minutes, to 110 degrees; do not stir. Add vanilla and walnuts. Beat until creamy. Spoon into buttered 8x8-inch dish. Chill until firm. Cut into squares. Yield: 1½ pounds.

Ann Neale, Texas

AVOCADO CHEESE PIE

8 oz. cream cheese, softened
1 can sweetened condensed
  milk
1 med. avocado, puréed
½ c. lime juice
¼ tsp. salt
Few drops green food coloring,
  (opt.)
1 9-in. graham cracker
  pie shell
Whipped cream

Beat cream cheese in mixer bowl until fluffy. Blend in condensed milk and avocado. Stir in lime juice, salt and food coloring. Spoon into pie shell. Chill for 4 hours or longer. Top with whipped cream. Yield: 8 servings.

Marilyn Peters, Utah

AVOCADO MOUSSE

1 avocado, chopped
⅔ c. lemon juice
1 can sweetened condensed
  milk

Combine avocado with lemon juice and condensed milk in blender container. Process until smooth. Spoon into dessert glasses. Chill until firm. Garnish with whipped cream. Yield: 4 servings.

Sheila Pendel, Idaho

BANANA

BAKED BANANA AMBROSIA

3 lg. bananas
1½ tbsp. melted butter
2 tbsp. lemon juice
⅓ c. shredded coconut

Cut bananas into halves crosswise, and then lengthwise. Arrange in greased 6x10-inch baking dish. Brush well with butter, then with lemon juice. Sprinkle with coconut. Bake at 375 degrees for 15 to 20 minutes, or until fork tender. Serve warm. Yield: 6 servings.

Mrs. Jean Downes, Ohio

BANANAS FLAMBÉ

4 lg. bananas
½ c. unsalted butter
½ c. sugar
⅓ c. dark rum
6 scoops vanilla ice cream

Cut bananas into halves lengthwise. Slice diagonally into 1½-inch pieces. Melt butter in skillet. Add sugar. Cook until golden, stirring constantly. Add bananas; stir and turn to coat well. Cook for 5 minutes or until tender, stirring and turning gently. Place rum in flame-proof container. Ignite. Pour over bananas. Spoon over vanilla ice cream when flame subsides. Yield: 6 servings.

Marsha Gloekler, Maryland

BANANA FRITTERS

3 lb. bananas
1 c. buttermilk baking mix
½ c. milk
1 egg
Hot oil for frying
Confectioners' sugar

Slice bananas into thirds; split lengthwise. Combine baking mix, milk and egg in bowl; mix well. Dip each banana piece in batter. Fry bananas in hot oil in skillet until brown on both sides. Remove from skillet; drain. Sprinkle with confectioners' sugar. Yield: 12 servings.

Inez Erickson, California

BANANA PUDDING

¼ c. melted butter
1½ c. packed brown sugar
2 tbsp. flour
⅛ tsp. salt
1 lg. can evaporated milk
3 eggs, separated
1 tsp. vanilla extract
30 vanilla wafers
4 bananas, sliced
2 tbsp. sugar

Mix first 4 ingredients in double boiler. Stir in evaporated milk and ¾ cup water. Cook for 15 minutes or until thickened, stirring constantly. Stir a small amount of hot mixture into beaten egg yolks; stir egg yolks into hot mixture. Cook until thick, stirring constantly; cool. Add vanilla. Line 1½-quart baking dish with vanilla wafers. Layer pudding and bananas over wafers. Beat egg whites and sugar until stiff. Spread over pudding, sealing to edges. Bake at 350 degrees until light brown.
Yield: 6 to 8 servings.

Blanch Lipscomb, West Virginia

BANANA CHIFFON CAKE

2¼ c. sifted cake flour
1 tbsp. baking powder
1 tsp. cinnamon
½ tsp. salt
1¼ c. sugar
½ c. oil
5 egg yolks
2 tbsp. lemon juice
1 c. mashed banana
1 c. egg whites
½ tsp. cream of tartar

Sift first 4 ingredients and 1 cup sugar into bowl. Add oil, egg yolks, lemon juice and banana; beat with spoon until smooth. Beat egg whites with cream of tartar until doubled in volume. Add remaining ¼ cup sugar gradually, beating until stiff. Fold in banana mixture gently. Spoon into ungreased 10-inch tube pan. Bake at 325 degrees for 1 hour and 10 minutes or until cake tests done. Invert on funnel to cool. Loosen cake from side of pan. Invert onto cake plate to cool. Yield: 16 servings.

Gena Wright, Georgia

BANANA-NUT CAKE

⅔ c. butter-flavored shortening
1⅔ c. sugar
3 eggs
2¼ c. sifted flour
1¼ tsp. baking powder
1¼ tsp. soda
1 tsp. salt
⅔ c. buttermilk
1½ c. lightly mashed bananas
⅔ c. chopped nuts
6 tbsp. margarine
1 c. packed brown sugar
¼ c. milk
2 c. (about) confectioners'
   sugar
1 tsp. vanilla extract

Cream shortening and sugar in mixer bowl until light and fluffy. Blend in eggs. Add next 4 dry ingredients and buttermilk; mix well. Stir in bananas and nuts. Pour into greased and floured 9x13-inch cake pan. Bake at 350 degrees for 45 to 50 minutes or until cake tests done. Cover with waxed paper; cool. Melt margarine in saucepan. Add brown sugar; bring to a boil. Cook for 1 to 2 minutes. Stir in milk. Bring to a boil again; remove from heat. Add confectioners' sugar gradually, mixing until of desired consistency. Stir in vanilla. Remove waxed paper from cake. Spread frosting over top. Yield: 16 servings.

Ruth Baker, Ohio

MICROWAVE BANANA CAKE

16 pecan halves
½ c. chopped pecans
2 tsp. light corn syrup
1 pkg. coconut-pecan
   frosting mix
1 c. packed dark brown sugar
1 c. flour
2 tsp. baking powder
2 eggs, beaten
½ c. butter, melted
1 c. mashed bananas

Place pecan halves in well-buttered 8-inch square glass baking dish. Sprinkle chopped pecans in prepared dish; drizzle with corn syrup. Combine frosting mix, brown sugar, flour and baking powder in mixer bowl; mix well. Add remaining ingredients; mix well.

Pour over pecans. Microwave on High for 10 to 12 minutes, turning dish 3 times. Let stand for 3 minutes. Invert onto serving plate. Yield: 9 servings.

SHAKERTOWN BANANA CAKE

2½ c. sifted flour
1⅔ c. sugar
1¼ tsp. baking powder
1¼ tsp. soda
1 tsp. salt
⅔ c. shortening
⅔ c. buttermilk
1¼ c. mashed banana
2 eggs

Sift dry ingredients into mixer bowl. Add shortening, buttermilk and banana. Mix just until moistened. Beat for 2 minutes. Add eggs; beat for 1 minute. Pour into 2 greased and waxed paper-lined 9-inch cake pans. Bake at 350 degrees for 25 to 30 minutes or until cake tests done. Cool in pans for 5 minutes. Invert onto wire racks to cool completely. Spread Banana-Nut Frosting between layers and on top of cake.

Banana-Nut Frosting

½ c. mashed banana
1 tsp. lemon juice
⅓ c. margarine, softened
2 16-oz. packages
   confectioners' sugar
1 c. toasted coconut
⅔ c. chopped nuts

Sprinkle banana with lemon juice. Cream margarine in bowl. Add confectioners' sugar and banana; beat until creamy. Add coconut and nuts; mix well.

Bonnie Sue Fisher, Texas

BANANA CREAM PIE

2½ c. milk
1 c. plus 2 tbsp. sugar
2 eggs, separated
¼ c. cornstarch
¼ tsp. salt
1 tbsp. vanilla extract
1 tbsp. butter
2 bananas
1 baked 9-in. pie shell
⅓ tsp. cream of tartar

Combine 2 cups milk and 1 cup sugar in top of double boiler. Add egg yolks and paste of cornstarch, salt and remaining ½ cup milk; mix well. Cook until thickened, stirring constantly. Stir in vanilla and butter. Pour over sliced bananas in pie shell. Beat egg whites with cream of tartar and remaining 2 tablespoons sugar until stiff peaks form. Spread over pie, sealing to edge. Bake at 375 degrees until golden brown.
Yield: 6 servings.

Ruth Logan, Ohio

BANANA SPLIT PIE

2¼ c. milk
1 c. sugar
1 tsp. salt
½ c. cornstarch
1 tbsp. butter
1 20-oz. can crushed
   pineapple
1 baked 9-in. pie shell
Pineapple slices
Bananas, sliced
Maraschino cherries, chopped

Bring 2 cups milk, ½ cup sugar and ½ teaspoon salt to a boil in saucepan. Add ¼ cup cornstarch dissolved in remaining ¼ cup milk. Cook over medium heat until thickened, stirring constantly. Remove from heat. Stir in butter; cool. Combine pineapple, remaining ½ cup sugar and ½ teaspoon salt in saucepan. Bring to a boil. Add remaining ¼ cup cornstarch dissolved in ¼ cup cold water. Cook over medium heat until thickened and clear, stirring constantly. Remove from heat; cool. Pour cream filling into pie shell. Top with pineapple filling. Arrange pineapple, bananas and maraschino cherries over filling. Chill until serving time. Garnish with whipped cream.
Yield: 6 servings.

Anita Bender, Oregon

Buy bananas when on special. Mash and sprinkle with ascorbic acid powder. Freeze in measured amounts. Bananas are ready to use in any recipe.

BANANA BARS

½ c. plus 2 tbsp. margarine,
  softened
1½ c. sugar
2 eggs
1½ c. milk
4 bananas, mashed
2 c. flour
1 tsp. baking powder
½ tsp. soda
1½ tsp. cinnamon
1 tsp. salt
2 c. confectioners' sugar
1 tsp. vanilla extract

Cream ½ cup margarine and sugar in mixer bowl until light and fluffy. Add eggs, milk and bananas; mix well. Add mixture of flour, baking powder, soda, cinnamon and salt; mix well. Spread into greased and floured 10x15-inch baking pan. Bake at 350 degrees for 20 minutes. Combine confectioners' sugar, vanilla, remaining 2 tablespoons margarine and 2 tablespoons hot water in bowl; mix well. Spread over warm layer. Cool. Cut into bars.
Yield: 2 to 3 dozen.

Gina Mondi, Pennsylvania

SPICE AND CRUMB BANANA BARS

½ c. butter
1½ c. sugar
¾ c. packed brown sugar
2 c. sifted flour
2 sm. bananas, thinly sliced
¾ c. coconut
½ c. sour cream
1 egg
1 tsp. salt
1 tsp. soda
1 tsp. cinnamon
1 tsp. nutmeg

Mix butter with sugars and flour in mixer bowl until crumbly. Reserve ½ cup for topping. Press 1½ cups mixture into lightly greased 9x13-inch pan. Add bananas, coconut, sour cream, egg, salt, soda and spices to remaining crumb mixture. Beat for 1 minute at medium speed. Pour over crumb layer. Top with reserved crumbs. Bake at 350 degrees for 30 to 40 minutes or until brown. Cool and cut into bars.
Yield: 2½ dozen.

Dawn Haug, Indiana

BERRIES

BOYSENBERRY COBBLER

¼ c. shortening
2 c. sugar
1¼ c. sifted flour
2 tsp. baking powder
½ c. milk
2 c. boysenberries
2 tbsp. butter

Beat shortening and 1 cup sugar in mixer bowl until light. Add flour and baking powder alternately with milk, mixing well after each addition. Pour into greased 9x13-inch baking pan. Sprinkle boysenberries and remaining 1 cup sugar over batter. Dot with butter. Bake at 350 degrees for 1 hour.
Yield: 10 servings.

Betty Stocking, Oregon

BOYSENBERRY MOUSSE

2 env. unflavored gelatin
½ c. sugar
3 eggs, separated
1 c. milk
2 c. boysenberry yogurt
1 c. whipping cream, whipped

Combine gelatin and ¼ cup sugar in saucepan. Add mixture of egg yolks and milk. Cook until gelatin dissolves, stirring constantly. Cool slightly. Add yogurt. Chill until partially set. Beat egg whites until soft peaks form. Beat in remaining ¼ cup sugar until stiff. Fold egg whites and whipped cream into boysenberry mixture. Spoon into 9-cup mold. Chill for several hours to overnight. Unmold onto serving plate.
Yield: 10 servings.

ELDERBERRY CRUMB PIE

3 c. elderberries
1¼ c. sugar
3 tbsp. cornstarch
1 tbsp. plus ¼ c. butter
1 unbaked 9-in. pie shell
½ c. flour
¼ tsp. cinnamon

Combine 1 cup elderberries, 1 cup sugar, cornstarch and ⅔ cup water in saucepan. Simmer until thickened, stirring constantly. Stir in remaining 2 cups berries and 1 tablespoon butter. Pour into pie shell. Mix flour, cinnamon and remaining ¼ cup butter and ¼ cup sugar in bowl until crumbly. Sprinkle over pie. Bake at 375 degrees for 30 minutes or until light brown.
Yield: 6 to 8 servings.

Mrs. Charles Hileman, Pennsylvania

GOOSEBERRY PIE

1 *c. sugar*
1 *tbsp. (heaping) flour*
1 *tsp. cinnamon*
⅛ *tsp. nutmeg*
½ *tsp. cloves*
¼ *tsp. salt*
1   *20-oz. can gooseberries*
1 *recipe 2-crust pie pastry*
1 *tbsp. butter*

Sift first 6 ingredients together into bowl. Add gooseberries; toss lightly. Spoon into pastry-lined pie plate. Dot with butter. Top with remaining pastry. Trim and seal edge; cut vents. Bake at 350 degrees for 25 minutes.
Yield: 6 servings.

Myrtle Balthrop, Texas

HUCKLEBERRY PIE

4 *c. huckleberries*
¼ *c. flour*
1 *c. sugar*
⅛ *tsp. salt*
1 *tbsp. lemon juice*
1 *recipe 2-crust pie pastry*
1 *tbsp. butter*

Mix huckleberries, flour, sugar, salt and lemon juice in bowl; mix gently. Pour into pastry-lined pie plate. Dot with butter. Top with remaining pastry; seal edge and cut vents. Bake at 450 degrees for 10 minutes. Reduce temperature to 350 degrees. Bake for 35 minutes or until brown. Yield: 8 servings.

Beryl Berringer, Washington

HUCKLEBERRY TART

1½ *c. mashed huckleberries*
2½ *c. sugar*
3 *tbsp. cornstarch*
2 *tbsp. lemon juice*
1½ *c. whole huckleberries*
1 *c. plus 2 tbsp. shortening*
3 *eggs*
3 *tsp. vanilla extract*
6½ *c. flour*
4 *tsp. baking powder*
1 *tsp. salt*
1 *c. milk*
2 *c. confectioners' sugar*
2 to 4 *tbsp. milk*

Combine mashed huckleberries and 1½ cups sugar in saucepan. Bring to a boil. Add mixture of cornstarch and ½ cup water. Cook until thickened. Stir in lemon juice and whole huckleberries. Let stand until almost cool. Cream remaining 1 cup sugar and 1 cup shortening in mixer bowl until light and fluffy. Add eggs and 2 teaspoons vanilla. Add mixture of flour, baking powder and salt to creamed mixture alternately with 1 cup milk, beating well after each addition. Reserve 1 cup dough. Pat remaining dough in greased 10x15-inch baking pan. Pour huckleberry filling over top. Crumble reserved dough over huckleberries. Bake at 350 degrees for 35 minutes. Drizzle warm tart with mixture of confectioners' sugar, milk, remaining 2 tablespoons shortening and 1 teaspoon vanilla. Yield: 12 to 18 servings.

Carole Zimmerman, Pennsylvania

MULBERRIES AND CREAM PIE

4 *c. fresh mulberries*
1 *unbaked 9-in. pie shell*
¾ *c. sugar*
¼ *c. flour*
¼ *tsp. salt*
½ *tsp. cinnamon*
1 *c. cream*

Place mulberries in pie shell. Pour mixture of remaining ingredients over mulberries. Bake at 400 degrees for 35 to 45 minutes or until light brown. Serve warm. Yield: 6 to 8 servings.

Dorothy Groves, Oregon

BLACKBERRY

FROZEN BLACKBERRY CREAM

2 *c. strained blackberry purée*
16 *lg. marshmallows*
1 *tbsp. lemon juice*
1 *c. sugar*
3 *c. whipped cream*

Mix blackberry purée with marshmallows, lemon juice and sugar in double boiler. Cook until marshmallows are melted, stirring constantly. Chill in refrigerator. Fold in whipped cream. Spoon into mold. Freeze until firm. Unmold on serving plate. Yield: 4 to 6 servings.

Teresa Allen, Oklahoma

BLACKBERRY PUDDING

¼ *c. margarine, softened*
1 *c. sugar*
1 *c. flour*
2 *tsp. baking powder*
¼ *tsp. salt*
½ *c. milk*
1 *c. blackberries*
1 *c. blackberry juice*

Cream margarine and ½ cup sugar in mixer bowl until light. Add sifted dry ingredients and milk; mix well. Pour into greased 2-quart casserole. Layer blackberries, remaining ½ cup sugar and blackberry juice over top. Do not stir. Bake at 375 degrees for 45 minutes or until brown. Yield: 4 servings.

Barbara A. Harman, West Virginia

BLACKBERRY SLUMP

2½ *c. blackberries*
½ *tsp. lemon juice*
⅓ *c. plus 2 tbsp. sugar*
1 *c. flour*
2 *tsp. baking powder*
¼ *tsp. salt*
1 *tbsp. butter*
½ *c. milk*

Combine blackberries, lemon juice, ⅓ cup sugar and 1 cup water in saucepan. Cook for 5 minutes. Combine remaining ingredients and remaining 2 tablespoons sugar in bowl; mix well. Drop by spoonfuls into simmering blackberries. Cook, covered, for 10 minutes. Serve warm. Yield: 4 to 6 servings.

J. A. Kruise, Pennsylvania

SPICY BLACKBERRY CAKE

¾ *c. butter, softened*
2 *c. sugar*
3 *eggs*
2 *c. plus 2 tbsp. flour*
1 *tsp. soda*
1 *tsp. cinnamon*
1 *tsp. cloves*
1 *tsp. allspice*
1 *c. drained blackberries*
½ *c. sour milk*
1 *c. blackberry juice*

Beat ½ cup softened butter and 1 cup sugar in mixer bowl. Add eggs; mix well. Sift 2 cups flour and next 4 dry ingredients together. Add to creamed mixture alternately with blackberries and sour milk, mixing well after each addition. Pour into greased and floured 9x13-inch cake pan. Bake at 350 degrees until cake tests done. Combine ¼ cup melted butter, blackberry juice and remaining 2 tablespoons flour in saucepan; mix well. Cook until thickened, stirring constantly. Pour over hot cake. Yield: 16 servings.

Joanna Williams, Indiana

BLACKBERRY CUSTARD PIE

1½ *c. (about) sugar*
1 *tbsp. flour*
2 *eggs, beaten*
1 *c. milk*
2 *c. fresh blackberries*
1 *unbaked 9-in. pie shell*
2 *tbsp. butter*

Combine sugar and flour in mixer bowl. Beat in eggs and milk. Mix in blackberries. Pour into pie shell. Dot with butter. Bake at 350 degrees for 1 hour or until set. Yield: 6 servings.

Libby Cordray, Alabama

BLACKBERRY PIES

1 c. sugar
3 tbsp. margarine
4 c. fresh blackberries
2 tbsp. cornstarch
1 sm. package blackberry
   gelatin
2 baked 9-in. pie shells

Simmer sugar, margarine and ½ cup water in saucepan until margarine melts and sugar dissolves, stirring constantly. Add fresh blackberries gradually. Cook until heated through, stirring constantly. Blend enough cold water with cornstarch to make thin paste. Stir into blackberries. Cook until thickened, stirring constantly. Dissolve gelatin in 1 cup boiling water. Stir into berry mixture. Spoon into pie shells. Chill for 2 hours or until set. Yield: 2 pies.

Jenny Grobusky, South Carolina

BLACKBERRY BARS

2¼ c. quick-cooking oats
2¼ c. flour
1 c. packed brown sugar
1½ tsp. baking powder
1⅓ c. margarine
1   20-oz. can blackberry
    pie filling

Combine oats, flour, brown sugar, baking powder and margarine in bowl. Mix with fingers until crumbly. Press ⅔ of the mixture into 9x13-inch baking pan. Spread with pie filling. Sprinkle with remaining crumb mixture. Bake at 350 degrees for 12 minutes. Cool on wire rack. Cut into bars.
Yield: 3 dozen.

Heather Nolan, Maryland

Select fresh blueberries that are plump, firm and deep blue in color. A reddish tinge indicates immature fruit. Blueberries will keep at room temperature for 2 to 3 days or in the refrigerator for about 1 week. Wash berries quickly in water just before serving.

BLUEBERRIES

BLUEBERRY CHEESECAKE

2 c. graham cracker crumbs
2 tbsp. plus 1 c. sugar
6 tbsp. margarine, softened
24 oz. cream cheese, softened
4 eggs, separated
1 tsp. vanilla extract
2 tsp. lemon juice
1   21-oz. can blueberry
    pie filling

Combine crumbs, 2 tablespoons sugar and margarine in bowl; mix well. Press over bottom of 8 or 9-inch springform pan. Combine cream cheese, egg yolks, vanilla and lemon juice in bowl; mix well. Beat egg whites in bowl until soft peaks form. Add remaining 1 cup sugar gradually, beating until stiff peaks form. Fold gently into cream cheese mixture. Spoon into prepared pan. Bake at 350 degrees for 30 minutes. Cool. Spoon blueberry pie filling over top.
Yield: 12 servings.

Catherine Dexter, California

BLUEBERRY COBBLER

½ c. plus 1 tbsp. sugar
1 tbsp. cornstarch
4 c. blueberries
1 tsp. lemon juice
1 c. flour
1½ tsp. baking powder
½ tsp. salt
3 tbsp. shortening
⅓ c. milk

Mix ½ cup sugar, cornstarch and blueberries in saucepan. Simmer for 1 minute or until mixture thickens, stirring constantly. Pour into 2-quart casserole; keep warm. Combine flour, remaining 1 tablespoon sugar, baking powder and salt in bowl. Cut in shortening until crumbly. Stir in milk until dough forms ball. Drop by spoonfuls onto hot fruit. Bake at 400 degrees for 25 to 30 minutes or until topping is brown.
Yield: 6 servings.

Rosemary Butler, Wisconsin

BLUEBERRY CRÊPES

2 c. sifted flour
½ tsp. salt
8 eggs, beaten
2⅔ c. milk
¼ c. melted butter
1   6-oz. can frozen orange
   juice concentrate
½ c. sugar
2 c. blueberries
½ c. slivered blanched almonds

Mix flour and salt in large mixer bowl. Add eggs, milk and butter. Beat at medium speed until smooth. Pour ¼ cup at a time into oiled 6-inch crêpe pan. Cook until light brown on both sides. Stack crêpes on plate, separating with waxed paper; keep warm. Combine orange juice concentrate, sugar, blueberries, almonds and ½ cup water in saucepan. Simmer for 10 minutes. Dip crêpes into sauce 1 at a time; fold into quarters. Place on serving plate. Serve remaining sauce over crêpes. Yield: 8 servings.

Eliza Olson, Georgia

BLUEBERRY PIZZA

1 2-layer pkg. white cake mix
1¼ c. quick-cooking oats
½ c. butter, softened
1 egg
1   21-oz. can blueberry
   pie filling
½ c. chopped nuts
¼ c. packed brown sugar
½ tsp. cinnamon

Combine cake mix, 1 cup oats and 6 tablespoons butter in mixer bowl; mix until crumbly. Reserve 1 cup crumbs. Blend remaining crumb mixture with egg. Press into greased 12-inch pizza pan. Bake at 350 degrees for 12 minutes. Cool slightly. Spread pie filling over baked layers. Combine reserved crumb mixture, remaining ¼ cup oats and 2 tablespoons butter, nuts, brown sugar and cinnamon; mix well. Sprinkle over pie filling. Bake at 350 degrees for 15 minutes or until golden. Cool. Cut into wedges. Yield: 10 servings.

Cynthia Kolberg, Indiana

BLUEBERRY BRUNCH CAKE

2 c. blueberries
1½ c. sugar
1 tbsp. cornstarch
½ c. plus 1 tbsp. butter,
   softened
3 oz. cream cheese, softened
2¼ c. cake flour
2 tsp. baking powder
1 tsp. salt
3 eggs
½ c. plus 2 tsp. milk
1 tsp. vanilla extract
1 tbsp. grated lemon rind
½ c. confectioners' sugar
¼ tsp. lemon extract

Combine first 3 ingredients and ½ cup water in saucepan. Cook until thickened, stirring frequently. Cool. Cut ½ cup butter and cream cheese into mixture of cake flour, remaining ½ cup sugar, baking powder and salt in bowl until crumbly. Reserve 1 cup crumbs for topping. Add eggs, ½ cup milk, vanilla and lemon rind to remaining crumbs, beat well. Pour into greased 9x13-inch cake pan. Spoon blueberries over batter. Sprinkle with reserved crumbs. Bake at 350 degrees for 35 to 45 minutes or until golden. Cool for 30 minutes. Combine remaining 1 tablespoon butter, confectioners' sugar, remaining 2 teaspoons milk and lemon extract in small bowl; mix well. Drizzle over warm cake. Cut into squares. Yield: 16 servings.

Alice Emery, New York

BLUEBERRY-CREAM CHEESE CAKE

3 eggs
8 oz. cream cheese, softened
1   2-layer pkg. butter cake mix
½ c. oil
1 can blueberries, drained

Beat eggs and cream cheese in bowl until light and fluffy. Add cake mix and oil; mix well. Add 1 cup water; mix well. Fold in blueberries gently. Pour into greased and floured 9x-13-inch cake pan. Bake at 350 degrees for 30 to 40 minutes or until cake tests done. Dust cooled cake with confectioners' sugar. Yield: 16 servings.

Reysa Yeager, Mississippi

COCONUT-BLUEBERRY CAKE

1¾ c. sugar
1 c. margarine, softened
4 eggs
3 c. flour
½ tsp. salt
1 tsp. baking powder
1 tsp. soda
1 tsp. cinnamon
1 c. milk
1 tsp. vanilla extract
2 c. blueberries
2 tbsp. butter, softened
1½ c. coconut

Cream 1 cup sugar and margarine in bowl until light. Beat in 3 eggs. Add mixture of flour, salt, baking powder, soda and cinnamon alternately with milk and vanilla, mixing well after each addition. Stir in blueberries. Pour into greased and floured 9x13-inch cake pan. Mix butter, remaining ¾ cup sugar and 1 egg in bowl. Stir in coconut. Spread over batter. Bake at 350 degrees for 45 to 50 minutes or until cake tests done. Cool in pan. Yield: 16 servings.

Jacquelyn M. Gabor, Pennsylvania

BLUEBERRY-MANDARIN PIE

1   11-oz. can mandarin
     oranges, well drained
1 qt. fresh blueberries, rinsed,
     drained
1 c. sugar
3 tbsp. quick-cooking tapioca
¼ tsp. salt
⅛ tsp. nutmeg
1 recipe 2-crust pie pastry
2 tbsp. butter
2 tbsp. cream

Reserve several orange segments and blueberries for garnish. Combine remaining oranges and blueberries in large bowl. Sprinkle with sugar, tapioca, salt and nutmeg; toss lightly until well mixed. Spoon fruit mixture into pastry-lined 9-inch pie plates. Dot with butter. Top with remaining pastry. Cut 4 or 5 slits near center. Trim and flute edges. Brush with cream. Bake at 400 degrees for 45 minutes or until golden. Cool on wire rack for 2 hours or longer. Garnish with reserved oranges and blueberries.

Photograph for this recipe on page 36.

BUTTERSCOTCH

BUTTERSCOTCH CHEESECAKE

⅓ c. melted butter
1½ c. graham cracker crumbs
⅓ c. packed brown sugar
1 can sweetened condensed
     milk
1 sm. package butterscotch
     pudding and pie filling mix
24 oz. cream cheese, softened
3 eggs
1 tsp. vanilla extract

Combine butter, crumbs and brown sugar in bowl. Press over bottom of 9-inch springform pan. Combine condensed milk, pudding mix and ¾ cup water in saucepan; mix well. Cook until thickened, stirring constantly. Beat softened cream cheese in mixer bowl until fluffy. Beat in eggs, vanilla and pudding. Pour into prepared pan. Bake at 375 degrees for 50 minutes or until golden around edge; center will be soft. Cool to room temperature. Chill in refrigerator. Yield: 12 servings.

BUTTERSCOTCH TORTE

2 sm. packages butterscotch
     pudding and pie filling mix
3 c. milk
½ c. margarine
1 c. flour
2 tbsp. sugar
1 c. chopped pecans
1 c. confectioners' sugar
8 oz. cream cheese, softened
16 oz. whipped topping

Combine pudding mix with milk in saucepan. Cook according to package directions. Cool. Combine margarine, flour, sugar and pecans in bowl; mix well. Press into 9x11-inch baking pan. Bake at 350 degrees for 20 minutes. Cool. Cream confectioners' sugar and cream cheese in bowl until light. Reserve ½ cup whipped topping. Blend remaining whipped topping into creamed mixture. Spread in prepared pan. Top with cooled pudding and reserved whipped topping. Chill. Yield: 12 servings.

Joan Hollingsworth, Maryland

BUTTERSCOTCH CAKE

1 3-oz. package butterscotch
   pudding and pie filling mix
2 c. milk
1 2-layer pkg. yellow cake mix
6 oz. butterscotch chips
¾ c. chopped pecans

Cook pudding mix with milk according to package directions. Add hot pudding to cake mix in bowl; mix well. Pour into greased and floured 9x13-inch pan. Sprinkle with butterscotch chips and pecans. Bakt at 350 degrees for 30 minutes or until cake tests done. Yield: 12 servings.

Bunny Cooper, Kentucky

BUTTERSCOTCH-RUM RIPPLE CAKE

1 c. butter, softened
2 c. sugar
1 c. sour cream
3 c. flour
1 tsp. soda
1 tsp. salt
1 tsp. vanilla extract
1 tsp. rum extract
6 eggs
1 sm. package butterscotch
   instant pudding mix
¾ c. butterscotch ice
   cream topping

Combine first 8 ingredients and 5 eggs in mixer bowl. Beat for 3 minutes. Mix 2 cups prepared batter, pudding mix, ice cream topping and remaining 1 egg in small mixer bowl. Beat for 1 minute. Spoon half the cake batter into greased and floured bundt pan. Add half the butterscotch batter. Cut with knife to marbleize. Repeat with remaining batters. Bake at 350 degrees for 1 hour and 15 minutes or until cake tests done. Cool in pan for 10 to 15 minutes. Remove to serving plate. Garnish with rum-flavored confectioners' sugar glaze. Yield: 12 servings.

Ruth Bartlett, Texas

Dust flour in greased cake pans with a new powder puff.

BUTTERSCOTCH PIE

1 c. packed brown sugar
½ c. flour
Pinch of salt
⅔ c. evaporated milk
2 egg yolks
1 tsp. vanilla extract
1 baked 9-in. pie shell
1 recipe meringue

Combine brown sugar, flour and salt in bowl. Add evaporated milk and egg yolks; mix well. Bring 1⅓ cups water to a boil in saucepan. Add brown sugar mixture. Bring to a boil, stirring constantly. Remove from heat. Stir in vanilla. Pour into pie shell. Top with meringue, sealing to edge. Bake at 350 degrees for 10 minutes or until light brown. Yield: 6 servings.

Kimberly Sayers, Pennsylvania

BUTTERSCOTCH PRALINE PIE

½ c. packed brown sugar
⅔ c. chopped pecans
¼ c. melted margarine
1 unbaked pie shell
2 c. milk
2 3-oz. packages butterscotch
   pudding and pie filling mix
1 c. whipped topping

Combine brown sugar, pecans and margarine in bowl; mix well. Cover bottom of pie shell with mixture. Bake at 400 degrees until crust is golden brown and pecan mixture is bubbly. Cool. Combine milk and pudding mix in bowl; mix until thick. Beat in whipped topping. Pour into cooled pie crust. Chill for 2 to 3 hours before serving. Serve with additional whipped topping. Yield: 6 to 8 servings.

Susie Masters, Iowa

BUTTERSCOTCH BARS

¾ c. melted butter
1 16-oz. package brown sugar
3 eggs
1 tsp. vanilla extract
3 c. flour
1 tbsp. baking powder
¾ tsp. salt
1 c. chopped nuts

Blend butter and brown sugar in bowl. Beat in eggs and vanilla. Add mixture of flour, baking powder and salt; mix well. Stir in nuts. Spread in greased 9x13-inch baking pan. Bake at 300 degrees until edges pull from sides of pan. Cut into bars while warm. Yield: 3 dozen.

Duane Billey, Oklahoma

BUTTERSCOTCH COOKIES

1 c. butter, softened
2 c. packed brown sugar
2 eggs
1 tbsp. vanilla extract
3½ c. flour
1 tsp. cream of tartar
1 tsp. soda
⅛ tsp. salt

Cream butter and brown sugar in mixer bowl until light and fluffy. Beat in eggs. Add remaining ingredients; mix well. Shape into 2 rolls. Chill, wrapped in waxed paper, for 4 hours to overnight. Slice rolls into cookies. Place on cookie sheet. Bake at 350 degrees for 10 to 12 minutes or until brown. Cool on wire rack. Yield: 3 dozen.

Jean Hamrick, Ohio

BUTTERSCOTCH PINWHEELS

6 oz. semisweet chocolate chips
¼ c. shortening
1 can sweetened condensed
   milk
1 c. flour
1 tsp. vanilla extract
6 oz. butterscotch chips
Confectioners' sugar
½ c. chopped walnuts

Melt chocolate chips and 2 tablespoons shortening in saucepan over low heat, stirring constantly. Remove from heat. Stir in condensed milk, flour and vanilla. Spread in greased and waxed paper-lined 10x15-inch baking pan. Bake at 325 degrees for 8 minutes. Melt butterscotch chips and remaining 2 tablespoons shortening in saucepan. Invert baked layer onto towel sprinkled with confectioners' sugar. Spread with butterscotch mixture; sprinkle with walnuts. Roll as for jelly roll from long side. Cool. Wrap in plastic wrap. Chill in refrigerator. Cut into ¼-inch slices. Yield: 4½ dozen.

Claire Gumert, Texas

ICED BUTTERSCOTCH COOKIES

¾ c. raisins
2½ c. packed brown sugar
1½ c. milk
1 c. shortening
½ c. sugar
3 eggs
3¾ c. flour
2 tsp. baking powder
1 tsp. soda
½ tsp. salt
½ c. butter
3 c. confectioners' sugar

Mix raisins with 1½ cups brown sugar and ¼ cup milk in bowl; let stand for several minutes. Cream shortening and sugar in mixer bowl until light and fluffy. Beat in eggs. Add ¾ cup milk, flour, baking powder, soda and salt; mix well. Stir in raisin mixture. Drop by teaspoonfuls onto greased cookie sheet. Bake at 350 degrees for 12 minutes. Boil butter and remaining 1 cup brown sugar in saucepan for 1 minute. Stir in remaining ½ cup milk. Pour over confectioners' sugar in bowl, mixing well. Spread on cooled cookies. Yield: 3 dozen.

Dorothy Eckert, Ohio

BUTTERSCOTCH CLUSTERS

6 oz. chocolate chips
6 oz. butterscotch chips
1   12-oz. jar salted peanuts
1   5-oz. can chow mein
   noodles

Melt chocolate and butterscotch chips in saucepan over low heat, stirring constantly. Stir in peanuts and noodles. Drop by spoonfuls onto waxed paper. Yield: 2 dozen.

Paula Heck, Missouri

MICROWAVE BUTTERSCOTCH FUDGE

1 7-oz. jar marshmallow creme
1 6-oz. can evaporated milk
6 tbsp. margarine
1¾ c. sugar
¼ tsp. salt
6 oz. butterscotch chips
1 c. chopped walnuts

Combine marshmallow creme, evaporated milk, margarine, sugar and salt in large glass bowl. Microwave on High for 6 minutes or until mixture comes to the boiling point, stirring twice. Microwave on Medium for 3 minutes, stirring once. Add butterscotch chips; stir until melted. Stir in walnuts. Spoon into buttered, foil-lined 8-inch square dish. Chill until firm. Cut into squares. Yield: 2 pounds.

Judy Adler, Texas

BUTTERSCOTCH-WALNUT LOG

6 oz. butterscotch chips
⅓ c. sweetened condensed milk
½ tsp. vanilla extract
⅔ c. coarsely chopped walnuts
1 egg white, beaten

Melt butterscotch chips in double boiler; remove from heat. Blend in condensed milk and vanilla. Stir in half the walnuts. Chill until firm. Shape into 12-inch log. Score with fork. Brush with egg white. Roll in remaining walnuts. Chill, wrapped, until firm. Cut into ½-inch slices. Store in refrigerator. Yield: 1 pound.

Becky Leonard, California

CARAMEL

CARAMEL DUMPLINGS

2 c. sugar
¼ c. butter, softened
⅛ tsp. salt
½ tsp. vanilla extract
1½ c. flour
2 tsp. baking powder
½ c. milk

Caramelize ½ cup sugar in heavy oven-proof skillet over medium heat. Add 1 cup sugar, 2 tablespoons butter, salt and 2 cups hot water; stir until sugar is dissolved. Simmer for 10 minutes, stirring frequently. Cream remaining 2 tablespoons butter and ½ cup sugar in mixer bowl until light and fluffy. Blend in vanilla. Add sifted mixture of flour and baking powder alternately with milk, mixing well after each addition. Drop by spoonfuls into hot syrup. Bake, covered, at 375 degrees for 20 minutes or until dumplings test done. Place dumplings in dessert dishes. Spoon caramel sauce over top. Yield: 9 servings.

Patricia Radford, West Virginia

CARAMEL FLAN

¾ c. sugar
4 eggs
1 can sweetened condensed milk
½ tsp. vanilla extract
⅛ tsp. salt

Heat sugar in heavy skillet over medium heat until melted and caramelized, stirring constantly. Pour into 9-inch round cake pan, tilting to coat bottom completely. Beat eggs in bowl. Stir in 1¾ cups water, sweetened condensed milk, vanilla and salt. Pour into prepared pan. Set in larger pan with 1 inch hot water. Bake at 350 degrees for 55 to 60 minutes or until knife inserted near center comes out clean. Cool. Chill in refrigerator. Loosen side of flan with knife. Invert onto serving plate with rim. Yield: 10 to 12 servings.

CARAMEL ICE CREAM

2 eggs
2 c. sugar
½ c. flour
1 qt. milk, scalded
1 pt. heavy cream
1 tsp. vanilla extract

Combine eggs and 1 cup sugar in bowl; beat until creamy. Blend in flour. Add hot milk gradually, stirring constantly until well blended. Place in top of double boiler over hot water.

Cook for 10 minutes, stirring constantly. Caramelize remaining 1 cup sugar in heavy skillet. Stir in cream. Add to milk mixture; cool. Stir in vanilla. Pour into freezer container. Freeze according to manufacturer's instructions.
Yield: ½ gallon.

Mrs. John Payne Harrison, Missouri

CARAMEL PUDDING

½ c. sugar
½ c. packed brown sugar
⅓ c. flour
⅛ tsp. salt
1½ c. milk
3 eggs, beaten
2 tbsp. butter
1 tsp. vanilla extract

Heat sugar in skillet until melted and golden brown. Blend in ½ cup boiling water gradually. Combine brown sugar, flour and salt in saucepan. Stir in carmelized sugar syrup and milk. Cook until thickened, stirring constantly. Stir a small amount of hot mixture into eggs; stir eggs into hot mixture. Add butter and vanilla; mix well. Spoon into dessert dishes. Yield: 4 servings.

CARAMEL SAUCE

1 c. sugar
1 c. heavy cream
2 tbsp. unsalted butter
1 tsp. vanilla extract

Combine sugar and 3 tablespoons water in a small heavy saucepan. Cook over low heat for 10 minutes or until light brown. Do not stir. Pour in cream very gradually. Stir in butter. Simmer for another 10 minutes; remove from heat. Stir in vanilla. Serve over ice cream or cake. Yield: 1¾ cups.

BURNT SUGAR CARAMEL CAKE

2½ c. sugar
½ c. butter, softened
3 eggs, separated
1 c. warm milk
2½ c. flour
2 tsp. baking powder
1 tsp. vanilla extract

Melt 1 cup sugar in heavy skillet over medium heat. Cook until light brown, stirring frequently. Add ½ cup boiling water; mix well. Cream butter in mixer bowl. Add remaining 1½ cups sugar gradually, beating until light and fluffy. Add egg yolks, milk, and 2 cups flour, beating well after each addition. Beat for 5 minutes. Add enough burnt sugar syrup to make of desired color. Add remaining ½ cup flour, baking powder and vanilla; mix well. Fold in stiffly beaten egg whites gently. Pour into 3 greased and floured 8-inch cake pans. Bake at 350 degrees for 25 minutes or until cake tests done. Cool in pans for 10 minutes. Remove to wire rack to cool completely. Frost as desired.
Yield: 16 servings.

Millie E. Patterson, Washington

FLUFFY CARAMEL-APPLE PIE

8 oz. vanilla caramels
1 tbsp. butter
1 baked 9-in. pie shell
4 tsp. unflavored gelatin
2 c. canned applesauce
¼ tsp. salt
2 tbsp. sugar
1 egg, beaten
2 tbsp. lemon juice
1 c. whipping cream, whipped

Melt half the caramels with 2 tablespoons hot water and butter in double boiler over hot water, stirring constantly. Pour into pie shell, spreading to cover bottom. Soften gelatin in ¼ cup cold water. Melt remaining caramels in 6 tablespoons hot water in double boiler, stirring constantly. Blend in applesauce and gelatin. Stir in salt, sugar and egg. Cook for 5 minutes or until smooth, stirring constantly. Cool until slightly thickened. Blend lemon juice into whipped cream. Whip applesauce mixture until fluffy. Fold in whipped cream. Spoon into pie shell. Chill until firm. Garnish with walnuts.
Yield: 6 servings.

Wanda Strassler, California

Always prick the bottom and side of a pie shell which is baked before filling. This will prevent puffing.

OLD-FASHIONED CARAMEL PIES

2 c. sugar
¼ c. butter, softened
5 eggs, separated
2 tbsp. (heaping) flour, sifted
1 tsp. salt
3 c. milk
1 tsp. vanilla extract
2 baked 9-in. pie shells

Blend 1 cup sugar and butter in a saucepan. Add egg yolks, flour and salt; mix until smooth. Stir in milk. Cook over medium heat until thick, stirring constantly. Blend in vanilla. Cook ½ cup sugar in iron skillet until melted and golden brown, shaking skillet several times. Do not stir. Pour slowly into custard mixture. Cook until blended, stirring constantly. Pour into 2 baked pie shells. Beat egg whites until soft peaks form. Add remaining ½ cup sugar gradually, beating until stiff peaks form. Spread over pies, sealing to edge. Bake at 300 degrees until browned.
Yield: 2 pies.

Nona Davis, Tennessee

CARAMEL SAND TARTS

½ c. butter or margarine, softened
1 c. packed brown sugar
1 egg
1 tsp. vanilla extract
1½ c. flour
2 tsp. baking powder
¼ tsp. salt
1 egg white
1 tbsp. sugar
¼ tsp. cinnamon
Pecan halves

Cream butter in mixer bowl. Add brown sugar gradually, beating well. Add egg and vanilla; mix well. Combine flour, baking powder and salt in bowl. Add to creamed mixture, mixing well. Chill, covered, for 1 to 2 hours. Roll dough to ⅛-inch thickness on lightly floured surface; cut with a 2½-inch round cutter. Brush each cookie lightly with egg white. Combine sugar and cinnamon; sprinkle lightly over cookies. Place 2 inches apart on lightly greased cookie sheet. Press pecan half gently into center of each. Bake at 350

degrees for 8 to 10 minutes or until light brown. Remove to wire racks to cool. Store in airtight containers.
Yield: 2½ dozen.

Anna Smith, Kentucky

CARAMEL BROWNIES

2 c. packed brown sugar
10 tbsp. oil
2 eggs
1 tsp. vanilla extract
1 c. flour
2 tsp. baking powder
1 tsp. salt
1 c. flaked coconut
1 c. chopped pecans

Combine brown sugar, 10 tablespoons oil, eggs and vanilla in bowl. Add mixture of flour, baking powder and salt; mix well. Stir in coconut and pecans. Pour into greased and floured 9x13-inch baking pan. Bake at 350 degrees for 30 minutes. Cut into squares. Yield: 3 dozen.

Martha Plunkett, Tennessee

CHERRY

CHERRY-ALMOND FRUIT FREEZE

1 20-oz. can pineapple tidbits, drained
1½ c. drained maraschino cherries, chopped
1 3-oz. package almonds, chopped
1 16-oz. can white cherries, drained, chopped
3 c. miniature marshmallows
¼ c. pineapple juice
¼ c. sugar
4 eggs, separated
1 pt. whipping cream, whipped

Combine first 5 ingredients in bowl, mixing well. Combine pineapple juice, sugar and egg yolks in saucepan. Cook over medium heat until thick, stirring constantly. Stir into fruit mixture. Fold in whipped cream and stiffly beaten egg whites. Pour into serving dish. Freeze until firm.
Yield: 24 servings.

CHERRY CRUMB GOODY

2 c. packed brown sugar
2 c. flour
2 c. quick-cooking oats
1 tsp. soda
1 c. margarine
3 to 4 c. cherry pie filling

Combine brown sugar, flour, oats and soda in bowl. Add margarine; mix with hands until crumbly. Press half the mixture into greased 9x13-inch baking pan. Spread evenly with pie filling. Sprinkle with remaining crumbs. Bake at 350 degrees for 35 minutes or until brown. Serve warm with ice cream. Yield: 12 servings.

CHERRIES JUBILEE

1/3 c. sugar
2 tsp. cornstarch
1/8 tsp. salt
1 c. cherry syrup
1½ c. drained canned
    pitted cherries
2 tsp. lemon juice
1/4 tsp. grated lemon rind
1/4 tsp. almond extract
1/3 c. Kirsch

Combine sugar, cornstarch, salt and cherry syrup in blazer pan of chafing dish. Place over direct heat. Cook until sauce is clear and slightly thickened, stirring constantly. Stir in cherries, lemon juice, lemon rind, almond extract and 2 tablespoons Kirsch. Cook until heated through. Place pan in water jacket to keep hot. Warm remaining Kirsch in small pan. Pour over sauce; ignite. Serve over vanilla ice cream when flame subsides. Yield: 6 servings.

Sarah Darnell, Tennessee

CHERRY-NUT CAKE

½ c. shortening
3/4 c. sugar
3 eggs
2¼ c. sifted cake flour
1 tbsp. baking powder
½ tsp. salt
1/4 c. cherry juice
½ c. milk
½ c. chopped cherries
½ c. chopped nuts

Cream shortening and sugar in mixer bowl until light and fluffy. Add eggs 1 at a time, beating well after each addition. Add mixture of flour, baking powder and salt alternately with cherry juice, mixing well after each addition. Fold in mixture of milk and cherries and nuts. Pour into greased and floured 7x11-inch cake pan. Bake at 375 degrees for 25 to 30 minutes or until cake tests done. Yield: 10 to 12 servings.

Penny Meckley, Pennsylvania

BLACK FOREST CHERRY CAKE

½ c. butter, softened
1½ c. sugar
2 eggs
2 c. flour
1¼ c. milk
1½ tsp. soda
3/4 tsp. salt
½ c. baking cocoa
½ tsp. red food coloring
1 tsp. vanilla extract
1 tbsp. cornstarch
2 c. black cherries in
    heavy syrup
2 c. (or more) whipping
    cream, whipped
12 maraschino cherries

Cream butter and sugar in mixer bowl until light and fluffy. Add eggs, flour, milk, soda, salt, cocoa, food coloring and vanilla 1 ingredient at a time, beating well after each addition. Beat at high speed for 3 minutes. Pour into 2 greased and floured round 9-inch cake pans. Bake at 350 degrees for 30 minutes or until cake tests done. Cool. Split cake layers in half horizontally. Combine cornstarch and black cherries in saucepan. Cook until clear and thickened, stirring constantly. Cool. Pipe whipped cream around outer edge and in center of bottom layer. Spread inner ring with cherry filling. Repeat process with second cake layer. Top with third layer. Frost top and side with whipped cream. Crumble fourth layer. Pat cake crumbs over side of cake. Decorate top with whipped cream rosettes. Top each rosette with maraschino cherry. Garnish with chocolate curls. Yield: 16 servings.

Janet Miller, Pennsylvania

31

CHERRY PIES

4 c. flour
2 tbsp. plus 2 c. sugar
1½ tsp. salt
2 c. shortening
1 tbsp. vinegar
1 egg
4 cans cherry pie filling
1 tsp. almond extract

Combine flour, 2 tablespoons sugar and salt in bowl. Cut in shortening until crumbly. Stir in mixture of 1 cup water, vinegar and egg. Divide into 8 portions. Roll ¼ inch thick on floured surface. Fit half the pastry into pie plates. Combine pie filling, almond extract and remaining 2 cups sugar in bowl; mix well. Spoon into prepared pie plates. Top with remaining pastry. Bake at 375 degrees for 45 to 60 minutes or until browned. Yield: 4 pies.

Kristie Mallatt, Indiana

CHERRY-CHEESE PIE

½ c. sugar
8 oz. cream cheese, softened
8 oz. whipped topping
1   9-in. graham cracker
    pie shell
1 can cherry pie filling

Cream sugar and cream cheese in mixer bowl until light and fluffy. Blend in whipped topping. Spoon into pie shell. Top with pie filling. Chill for 3 hours or longer. Yield: 6 servings.

Bridget White, Pennsylvania

CHERRY MELBA MERINGUE PIE

1 tbsp. cornstarch
1   8-oz. jar maraschino
    cherries, puréed
½ c. currant jelly
4 tsp. lemon juice
¼ tsp. grated lemon rind
4 egg whites
½ tsp. vanilla extract
¼ tsp. salt
¼ tsp. cream of tartar
1⅓ c. sugar
8 fresh peach halves, chilled
1 qt. vanilla ice cream

Blend cornstarch with 1 tablespoon cold water in saucepan. Add cherries, jelly, lemon juice and rind. Cook over medium heat until thick, stirring constantly. Chill. Combine egg whites, vanilla, salt and cream of tartar in mixer bowl. Beat until soft peaks form. Add sugar gradually, beating until stiff peaks form. Spread in pie plate, shaping to form pie shell. Bake at 250 degrees for 45 minutes. Turn off oven. Let stand in closed oven for 30 minutes. Arrange peach halves in meringue shell. Top with ice cream. Spoon cherry sauce over top. Yield: 6 to 8 servings.

CHERRY BARS

1¼ c. flour
1¼ c. confectioners' sugar
½ c. margarine, softened
¾ c. sugar
½ tsp. baking powder
2 eggs, beaten
½ c. chopped nuts
½ c. chopped maraschino
    cherries
½ c. coconut
Maraschino cherry juice

Mix 1 cup flour and ¼ cup confectioners' sugar in bowl. Cut in margarine until crumbly. Press into ungreased 8x8-inch baking pan. Bake at 350 degrees for 10 minutes. Combine remaining ¼ cup flour, sugar and baking powder in bowl. Blend in eggs. Stir in nuts, cherries and coconut. Spread over crust. Bake for 30 minutes. Blend remaining 1 cup confectioners' sugar with a small amount of cherry juice. Spread over hot baked layer. Cool. Cut into bars. Yield: 1½ dozen.

Pat Duncan, Texas

CHERRY DROPS

1 c. shortening
3 oz. cream cheese, softened
1 c. sugar
1 egg
1 tsp. almond extract
2½ c. flour
¼ tsp. soda
½ tsp. salt
1¼ c. finely chopped pecans
72 maraschino cherry halves

Cream shortening and cream cheese in bowl until light and fluffy. Add sugar gradually, beating until light and fluffy. Add egg and flavoring; mix well. Add combined dry ingredients; mix well. Chill for 1 hour. Shape into 1-inch balls. Roll in pecans. Place on greased cookie sheet. Press cherry half into center of each cookie. Bake at 350 degrees for 12 minutes or until golden brown. Cool on wire rack.
Yield: 6 dozen.

Daresa Dell, Oklahoma

CHERRY SWIRLS

1½ c. sugar
½ c. margarine, softened
½ c. shortening
4 eggs
1 tsp. vanilla
1 tsp. almond extract
3 c. flour
1½ tsp. baking powder
1 can cherry pie filling
¾ c. confectioners' sugar
1 to 2 tbsp. milk

Cream sugar, margarine, shortening, eggs and flavorings in large mixer bowl. Beat at high speed for 3 minutes. Stir in flour and baking powder. Spread ⅔ of the batter in greased 9x13-inch baking pan. Spread pie filling over batter. Bake at 350 degrees for 45 minutes. Blend confectioners' sugar with a small amount of milk. Drizzle over warm cake. Cut into squares. Yield: 2 dozen.

Nancy Finck, Vermont

CHOCOLATE-COVERED CHERRIES

1 lb. dark chocolate
2 to 3 tbsp. melted paraffin
1 16-oz. package
    confectioners' sugar
2 tbsp. evaporated milk
1 tsp. vanilla extract
1 lg. jar maraschino
    cherries with stems, drained

Melt chocolate in double boiler. Blend in paraffin. Mix confectioners' sugar, evaporated milk and vanilla in bowl. Shape by spoonfuls into balls around cherries. Dip into chocolate to coat. Place in paper bonbon cups.
Yield: 5 dozen.

Marian Hart, Arizona

CHESS

CHESS CAKE

1 2-layer pkg. butter recipe
    yellow cake mix
½ c. melted margarine
4 eggs
8 oz. cream cheese, softened
1 16-oz. package
    confectioners' sugar
1 tsp. vanilla extract

Combine cake mix, margarine and 1 egg in bowl; mix well. Press into 9x13-inch baking pan. Combine remaining 3 eggs, cream cheese, confectioners' sugar and vanilla in bowl; beat until creamy. Pour into prepared pan. Bake at 350 degrees for 35 to 40 minutes or until lightly browned. Yield: 20 servings.

Kim Neitch, Virginia

CHOCOLATE CHESS PIE

1 c. sugar
3 tbsp. cornmeal
3 tbsp. baking cocoa
3 eggs, well beaten
½ c. melted margarine
½ c. light corn syrup
1 tsp. vanilla extract
1 unbaked 9-in. pie shell

Mix sugar, cornmeal and cocoa in bowl. Combine eggs, margarine, corn syrup and vanilla in bowl; mix well. Add to sugar mixture; mix until smooth. Pour into pie shell. Bake at 350 degrees for 45 minutes or until set.
Yield: 8 servings.

Joanne Varner, Wyoming

Chess pies freeze well for up to 3 months. Freeze pies, unwrapped, until almost firm. Then wrap well in moisture-proof paper.

LEMON CHESS PIE

2 c. sugar
4 eggs, beaten
1 tbsp. flour
1 tbsp. cornmeal
¼ c. milk
¼ c. melted butter
¼ c. lemon juice
3 tbsp. grated lemon rind
1 unbaked 9-in. pie shell

Beat sugar, eggs, flour and cornmeal in bowl until blended. Add next 4 ingredients; mix well. Pour into pie shell. Bake at 400 degrees for 10 minutes. Reduce temperature to 300 degrees. Bake for 30 minutes longer or until set. Yield: 8 servings.

OLD-FASHIONED CHESS PIE

2 c. sugar
2 tbsp. (heaping) flour
1 tbsp. (heaping) cornmeal
½ c. melted butter
3 eggs, beaten
½ c. buttermilk
2 tsp. vanilla extract
1 unbaked 10-in. pie shell

Mix sugar, flour and cornmeal in bowl. Stir in butter, eggs, buttermilk and vanilla; mix well. Pour into pie shell. Bake at 425 degrees for 10 minutes. Reduce temperature to 325 degrees. Bake for 30 minutes longer or until set. Yield: 8 servings.

Jean Ellington, Oklahoma

CHESS TARTLETS

¾ c. butter, softened
2 c. sugar
6 eggs
1 tbsp. cream
2 tbsp. cornmeal
1 tbsp. vanilla extract
1 tbsp. vinegar
12 unbaked 3-in. tart shells

Cream butter and sugar in bowl. Add eggs 1 at a time, beating well after each addition. Add next 4 ingredients; mix well. Spoon into tart shells. Bake at 350 degrees until set. Yield: 1 dozen.

Melinda Pitts, Arizona

CHOCOLATE

TRI-CHOCOLATE BAVARIAN

1 tbsp. unflavored gelatin
5 egg yolks
½ c. sugar
1 c. half and half, scalded
3 oz. white chocolate, grated
3 oz. semisweet chocolate, grated
3 oz. milk chocolate, grated
1¾ c. whipping cream

Soften gelatin in ¼ cup cold water. Beat egg yolks and sugar in mixer bowl until mixture is very light and thick. Whisk in hot half and half. Pour into non-aluminum saucepan. Cook over low heat for 8 to 10 minutes or until mixture coats spoon, stirring constantly. Remove from heat; stir in gelatin until dissolved. Strain mixture if necessary. Divide into 3 portions. Stir 1 variety chocolate into each portion until melted. Chill, covered with plastic wrap, until thickened. Whip 1 cup whipping cream in bowl until soft peaks form. Fold half the whipped cream into white chocolate mixture. Pour into oiled 6-cup soufflé dish. Freeze, covered, for 10 minutes. Repeat with remaining whipped cream and milk chocolate mixture. Whip remaining cream in bowl. Fold into semisweet chocolate mixture. Pour over milk chocolate; smooth top. Chill, covered, overnight. Unmold onto serving plate. Spoon Bittersweet Chocolate Sauce onto dessert plates. Cut Bavarian into wedges. Serve on sauce. Yield: 8 servings.

Bittersweet Chocolate Sauce

½ c. sugar
2 oz. unsweetened chocolate
6 oz. bittersweet chocolate
¼ c. lightly salted butter, sliced
1 tbsp. Cognac

Mix 1 cup water and sugar in 1-quart non-aluminum saucepan. Bring to a simmer over low heat. Simmer, covered, for 5 minutes. Remove cover. Cool mixture to lukewarm. Melt unsweetened and bittersweet chocolate with butter in double boiler. Blend in sugar syrup and Cognac gradually. Keep warm until serving time. Do not refrigerate.

CHOCOLATE BREAD PUDDING

1½ oz. baking chocolate,
    chopped
3 c. milk
3 eggs, separated
⅓ c. plus 6 tbsp. sugar
¼ c. packed brown sugar
2½ tsp. vanilla extract
½ tsp. salt
2 to 2½ c. stale bread cubes
¼ tsp. cream of tartar

Combine chocolate and milk in saucepan. Cook over low heat until chocolate is melted, stirring constantly. Beat egg yolks slightly. Add ⅓ cup sugar, brown sugar, 2 teaspoons vanilla and salt; mix well. Stir chocolate mixture into egg yolk mixture. Arrange bread in buttered 8-inch square pan. Pour chocolate mixture over bread. Place in pan of hot water. Bake at 350 degrees for 1 hour or until set. Beat egg whites until frothy. Add cream of tartar and remaining 6 tablespoons sugar gradually, beating until stiff and glossy. Stir in remaining ½ teaspoon vanilla. Mound meringue over pudding. Bake for 10 minutes longer or until meringue is browned. Serve with cream. Yield: 8 servings.

Marie E. Dierks, Montana

TWO CHOCOLATE CHEESECAKE

3 tbsp. melted butter
1¼ c. chocolate wafer crumbs
24 oz. cream cheese, softened
12 oz. semisweet chocolate
    chips, melted
4 eggs, beaten
1   14-oz. can sweetened
    condensed milk
2 tsp. vanilla extract

Combine melted butter and crumbs in bowl; mix well. Press over bottom and side of buttered 9-inch springform pan. Chill. Beat cream cheese in mixer bowl until light and fluffy. Blend in melted chocolate, eggs, condensed milk and vanilla 1 at a time, beating well after each addition. Pour into prepared pan. Bake at 325 degrees for 1 hour or until set. Cool. Chill in refrigerator. Place on serving plate; remove side of pan. Yield: 12 servings.

CHOCOLATE CREAM PUFF FILLING

2 tbsp. flour
6 tbsp. sugar
Dash of salt
¾ c. milk
1 oz. baking chocolate, melted
1 tbsp. butter
1 tsp. vanilla extract
½ c. whipping cream, whipped
½ c. chopped walnuts
12 cream puffs
Chocolate syrup

Mix flour, sugar and salt in double boiler. Add milk and chocolate. Cook over hot water until thick, stirring constantly. Add butter and vanilla; cool. Fold in whipped cream and walnuts. Spoon into puffs. Drizzle syrup over top. Yield: 1 dozen.

Frances Grimes, Oklahoma

DOUBLE CHOCOLATE ICE CREAM

3 eggs, beaten
2   12-oz. cans evaporated
    milk
3 c. sugar
3 c. whipping cream
1 can chocolate syrup
1   6-oz. package chocolate
    instant pudding mix
2½ c. milk
Dash of salt
2 tbsp. vanilla extract
1 c. chopped pecans
Milk

Combine first 3 ingredients in large bowl; mix well. Add cream and chocolate syrup. Combine pudding mix with 2½ cups milk in bowl. Add to cream mixture. Add salt, vanilla and pecans; mix well. Pour into 1½-gallon ice cream freezer container. Add milk to within 4 inches of top of container. Freeze using manufacturer's directions. Yield: 12 servings.

Sue Pew, Arizona

To melt chocolate, bring water to a simmer in bottom of double boiler and remove from heat. Place chocolate in top of double boiler over heated water and stir with rubber spatula until melted.

BROWNIE FUDGE PUDDING

1 **17-oz. package brownie mix**
½ **c. chopped pecans**
¾ **c. packed brown sugar**
¾ **c. sugar**
⅓ **c. baking cocoa**
1¼ **c. cold coffee**

Prepare brownie mix using package directions for cake-type brownies. Stir in pecans. Pour into greased 9x13-inch baking pan. Mix brown sugar, sugar and cocoa in bowl. Sprinkle over brownie mixture. Drizzle coffee over top. Bake using package directions. Serve warm with ice cream. Yield: 12 servings.

Michelle Epps, Texas

HOT FUDGE SAUCE

2 **oz. semisweet chocolate**
2 **tbsp. unsalted butter**
¼ **c. corn syrup**
1 **c. sugar**
⅛ **tsp. salt**
1 **tsp. vanilla extract**
6 **oz. semisweet chocolate chips**

Combine chocolate, butter and ⅓ cup water in heavy saucepan. Cook over low heat until chocolate has melted, stirring constantly. Stir in corn syrup, sugar and salt. Cook over low heat for 10 minutes or until smooth. Remove from heat. Stir in vanilla. Stir in chocolate chips. Serve over ice cream.

CHOCOLATE MERINGUE TORTE

12 **egg whites**
½ **tsp. cream of tartar**
¾ **c. sugar**
1¾ **c. confectioners' sugar**
⅓ **c. baking cocoa**
13 **oz. semisweet chocolate, melted**
24 **oz. whipping cream**
1½ **tsp. vanilla extract**

Beat 5 egg whites and ¼ teaspoon cream of tartar until soft peaks form. Add sugar gradually, beating constantly until stiff peaks form. Sift confectioners' sugar and cocoa together. Fold gently into egg whites. Shape into three 8-inch squares on parchment-lined baking sheet. Bake at 300 degrees for 1 hour. Cool on wire rack. Beat remaining 7 egg whites and ¼ teaspoon cream of tartar until stiff peaks form. Fold in chocolate. Whip cream with vanilla in bowl until soft peaks form. Fold gently into egg whites. Spread ⅔ of the chocolate mousse between meringues. Place on serving plate. Pipe remaining mousse on torte. Chill, loosely covered, for 4 hours or longer. Yield: 9 servings.

Nancy Van Ogtrop, Virginia

CHOCOLATE-FILLED ANGEL CAKE

1 **pkg. angel food cake mix**
2 **tbsp. sugar**
1½ **c. semisweet chocolate chips**
4 **eggs, separated**
1 **tsp. vanilla extract**
2 **c. whipping cream, whipped**

Prepare and bake cake mix using package directions. Invert on funnel to cool completely. Combine sugar, chocolate chips and 2 tablespoons water in double boiler. Heat until chocolate melts, stirring to blend well. Stir a small amount of chocolate mixture into beaten egg yolks. Stir egg yolks into chocolate mixture. Cook for 2 minutes, stirring constantly; cool. Fold in stiffly beaten egg whites and vanilla. Loosen cake from side of pan. Invert onto cake plate. Slice top ⅓ from cake. Scoop out center evenly to within 1 inch of side and bottom. Combine cake pieces and chocolate mixture; spoon into cake. Replace top layer. Flavor whipped cream as desired. Spread over cake. Chill for several hours. Yield: 16 servings.

Nancy Youden, Maryland

CHOCOLATE WALNUT TORTE

12 **eggs, separated**
1½ **c. sugar**
¼ **c. baking cocoa**
1 **c. ground walnuts**
½ **tsp. vanilla extract**

Combine egg yolks, sugar and cocoa in mixer bowl. Beat for 10 minutes. Add walnuts and vanilla; mix well. Beat egg whites until stiff peaks form. Fold gently into egg yolk mixture. Spoon into 3 greased and floured 9-inch round baking pans. Bake at 325 degrees for 1 hour. Invert pans onto wire rack to cool. Loosen layers from baking pans with spatula. Spread Chocolate Filling between layers and over top and side of torte. Sprinkle with additional chopped walnuts. Yield: 16 servings.

Chocolate Filling

1 *c. unsalted butter, softened*
8 *oz. milk chocolate, melted*
½ *c. sugar*
2 *eggs*

Combine butter, chocolate and sugar in mixer bowl; mix well. Add eggs. Beat until of spreading consistency. Spread between layers and on top of torte.

Jean Worley, Kentucky

DEVIL'S FOOD CAKE

1 *c. butter, softened*
6 *oz. baking chocolate, melted*
2 *c. sugar*
5 *eggs, separated*
½ *c. packed light brown sugar*
1 *tsp. soda*
1 *c. buttermilk*
1 *tbsp. vanilla extract*
3 *c. cake flour*
1 *tsp. baking powder*
¼ *tsp. salt*

Cream butter and chocolate in mixer bowl until light. Add sugar gradually, beating until fluffy. Add beaten egg yolks and brown sugar; mix well. Dissolve soda in ½ cup water. Combine with buttermilk and vanilla in small bowl. Add sifted dry ingredients alternately with buttermilk mixture, mixing well after each addition. Fold in stiffly beaten egg whites. Pour into 3 greased and floured 9-inch cake pans. Bake at 350 degrees for 30 to 35 minutes or until cake tests done. Remove to wire rack to cool. Frost as desired. Yield: 16 servings.

Sallie Hyde, Michigan

GERMAN CHOCOLATE CAKE

1 *oz. sweet baking chocolate*
1 *c. butter or margarine,*
   softened
2 *c. sugar*
4 *eggs, separated*
1 *tsp. vanilla extract*
2½ *c. sifted cake flour*
1 *tsp. soda*
Pinch of salt
1 *c. buttermilk*

Melt chocolate with ½ cup water in double boiler. Cool. Line 3 greased 8-inch cake pans with waxed paper. Cream butter and sugar in mixer bowl until light and fluffy. Add egg yolks 1 at a time, mixing well after each addition. Stir in chocolate mixture and vanilla. Add sifted dry ingredients alternately with buttermilk, mixing well after each addition. Fold in stiffly beaten egg whites. Spoon into prepared pans. Bake at 350 degrees for 30 to 40 minutes or until cake tests done. Remove to wire rack to cool. Spread Coconut-Pecan Frosting between layers and over top and side of cake. Yield: 16 servings.

Coconut-Pecan Frosting

1 *c. evaporated milk*
1 *c. sugar*
3 *egg yolks*
½ *c. margarine*
1 *tsp. vanilla extract*
1⅓ *c. coconut*
1 *c. chopped pecans*

Combine evaporated milk, sugar, egg yolks, margarine and vanilla in saucepan. Cook over medium heat for 12 minutes or until thickened, stirring constantly. Stir in coconut and pecans. Beat until cool and of spreading consistency.

Lynelle Sykes, South Carolina

Keep the serving plate clean while frosting a cake by placing strips of waxed paper over edge of plate. Place cake on these strips. Remove carefully after frosting.

CHOCOLATE UPSIDE-DOWN CAKE

1 *c. chopped pecans*
1 *c. coconut*
1 *2-layer pkg. German chocolate cake mix*
1 *c. melted margarine*
8 *oz. cream cheese, softened*
1 *16-oz. package confectioners' sugar*

Sprinkle pecans and coconut in buttered 9x13-inch cake pan. Prepare cake mix according to package directions. Spoon into prepared pan. Combine remaining ingredients in mixer bowl; beat until smooth. Spoon evenly over cake, leaving 1-inch edge. Bake at 350 degrees for 50 minutes. Cream cheese mixture will sink to bottom during baking to form frosting. Cool in pan. Cut into squares. Invert squares onto serving plates.
Yield: 16 servings.

Suegenia Tolbird, Kentucky

CHOCOLATE MERINGUE PIE

2 *oz. baking chocolate*
2½ *c. milk*
1 *c. sugar*
6 *tbsp. flour*
½ *tsp. salt*
3 *eggs, separated*
2 *tbsp. butter*
1 *tsp. vanilla extract*
1 *baked 9-in. pie shell*

Melt chocolate with milk in double boiler over boiling water; blend well. Mix ¾ cup sugar, flour and salt in bowl. Add to chocolate mixture; mix well. Cook until thickened, stirring constantly. Cook over low heat for 8 minutes longer, stirring frequently. Stir a small amount of hot mixture into beaten egg yolks; stir egg yolks into hot mixture. Cook for 2 minutes or until thickened, stirring constantly; remove from heat. Blend in butter and vanilla. Let stand, covered, until cool. Spoon into pie shell. Beat egg whites until foamy. Add remaining ¼ cup sugar gradually, beating until stiff peaks form. Spoon over filling. Bake at 350 degrees for 15 minutes or until light brown.
Yield: 6 to 8 servings.

CHOCOLATE CAKE ROLL

3 *eggs*
1 *c. sugar*
1 *tsp. vanilla extract*
1 *c. sifted flour*
1 *tsp. baking powder*
¼ *c. baking cocoa*
¼ *tsp. salt*
Confectioners' sugar
1 *c. whipped cream*
1 *oz. baking chocolate*
1 *tsp. butter*

Beat eggs in mixer bowl until thick. Add sugar gradually, beating until lemon-colored. Blend in ⅓ cup water and vanilla. Add sifted mixture of flour, baking powder, cocoa and salt; mix well. Pour into waxed paper-lined 10x15-inch pan. Bake at 375 degrees for 12 to 15 minutes or until cake tests done. Loosen edges with knife. Invert onto towel sprinkled with confectioners' sugar. Roll cake in towel; cool. Unroll cake. Spread with whipped cream. Roll as for jelly roll. Chill in refrigerator. Melt chocolate and butter in double boiler; mix well. Add 1 cup confectioners' sugar and 2 tablespoons boiling water; beat until cool and smooth. Spread on cake roll. Store in refrigerator.
Yield: 12 servings.

HUNDRED-DOLLAR BROWNIES

¾ *c. butter*
5 *sq. baking chocolate*
2 *c. sugar*
5 *eggs*
1 *c. sifted flour*
½ *tsp. salt*
2½ *tsp. vanilla extract*
2¼ *c. confectioners' sugar*
1½ *tsp. lemon juice*
1 *c. chopped pecans*

Melt ½ cup butter and 4 squares chocolate over low heat in heavy saucepan. Cool. Stir in sugar. Add 4 eggs 1 at a time, mixing well after each addition. Add flour, salt and 1 teaspoon vanilla; mix well. Pour into greased and floured 10x15-inch baking pan. Bake at 350 degrees for 20 minutes or just until firm. Do not overbake. Melt remaining ¼ cup butter and 1 square chocolate over low heat in heavy saucepan. Stir in confectioners' sugar, blending well. Remove from heat. Add remaining egg; beat well. Add remaining 1½ teaspoons vanilla and lemon juice; mix well. Stir in pecans. Add enough additional confectioners' sugar to make of spreading consistency. Spread frosting over warm brownies. Cool. Cut into squares. Yield: 5 dozen.

Helen Exum, Tennessee

SUPER COOKIES

    2 c. butter, softened
    2 c. sugar
    2 c. packed brown sugar
    5 c. oats
    4 c. flour
    1 tsp. salt
    2 tsp. baking powder
    2 tsp. soda
    24 oz. semisweet chocolate
      chips
    3 c. chopped pecans

Cream butter and sugars in bowl until light and fluffy. Process mixture of oats and flour, a small amount at a time, in blender until pulverized. Combine with salt, baking powder and soda. Add to creamed mixture; mix well. Stir in chocolate chips and pecans. Shape into golf ball-sized cookies. Place 2 inches apart on ungreased cookie sheet. Bake at 375 degrees for 6 minutes. Cool on wire rack. Yield: 9 dozen.

Doris Ann Love, Illinois

FANTASY FUDGE

    3 c. sugar
    ¾ c. margarine
    ⅔ c. evaporated milk
    1 c. chopped nuts
    12 oz. semisweet chocolate
      chips
    1   7-oz. jar marshmallow
      creme
    1 tsp. vanilla extract

Combine sugar, margarine and evaporated milk in saucepan. Bring to the boiling point, stirring constantly to dissolve sugar completely. Cook, covered, for 2 to 3 minutes or until steam washed sugar crystals from side of pan. Cook, uncovered, over medium heat for

5 minutes. Remove from heat. Add remaining ingredients. Beat until mixture thickens and loses its luster. Pour into buttered 9x13-inch dish. Let stand until firm. Cut into squares. Yield: 3½ pounds.

Kim Rubbino, Florida

CHOCOLATE TRUFFLES

    ½ c. whipping cream
    ⅓ c. sugar
    6 tbsp. butter
    12 oz. miniature chocolate
      chips
    1 tsp. vanilla extract
    1 tbsp. shortening
    Finely chopped nuts
    Shaved chocolate
    Confectioners' sugar

Combine whipping cream, sugar and butter in saucepan. Bring to a boil; remove from heat. Add 1 cup chocolate chips immediately; stir until chips are melted. Add vanilla. Pour into bowl. Let stand until cool; stir occasionally. Chill, covered, for several hours. Melt remaining chocolate chips and shortening in saucepan. Shape chilled mixture into ½-inch balls. Roll in chopped nuts, shaved chocolate or confectioners' sugar or coat with melted chocolate. Yield: 3 dozen.

Barbara Grimes, Illinois

COCONUT

BLENDER COCONUT CUSTARD

    2 c. milk
    ½ c. honey
    1 c. coconut
    4 eggs
    ½ c. flour
    6 tbsp. butter
    ¼ tsp. salt
    1 tsp. vanilla extract

Combine all ingredients in blender container. Process until smooth. Pour into greased and lightly floured 9-inch pie plate. Bake at 325 degrees for 45 minutes. Yield: 6 servings.

Mary I. Grafton, Ohio

COCONUT SAUCE

1 *can sweetened condensed*
  milk
2 *egg yolks, beaten*
¼ *c. margarine*
½ *c. flaked coconut*
½ *c. chopped pecans*
1 *tsp. vanilla extract*

Combine sweetened condensed milk, egg yolks and margarine in 1-quart glass measure. Microwave on Medium-High for 3 minutes; stir. Microwave for 1 to 2 minutes longer. Stir in remaining ingredients. Serve warm over ice cream or cake. Yield: 2 cups.

FROZEN COCONUT SURPRISE

2 *c. sour cream*
1 *3-oz. package vanilla*
   instant pudding mix
1⅓ *c. shredded coconut*
1 *7-oz. can crushed pineapple*
½ *c. chopped maraschino*
   cherries

Mix sour cream with pudding mix in bowl. Add coconut, pineapple and cherries; mix well. Spoon into loaf pan. Freeze for 3 hours or until firm. Slice and serve. Yield: 12 servings.

Jo Anne M. Stringer, Ohio

COCONUT CAKE

1 *2-layer pkg. yellow cake mix*
1 *3-oz. package vanilla*
   instant pudding mix
4 *eggs*
¼ *c. oil*
4 *c. coconut*
1 *c. chopped walnuts*
¼ *c. butter*
8 *oz. cream cheese, softened*
3½ *c. sifted confectioners'*
   sugar
2 *tsp. milk*
½ *tsp. vanilla extract*

Combine cake mix, pudding mix, eggs, oil and 1⅓ cups water in mixer bowl. Beat at medium speed for 4 minutes. Stir in 2 cups coconut and walnuts. Spoon into 3 greased and floured 8-inch cake pans. Bake at 350

degrees for 35 minutes. Cool in pans for 15 minutes. Remove to wire rack to cool completely. Melt 2 tablespoons butter in skillet. Add 2 cups coconut. Cook over low heat until golden brown, stirring constantly. Spread on paper towel. Cool. Cream remaining 2 tablespoons butter and cream cheese in mixer bowl until light. Add confectioners' sugar alternately with milk, mixing well after each addition. Stir in vanilla and 1¾ cups toasted coconut. Spread between layers and over top and side of cake. Sprinkle with remaining toasted coconut. Yield: 16 servings.

Norma Jean McDonald, Kentucky

ITALIAN COCONUT CREAM CAKE

½ *c. shortening*
½ *c. margarine, softened*
2 *c. sugar*
2 *tbsp. vanilla extract*
5 *eggs, separated*
2 *c. flour*
1 *tsp. soda*
½ *tsp. salt*
1 *c. buttermilk*
2 *c. coconut*
1 *c. chopped pecans*
¼ *c. margarine, softened*
8 *oz. cream cheese, softened*
1 *16-oz. package*
   confectioners' sugar

Cream first 3 ingredients and 1 tablespoon vanilla in bowl until fluffy. Beat in egg yolks 1 at a time. Add mixture of flour, soda and salt alternately with buttermilk, mixing well after each addition. Stir in coconut and pecans. Fold in stiffly beaten egg whites gently. Pour into 3 greased and floured 9-inch cake pans. Bake at 350 degrees for 30 to 40 minutes or until cake tests done. Cool in pans for 10 minutes. Remove to wire rack to cool completely. Cream ¼ cup margarine, cream cheese and remaining 1 tablespoon vanilla in bowl until light. Add confectioners' sugar, beat until smooth. Spread between layers and over top and side of cake. Garnish with additional coconut. Yield: 15 servings.

Amy Stitt, Oregon

CHOCOLATE-COCONUT CAKE

½ c. shortening
3 oz. baking chocolate, melted
1¾ c. cake flour
1¼ c. sugar
¼ tsp. baking powder
¾ tsp. each soda, salt
¼ tbsp. cloves
1 c. buttermilk
1 tsp. vanilla extract
2 eggs
1 c. coconut

Cream shortening with melted chocolate in mixer bowl until light and fluffy. Combine dry ingredients in bowl. Add to creamed mixture alternately with buttermilk and vanilla, mixing well after each addition. Beat in eggs 1 at a time. Stir in coconut. Pour into 2 greased and floured 9-inch cake pans. Bake at 350 degrees for 30 minutes. Remove to wire rack to cool. Frost with fluffy white frosting and garnish with additional coconut. Yield: 16 servings.

COCONUT CREAM PIE

1 c. plus 6 tbsp. sugar
¼ c. cornstarch
¼ tsp. salt
2 c. milk
3 eggs, separated
1 tbsp. butter
1 3½-oz. can coconut
¼ tsp. coconut extract
1 baked 9-in. pie shell
¼ tsp. cream of tartar

Combine 1 cup sugar, cornstarch, salt and milk in double boiler. Cook over boiling water until thickened, stirring constantly. Stir a small amount of hot mixture into beaten egg yolks; stir egg yolks into hot mixture. Cook for 4 minutes longer, stirring constantly. Remove from heat. Add butter, coconut and coconut flavoring. Pour into pie shell. Beat egg whites and cream of tartar in mixer bowl until soft peaks form. Add remaining 6 tablespoons sugar gradually, beating until stiff peaks form. Spread over coconut filling, sealing to crust. Bake at 350 degrees for 15 minutes or until golden.
Yield: 6 servings.

Mae Flanery, Kentucky

IMPOSSIBLE COCONUT PIE

4 eggs, beaten
2 c. milk
1 tsp. vanilla extract
½ c. flour
Pinch of salt
½ c. margarine, softened
⅔ c. sugar
1 c. flaked coconut
1 tsp. baking powder

Combine all ingredients in blender container; process for 1 minute. Pour into greased 10-inch pie plate. Bake at 350 degrees for 45 minutes or until golden brown and set. Yield: 8 servings.

Catherine Athanasion, New Hampshire

GRANDMA'S COCONUT COOKIES

½ c. butter, softened
1 c. packed brown sugar
1 egg
1 c. whole wheat flour
½ tsp. baking powder
½ tsp. soda
¼ tsp. salt
1 c. quick-cooking oats
1 c. flaked coconut
1 c. chopped nuts

Cream butter and brown sugar in mixer bowl until light and fluffy. Add egg; mix well. Add mixture of flour, baking powder, soda and salt; mix well. Stir in remaining ingredients. Drop by teaspoonfuls 2 to 3 inches apart onto lightly greased cookie sheet. Bake at 375 degrees for 6 to 8 minutes or until brown. Cool on cookie sheet for 1 minute. Remove to wire rack to cool completely. Yield: 6 dozen.

Bobbi Jo Wendel, Pennsylvania

For fresh coconut, select a coconut that feels heavy and sounds full of liquid when shaken. Puncture the eyes with an ice pick and hammer. Drain juice and reserve for future use. Crack shell with hammer. Pry out meat in pieces with sharp knife. Peel off brown skin. Shred meat with coarse grater.

COCONUT MACAROONS

2 egg whites
½ tsp. vanilla extract
¾ c. sugar
2 c. cornflakes
½ c. chopped nuts
¾ c. shredded coconut

Beat egg whites and vanilla in mixer bowl until frothy. Add sugar gradually, beating constantly until stiff peaks form. Fold in cornflakes, nuts and coconut gently. Drop by tablespoonfuls onto well-greased cookie sheet. Bake at 350 degrees for 12 minutes. Remove to wire rack immediately. Yield: 3 dozen.

ROYAL COCONUT COOKIES

1¼ c. sifted flour
1 tsp. baking powder
1 tsp. soda
½ tsp. salt
½ c. sugar
½ c. packed brown sugar
½ c. margarine, softened
1 egg
½ tsp. vanilla extract
1 c. oats
1 c. coconut

Sift flour, baking powder, soda and salt together into bowl. Add sugar, brown sugar, margarine, egg and vanilla. Beat for 2 minutes or until smooth. Stir in oats and coconut. Shape into small balls; place on greased cookie sheets. Bake at 350 degrees for 12 to 15 minutes or until brown. Cool on wire rack. Yield: 3 dozen.

Misty Lyons, Indiana

COCONUT SQUARES

6 tbsp. butter, softened
¼ c. sugar
¾ tsp. salt
1 c. plus 2 tbsp. flour
2 eggs, slightly beaten
1 tsp. vanilla extract
1 c. packed brown sugar
1 c. flaked coconut
½ c. chopped walnuts

Cream butter, sugar and ¼ teaspoon salt in mixer bowl. Add 1 cup flour; mix well. Press into 9x9-inch pan. Bake at 350 degrees for 15 minutes. Mix eggs and vanilla in bowl. Beat in brown sugar, remaining 2 tablespoons flour and ½ teaspoon salt gradually. Stir in coconut and walnuts. Spread over baked layer. Bake at 350 degrees for 20 minutes or until toothpick inserted in center comes out clean. Cut into squares when cool. Yield: 1½ dozen.

Brooke Lawson, Indiana

COCONUT POTATO CANDY

¾ c. cold mashed potatoes
4 c. confectioners' sugar
4 c. shredded coconut
1½ tsp. vanilla extract
½ tsp. salt
8 oz. baking chocolate, melted

Combine mashed potatoes and confectioners' sugar in bowl. Add coconut, vanilla and salt; mix well. Press into ½-inch layer in large pan. Spread melted chocolate over top. Cool. Cut into squares. Yield: 3 dozen.

Nicky Peters, Georgia

CRANBERRY

CRANBERRY CHEESECAKE

1½ c. graham cracker crumbs
2¾ c. sugar
½ tsp. cinnamon
⅓ c. melted butter
24 oz. cream cheese, softened
5 eggs
¼ tsp. salt
1 tsp. vanilla extract
1 tbsp. cornstarch
1½ c. cranberries, rinsed,
    drained

Combine cracker crumbs, ¾ cup sugar and cinnamon in bowl. Add butter; mix well. Press over bottom of springform pan. Beat cream cheese and 1 cup sugar in bowl until light and fluffy. Add eggs 1 at a time, beating well after each addition. Blend in salt and vanilla. Pour into prepared pan. Bake at 350 degrees for 45 minutes or until firm. Cool in oven. Chill in refrigerator. Combine cornstarch, cranberries, remaining 1 cup sugar and ½ cup water in saucepan. Cook over low heat until thickened, stirring constantly. Simmer for 2 minutes longer. Cool. Spread over cheesecake. Chill until serving time. Yield: 12 servings.

Tracy Mills, Ohio

CRANBERRY CHIFFON MOLD

8 c. cranberries
1 6-oz. package orange gelatin
3 eggs, separated
¾ c. sugar
¼ tsp. salt

Cook cranberries in 1 cup water in saucepan until cranberries pop. Force through strainer. Dissolve gelatin in ¾ cup boiling water. Beat egg yolks until light. Beat in ¼ cup sugar. Add hot gelatin gradually, beating constantly. Stir in salt and cranberries. Chill until partially set, stirring occasionally. Beat egg whites until foamy. Add remaining ½ cup sugar gradually, beating constantly until soft peaks form. Fold into gelatin mixture, leaving marbleized effect. Spoon into 1½-quart mold. Chill until firm. Unmold on serving plate. Yield: 6 to 8 servings.

Neva Montgomery, Ohio

CRANBERRY-APPLE CRISP

3 c. apple slices
2 c. whole cranberries
2 tbsp. honey
1 c. oats
½ c. whole wheat flour
¾ c. packed brown sugar
½ c. butter
½ c. chopped nuts
½ tsp. vanilla extract

Combine apple slices and cranberries in bowl. Drizzle with honey. Toss lightly to coat. Combine oats, flour and brown sugar in bowl. Cut in butter until crumbly. Stir in nuts and vanilla. Place apples and cranberries in greased 7x11-inch baking dish. Top with oats mixture. Bake at 350 degrees for 50 minutes or until browned and bubbly. Serve warm or cool with whipped cream. Yield: 6 to 8 servings.

CRANBERRY FREEZE

⅔ c. graham cracker crumbs
2 tbsp. sugar
¼ c. melted butter
8 oz. cream cheese, softened
¼ c. sugar
1 pt. vanilla ice cream, softened
1 16-oz. can whole cranberry
   sauce

Combine graham cracker crumbs, 2 tablespoons sugar and butter in bowl; mix well. Press into bottom of 8-inch springform pan. Beat cream cheese with ¼ cup sugar in bowl until fluffy. Add ice cream by tablespoonfuls, beating to blend quickly. Pour over crust. Stir cranberry sauce with fork. Drop by spoonfuls over ice cream mixture. Freeze, covered, for 4 hours or until firm. Yield: 8 servings.

Jessica Winkler, Michigan

CRANBERRY CAKE

2½ c. flour
1 tsp. salt
1 tsp. baking powder
1 tsp. soda
1½ c. sugar
1 c. chopped dates
1 c. whole cranberries
1 c. chopped pecans
2 eggs
1 c. buttermilk
¾ c. oil
½ c. orange juice

Sift first 4 ingredients and 1 cup sugar into bowl. Stir in dates, cranberries and pecans; make well in mixture. Place eggs, buttermilk and oil in well; mix well. Pour into ungreased tube pan. Bake at 325 degrees for 1 hour. Mix remaining ½ cup sugar with orange juice. Pour over hot cake in pan. Cool completely before removing from pan. Yield: 12 servings.

CRANBERRY RIPPLE CAKE

½ c. butter, softened
1 c. sugar
½ tsp. almond extract
2 eggs
2 c. flour
1 tsp. baking powder
1 tsp. soda
8 oz. sour cream
1 8-oz. can whole
   cranberry sauce
½ c. chopped pecans

Beat butter, sugar and almond flavoring in large mixer bowl until fluffy. Add eggs 1 at a time, beating well after each addition. Add mixture of dry ingredients alternately with sour cream, beating well after each addition. Spread half the batter in greased and floured tube pan. Spoon half the cranberry sauce over batter. Spread remaining batter to cover sauce. Top with remaining sauce and pecans. Bake at 350 degrees for 40 to 50 minutes or until cake tests done. Cool in pan for 10 minutes before removing to wire rack to cool completely. Yield: 16 servings.

Wendy Thomas, Indiana

CRANBERRY ICE CREAM PIE

1 c. oats
½ c. packed brown sugar
½ c. coconut
⅓ c. melted butter
1 qt. vanilla ice cream, softened
2 c. fresh cranberries
1 c. sugar

Spread oats in shallow pan. Bake at 350 degrees for 10 minutes. Combine with brown sugar, coconut and butter in bowl; mix well. Press over bottom and side of 9-inch pie pan. Chill. Spoon ice cream into crust. Cover with aluminum foil; freeze until firm. Cook cranberries in ½ cup water in saucepan until cranberries pop. Stir in sugar until dissolved. Cool for 10 minutes or until mixture thickens. Cool. Spread over ice cream. Serve immediately or freeze until serving time. Yield: 6 to 8 servings.

Marilyn J. Ziegler, Indiana

CRANBERRY CHEWS

4 eggs, beaten
2 c. sugar
Juice of 1 lemon
½ tsp. lemon extract
½ tsp. almond extract
3 c. flour
1 tbsp. baking powder
½ tsp. salt
1 16-oz. can jellied
   cranberry sauce
1½ c. chopped pecans
3 c. confectioners' sugar
6 to 8 tbsp. milk
¼ c. butter, softened
1 tsp. vanilla extract

Beat eggs and sugar in mixer bowl until thick and smooth. Blend in lemon juice, lemon extract and almond extract. Add sifted flour, baking powder and salt; mix well. Chop cranberry sauce into ¼-inch cubes. Fold cranberry cubes and pecans into batter. Spread in 2 greased 10x15-inch baking pans. Bake at 350 degrees for 30 minutes. Combine confectioners' sugar and remaining ingredients in bowl; mix until smooth and creamy. Spread on warm cranberry layer. Cut into squares while warm. Yield: 6 to 7 dozen.

Violet R. Nolfi, California

CRANBERRY CRUNCH SQUARES

1 c. quick-cooking oats
½ c. flour
¾ c. packed brown sugar
½ c. coconut
⅓ c. margarine
1 16-oz. can whole
   cranberry sauce
1 tbsp. lemon juice

Combine oats, flour, brown sugar and coconut in bowl. Cut in margarine until crumbly. Press half the mixture into greaed 8x8-inch baking pan. Mix cranberry sauce and lemon juice in bowl. Spread over crumb layer. Top with remaining crumbs. Bake at 350 degrees for 30 to 40 minutes or until brown. Cut into squares. Serve with whipped cream or ice cream. Yield: 9 servings.

Mildred Anderson, Ohio

CRANBERRY FUDGE

2 c. sugar
¼ c. light corn syrup
1⅓ c. milk
⅓ c. light cream
1 tsp. vanilla extract
1 tbsp. butter
1¼ c. coarsely chopped pecans
1 c. cranberries, coarsely
   chopped

Combine first 4 ingredients in large saucepan. Cook over medium heat until sugar dissolves, stirring constantly. Cook over medium-low heat to 238 degress on candy thermometer, soft-ball stage, stirring down only if necessary. Remove from heat. Add vanilla and butter; do not stir. Cool to lukewarm, 110 degrees; do not stir. Beat until thickened and mixture loses its luster. Stir in pecans and cranberries. Pour into 8-inch square dish. Let stand until firm. Cut into 1-inch squares. Yield: 2½ pounds.

CURRANT

CURRANT CHEESECAKE

1 c. butter or margarine
1½ c. flour
4 eggs
24 oz. cream cheese, softened
¾ c. sugar
1 tsp. vanilla extract
1 tsp. nutmeg
½ c. dried currants

Cut ½ cup butter into flour in bowl until crumbly. Add mixture of 1 egg and 1 tablespoon cold water. Mix with fork until mixture forms dough. Roll to 12-inch circle on floured surface. Fit into 9-inch springform pan. Line with foil; weight with dried beans. Bake at 400 degrees for 15 minutes. Remove and discard beans and foil liner. Cool. Cream remaining ½ cup softened butter and cream cheese in mixer bowl until fluffy. Blend in remaining 3 eggs, sugar, vanilla, nutmeg and currants. Bake at 350 degrees for 30 minutes. Turn off oven. Let cheesecake stand in oven for 30 minutes. Cool on wire rack. Place on serving plate; remove side of pan. Yield: 12 servings.

CURRANT CAKE

2 c. currants
2 c. sugar
4 c. flour
1 tsp. salt
2 tsp. soda
1 tsp. nutmeg
1 c. oil
2 tsp. vanilla extract
1½ c. chopped nuts

Combine currants with water to cover in saucepan. Cook over medium heat for 15 minutes; cool. Drain, reserving liquid. Add enough water to reserved liquid to measure 2 cups. Combine dry ingredients in bowl. Add oil, currant liquid and vanilla; mix well. Stir in currants and nuts. Pour into greased and floured 9x13-inch cake pan. Bake at 325 degrees for 1 hour or until cake tests done. Frost as desired.
Yield: 16 servings.

Robin Slocum, Rhode Island

CURRANT TARTLETS

4 eggs
½ c. melted butter
1 lb. brown sugar
2 tbsp. milk
1 tsp. vanilla extract
1　8-oz. package currants
1 c. chopped walnuts
24 unbaked tartlet shells

Combine eggs, butter, brown sugar, milk and vanilla in bowl; mix well. Stir in currants and walnuts. Place tart shells in ungreased muffin cups. Spoon currant mixture into shells. Bake at 375 degrees for 20 minutes or until golden brown. Cool on wire rack.
Yield: 2 dozen.

Janet Burns, Michigan

Fresh currants resemble gooseberries. Dried currants are usually used in desserts and are packaged like raisins. Plumping currants before baking enhances their appearance and flavor. To plump currants, soak in warm water or juice for 10 to 15 minutes. Drain well before using.

CURRANT COOKIES

4 c. flour
1½ c. sugar
1 tbsp. baking powder
¾ tsp. salt
1 tsp. nutmeg
1 c. shortening
¼ c. (about) milk
3 eggs, beaten
1 c. currants

Mix first 5 ingredients in bowl. Cut in shortening until crumbly. Add enough milk to eggs to measure 1 cup. Stir into flour mixture. Add currants; mix well. Chill in refrigerator. Roll on floured surface. Cut into circles. Bake on medium-hot griddle until brown on both sides. Cool on wire rack. Yield: 3 dozen.

Phyllis McNamara, Pennsylvania

DATE

DATE PUDDING

4 egg whites
¼ c. (heaping) sugar
3 tbsp. flour
Pinch of salt
1 tsp. baking powder
2 c. chopped dates
1 c. chopped nuts
1 tsp. vanilla extract

Beat egg whites in bowl until stiff peaks form. Add sugar gradually, beating until very stiff peaks form. Sift flour, salt and baking powder together into bowl. Fold gently into egg whites. Fold in remaining ingredients. Pour into greased 9x11-inch baking pan. Bake at 325 degrees for 1 hour or until set. Serve warm or cold. Yield: 6 to 8 servings.

Hazel Shelberg, Washington

DATE AND BREAD PUDDING

½ c. chopped dates
½ c. chopped nuts
½ c. flour
¼ tsp. salt
1 tsp. baking powder
¾ c. honey
2 eggs, beaten
½ c. whole wheat bread crumbs

Dust dates and nuts with a small amount of flour. Sift remaining flour with salt and baking powder. Add honey to eggs in a fine stream in bowl, beating constantly. Add crumbs, sifted dry ingredients, dates and nuts; mix well. Pour into greased 9-inch baking dish. Bake at 350 degrees for 20 minutes. Serve warm. Yield: 6 servings.

DATE AND CHOCOLATE CHIP CAKE

1 c. chopped dates
1 c. margarine, softened
1½ c. flour
3 tbsp. baking cocoa
1 tsp. soda
½ tsp. salt
2 eggs, slightly beaten
1 c. sugar
1 tsp. vanilla extract
½ c. chopped nuts
½ c. semisweet chocolate chips
1 c. packed brown sugar

Combine dates with 1 cup boiling water in bowl. Add margarine, flour, cocoa, soda and salt; mix well. Stir in eggs, sugar and vanilla. Pour into greased and floured 9x13-inch cake pan. Sprinkle with mixture of nuts, chocolate chips and brown sugar. Bake at 350 degrees for 40 minutes or until cake tests done. Cool in pan. Yield: 18 servings.

DATE PIE

2 tbsp. sesame seed, toasted
1 unbaked 9-in. pie shell
1 env. unflavored gelatin
2 eggs, separated
1 c. milk
5 tbsp. sugar
¼ tsp. salt
1 c. finely chopped dates
1 c. whipping cream
1 tsp. vanilla extract

Sprinkle sesame seed over pie shell; press in gently. Prick with fork. Bake at 425 degrees for 10 minutes or until light brown. Soften gelatin in ¼ cup cold water. Beat egg yolks in double boiler. Stir in milk, ¼ cup sugar and salt. Cook over hot water for 10 minutes, stirring constantly. Remove from heat. Add gelatin; mix well. Add dates. Chill until syrupy. Whip cream in bowl until soft

peaks form. Add vanilla. Stir into gelatin mixture. Beat egg whites with remaining 1 tablespoon sugar until stiff peaks form. Fold into gelatin mixture. Pour into pie shell. Chill.
Yield: 6 to 8 servings.

Margaret J. Williams, California

DATE CHIFFON PIE

1 *env. unflavored gelatin*
½ *c. sugar*
2 *eggs, separated*
½ *c. orange juice*
⅓ *c. lemon juice*
½ *c. light cream*
Pinch of salt
⅔ *c. chopped dates*
1 *baked 8-in. pie shell*

Mix gelatin and ¼ cup sugar in saucepan. Beat egg yolks, orange juice and lemon juice in bowl. Stir into gelatin mixture. Cook over low heat until gelatin dissolves and mixture thickens, stirring constantly. Cool. Stir in cream. Beat egg whites with salt until soft peaks form. Add remaining ¼ cup sugar; beat until stiff peaks form. Fold into custard. Fold in dates. Spoon into pie shell. Chill for 3 hours or longer.

Jamie Gore, Connecticut

DATE BARS

½ *c. melted butter*
1 *c. sugar*
2 *eggs, well beaten*
¾ *c. flour*
¼ *tsp. baking powder*
⅛ *tsp. salt*
1 *c. finely chopped nuts*
1 *c. finely chopped dates*
¼ *c. confectioners' sugar*

Blend butter, sugar and eggs in bowl. Sift flour with baking powder and salt. Add to egg mixture; mix well. Stir in nuts and dates. Spread in greased 8x10-inch baking pan. Bake at 350 degrees for 30 minutes. Cut into 2-inch bars. Sprinkle with confectioners' sugar while warm. Yield: 2 dozen.

Megan Rusk, Texas

DATE PINWHEELS

2½ *c. chopped dates*
2 *c. sugar*
1 *c. chopped nuts*
1 *c. shortening*
1 *c. packed brown sugar*
3 *eggs, beaten*
4 *c. flour*
1 *tsp. soda*
¾ *tsp. salt*

Simmer dates with 1 cup water and 1 cup sugar in saucepan until tender. Stir in nuts. Cool. Cream shortening, brown sugar and remaining 1 cup sugar in bowl until fluffy. Add eggs; mix well. Add mixture of flour, soda and salt; mix well. Divide into 4 portions. Roll each into 9x11-inch rectangle on floured surface. Spread with cooled date mixture. Roll as for jelly roll. Cut into 1-inch slices. Place on ungreased cookie sheet. Bake at 350 degrees for 10 to 12 minutes or until golden. Cool on wire rack.
Yield: 12 dozen.

STUFFED DATE DROPS

40 *pitted dates*
40 *walnut quarters*
6 *tbsp. butter, softened*
⅓ *c. packed light brown sugar*
1 *egg*
¾ *c. flour*
¼ *tsp. baking powder*
¼ *tsp. soda*
¼ *tsp. nutmeg*
¼ *c. sour cream*
1¼ *c. confectioners' sugar*
¼ *tsp. vanilla extract*

Stuff dates with walnuts. Cream 2 tablespoons softened butter and brown sugar in bowl until light. Beat in egg. Add mixture of flour, baking powder, soda and nutmeg alternately with sour cream. Fold in stuffed dates. Drop coated dates 1 at a time onto greased cookie sheet. Bake at 400 degrees for 8 to 10 minutes. Cool on wire rack. Heat remaining ¼ cup butter in saucepan until golden, stirring constantly. Remove from heat. Beat in confectioners' sugar, vanilla and enough water to make of spreading consistency. Frost cooled cookies. Yield: 3⅓ dozen.

EGGNOG

EGGNOG CUP

2 env. unflavored gelatin
¼ c. sugar
4 c. commercial eggnog
4 tsp. rum extract
2 c. whipped cream

Mix gelatin and sugar with 1 cup eggnog in double boiler. Let stand until gelatin is softened. Heat until gelatin and sugar are dissolved, stirring constantly. Remove from heat. Stir in remaining eggnog and flavoring. Chill until set. Beat until light and fluffy. Fold in whipped cream. Spoon into dessert dishes. Yield: 12 servings.

Nancy Tosetti, Illinois

EGGNOG FLUFF

2 env. unflavored gelatin
4 c. commercial eggnog
¼ tsp. orange bitters
2 tsp. grated orange rind
¼ tsp. cardamom
3 tbsp. Cointreau
2 c. whipped cream
1 6-oz. can frozen orange
   juice concentrate, thawed
1¼ c. sugar
2 tsp. cornstarch
4 c. cranberries

Soften gelatin in 2 cups eggnog in 1½-quart saucepan. Cook over low heat until gelatin is dissolved, stirring constantly. Add bitters, orange rind and cardamom dissolved in 1 tablespoon eggnog; mix well. Remove from heat. Stir in remaining eggnog and Cointreau. Chill until partially set. Fold in whipped cream. Spoon into 7-cup mold. Chill until set. Mix orange juice concentrate with enough water to measure 1 cup. Blend into mixture of sugar and cornstarch in saucepan. Stir in cranberries. Cook until thickened, stirring constantly. Simmer, covered, for 5 minutes, stirring occasionally. Chill. Unmold congealed mixture onto serving plate. Serve with cranberry sauce. Yield: 8 to 10 servings.

EGGNOG RING

1 sm. package lemon gelatin
¼ tsp. rum extract
¾ c. commercial eggnog
1 11-oz. can mandarin
   oranges
1 16-oz. can pears
1 sm. package cherry gelatin
1½ c. pecans

Dissolve lemon gelatin in 1 cup boiling water in bowl. Stir in ¼ cup cold water and flavoring. Reserve ½ cup mixture for second layer. Stir eggnog into remaining mixture. Pour into 6-cup ring mold. Chill until partially set. Drain fruit, reserving juices. Arrange orange sections around edge of mold, pressing into partially congealed eggnog mixture. Chop pears. Dissolve cherry gelatin in 1 cup boiling water in bowl. Stir in reserved juices and reserved lemon gelatin. Chill until partially set. Stir in pears. Spoon over eggnog mixture. Chill until set. Unmold onto serving plate. Fill center with pecans. Garnish with maraschino cherries. Yield: 10 servings.

Corinne Rivest, Alberta, Canada

EGGNOG CAKE

¾ c. butter, softened
2½ c. confectioners' sugar
4 egg yolks
1 tsp. almond extract
¼ c. milk
1 c. chopped toasted almonds
1 angel food cake
8 oz. whipping cream,
   whipped

Cream butter and confectioners' sugar in mixer bowl until light and fluffy. Add egg yolks 1 at a time, mixing well after each addition. Stir in almond flavoring, milk and ¾ cup almonds. Cut cake into 3 layers. Spread almond filling between layers. Chill cake, covered with waxed paper, 24 hours. Spread whipped cream over top and side of cake. Sprinkle remaining ¼ cup almonds over top. Garnish with chocolate curls. Chill until serving time. Yield: 16 servings.

Frances Harrison, Louisiana

EGGNOG CHIFFON PIE

1 env. unflavored gelatin
1½ c. milk
5 tbsp. plus ¼ c. sugar
½ tsp. salt
4 egg yolks, beaten
1 c. whipping cream
1 tsp. nutmeg
2 egg whites
2 tbsp. rum
2 tsp. vanilla extract
1 baked 10-in. pie shell

Soften gelatin in ¼ cup cold water. Combine milk, 5 tablespoons sugar and salt in double boiler. Heat over simmering water until scalded. Stir 3 tablespoons hot mixture into egg yolks; stir egg yolks into hot mixture. Cook until thick, stirring constantly. Stir in gelatin until dissolved. Chill until partially set. Beat whipping cream in bowl until soft peaks form. Beat remaining ¼ cup sugar and ½ teaspoon nutmeg gradually into softly beaten egg whites, beating until stiff. Fold whipped cream, egg whites, rum and vanilla into gelatin mixture. Spoon into pie shell. Sprinkle with remaining ½ teaspoon nutmeg. Chill until firm. Yield: 6 to 8 servings.

Anita King, Wisconsin

FIG

FIGS FLAMBÉ

1 can Kadota figs
1 tsp. cornstarch
2 thin lemon slices
6 tbsp. Brandy
½ pt. heavy cream
Lemon wafers

Drain syrup from figs into chafing dish. Add cornstarch; stir until thickened. Add figs, lemon slices and 2 tablespoons Brandy. Heat to serving temperature. Heat remaining ¼ cup Brandy in saucepan. Ignite Brandy. Pour over figs when flames subside. Serve at once with cream and lemon wafers. Yield: 4 servings.

Mrs. Raymond M. Harris, Virginia

FESTIVE FIG CAKES

3 c. flour
1 tbsp. baking powder
1 tsp. mace
½ tsp. soda
½ tsp. salt
⅓ c. ground walnuts
¼ c. butter
1½ c. sugar
4 eggs, separated
8 oz. sour cream
⅓ c. milk
⅓ Kirsch
¼ tsp. cream of tartar
1½ c. chopped dried figs
1 c. chopped walnuts

Combine flour, baking powder, mace, soda and salt; set aside. Grease and lightly flour two 4x8-inch loaf pans. Sprinkle with ground walnuts. Beat butter in mixer bowl for 30 seconds. Add 1 cup sugar, gradually beating until fluffy. Add egg yolks and sour cream; mix well. Add dry ingredients alternately with milk and Kirsch, beating after each addition just until blended. Beat egg whites and cream of tartar until soft peaks form. Add remaining ½ cup sugar gradually, beating until stiff peaks form. Fold egg whites into yolk mixture. Fold in figs and walnuts. Pour into prepared pans. Bake at 325 degrees for 1 hour or until cakes test done. Cool in pan for 10 minutes. Invert onto wire rack to cool completely. Garnish with confectioners' sugar. Yield: 12 to 16 servings.

LATTICED FIG PIE

5 c. firm ripe figs, peeled
1 recipe 2-crust pie pastry
6 tbsp. sugar
Juice of 1 lemon
6 tbsp. butter

Place figs in pastry-lined 9-inch pie plate. Sprinkle with sugar and lemon juice. Dot with butter. Cut remaining pastry into strips. Weave into lattice on top of pie. Bake at 425 degrees for 30 to 40 minutes or until brown. Yield: 6 servings.

Katherine Taylor, Texas

FRESH FIG PIE

2 env. unflavored gelatin
2 eggs, separated
6 tbsp. sugar
⅛ tsp. salt
¾ c. milk, scalded
1 tbsp. grated orange rind
2 tbsp. orange juice
2 c. chopped ripe figs
½ c. heavy cream, whipped
1   9-in. graham cracker
     pie shell

Soften gelatin in ¼ cup cold water. Beat egg yolks with 4 tablespoons sugar and salt in small bowl. Stir a small amount of hot milk into egg yolks; stir egg yolks into hot milk in saucepan. Cook over low heat until thickened, stirring constantly. Stir in gelatin until dissolved; remove from heat. Stir in orange rind and juice. Cool until partially set. Beat egg whites with remaining 2 tablespoons sugar until stiff. Fold figs, egg whites and whipped cream gently into cooked mixture. Spoon into pie shell. Chill until set. Yield: 6 servings.

Amy French, Minnesota

ITALIAN FIG PASTRIES

3 lb. white Calimyrna figs
3 lb. raisins
1 lb. toasted almonds
1 lb. walnuts
1 sm. jar orange marmalade
2 c. honey
1 c. sweet wine
1 tbsp. allspice
1 tbsp. cinnamon
1½ tsp. nutmeg
9 c. flour
¼ c. baking powder
4 c. sugar
1 tsp. salt
2 c. shortening
6 eggs, beaten
1 tbsp. plus 2 tsp. vanilla
    extract
1 lg. can evaporated milk
1 lb. confectioners' sugar
¼ c. butter, melted
3 tbsp. milk

Put figs, raisins and nuts through food grinder. Combine with marmalade, honey, wine and spices in bowl; mix well. Sift flour, baking powder, sugar and salt into bowl. Cut in shortening until crumbly. Add eggs, 1 tablespoon vanilla and evaporated milk; mix well. Divide into several portions. Roll each into strip on floured surface. Spread fig mixture down 1 side of strip. Fold dough over to enclose filling; seal edges. Place on ungreased baking sheet. Repeat with remaining dough and filling. Bake at 350 degrees for 10 minutes or until brown. Cool. Combine confectioners' sugar, butter, milk and remaining 2 teaspoons vanilla in bowl; beat until smooth. Spread over cooled strips. Cut into bars. Yield: 12 dozen.

Rose Burkley, Tennessee

FIG COOKIES

1 c. dried figs
½ c. shortening
¾ c. sugar
2 eggs
½ c. honey
2 tbsp. milk
2¾ c. sifted flour
1 tbsp. baking powder
½ tsp. salt
3 tbsp. grated orange rind
1½ c. coconut
1 tsp. lemon extract

Combine figs and water to cover in saucepan. Simmer for 10 minutes. Drain and chop. Cream shortening and sugar in large bowl until light and fluffy. Add eggs 1 at a time, beating well after each addition. Add honey in a fine stream, stirring constantly. Add milk; mix well. Sift flour, baking powder and salt into creamed mixture; mix well. Add figs, orange rind, coconut and lemon flavoring; mix well. Drop by teaspoonfuls onto greased cookie sheet. Bake at 425 degrees for 12 minutes or until light brown. Cool on wire rack. Yield: 3 dozen.

Janeene Shields, Texas

FIG FUDGE

3 c. sugar
1 c. milk
2 tbsp. light corn syrup
3 tbsp. butter
1 tsp. vanilla extract
½ c. chopped dried figs
½ c. chopped pecans

Bring sugar, milk and corn syrup to a boil in saucepan, stirring until sugar is dissolved. Cook, covered, for 2 to 3 minutes or until steam washes sugar crystals from side of pan. Cook to 234 to 240 degrees on candy thermometer, soft-ball stage. Add butter and vanilla extract; do not stir. Cool to 110 degrees. Beat with wooden spoon until fudge becomes thick and loses its luster. Stir in figs and pecans. Pour into buttered 8x8-inch pan. Do not scrape saucepan. Cut into squares. Store in covered container. Yield: 2 pounds.

GRAPE

GRAPE AMBROSIA

2 c. seedless green grape halves
2 c. Concord grape halves
2 c. seedless red grape halves
1 c. sour cream
½ c. honey
½ c. shredded coconut

Combine grapes in bowl. Chill until serving time. Spoon into individual serving dishes. Spoon sour cream over top. Drizzle with honey; sprinkle with coconut. Yield: 8 servings.

Terri MacPhee, Oregon

STEAMED GRAPE PUDDING

½ c. butter, softened
1½ c. grape jelly
2 eggs
1 c. whole wheat flour
¾ c. all-purpose flour
¼ c. wheat germ
2½ tsp. baking powder
1 tsp. pumpkin pie spice
½ c. milk
½ c. chopped walnuts
½ c. raisins

Cream butter in mixer bowl until light. Blend in 1¼ cups grape jelly and eggs. Add combined dry ingredients alternately with milk, mixing well after each addition. Fold in walnuts and raisins. Pour into greased and floured 1½-quart pudding mold; cover tightly. Place on rack in deep saucepan. Add enough boiling water to cover half the mold. Steam for 1½ hours or until pudding tests done. Cool in mold for 5 minutes. Loosen from side of mold. Invert onto serving plate. Melt remaining ¼ cup jelly in saucepan over low heat. Brush over pudding. Garnish with fresh grapes and walnuts. Yield: 8 servings.

Sheryl Meigs, Indiana

GRAPE TARTS

10 oz. blanched almonds,
    finely chopped
1 c. unsalted butter, softened
3 c. flour
1 egg, beaten
1 tsp. almond extract
12 c. seedless red or green
    grape halves
2 tbsp. unflavored gelatin
½ c. white grape juice
1   12-oz. jar apple-grape jelly
1 pt. whipping cream

Mix almonds, butter, flour, egg and almond extract in mixer bowl. Divide into 2 portions. Press into 2 buttered 9-inch springform tart pans. Chill for 30 minutes. Bake at 350 degrees for 15 to 20 minutes or until golden brown. Cool. Arrange grapes in tarts. Soften gelatin in grape juice. Melt jelly over low heat in saucepan. Add gelatin mixture. Cook until gelatin is dissolved, stirring constantly. Spoon mixture evenly over grapes. Chill for 4 hours or longer. Place on serving plates. Remove sides of pans. Whip cream in bowl until soft peaks form. Cut tarts into thin wedges. Top each wedge with whipped cream. Yield: 20 servings.

Celeste Riggs, Missouri

To whip cream successfully, use chilled cream, mixer bowl and beaters.

CONCORD GRAPE PIE

6 c. Concord grapes
1½ c. sugar
3 tbsp. Minute tapioca
1 tsp. butter
⅛ tsp. salt
½ c. chopped pecans
1 recipe 2-crust pie pastry

S lip grape skins from pulp, reserving skins. Bring pulp to a simmer in saucepan. Put through sieve to remove seeds. Add enough reserved skins to pulp to measure 3½ cups. Mix grape mixture with sugar, tapioca, butter, salt and pecans. Spoon into pastry-lined 9-inch pie plate. Top with remaining pastry; seal edge and cut vents. Bake at 425 degrees for 15 minutes. Reduce temperature to 400 degrees. Bake for 30 minutes longer. Yield: 6 to 8 servings.

Zelda Frampton, Pennsylvania

PURPLE PASSION PIE

1 tsp. gelatin
4 eggs, separated
½ c. lemon juice
¼ tsp. salt
1   6-oz. can frozen grape juice
    concentrate, thawed
½ c. sugar
2 or 3 drops of red food coloring
Dash of cinnamon
1 baked 9-in. pie shell

S often gelatin in ½ cup cold water. Combine well-beaten egg yolks, lemon juice and salt in double boiler. Add grape juice mixed with enough water to measure 1 cup; mix well. Cook over hot water for 10 minutes or until mixture coats spoon, stirring frequently. Stir in gelatin until dissolved. Let stand for 10 minutes. Beat sugar into stiffly beaten egg whites. Tint with food coloring. Fold in cinnamon. Fold gently into grape juice mixture. Chill for 1 hour. Pour into pie shell. Chill for 4 hours. Garnish with whipped cream flavored with almond extract.
Yield: 6 to 8 servings.

Jodi Mills, New Jersey

GRAPEFRUIT

GRAPEFRUIT BAKED ALASKA

3 lg. grapefruit
Sugar
3 egg whites
⅛ tsp. salt
½ tsp. vanilla extract
1 pt. vanilla ice cream

S lice grapefruit into halves; remove cores. Cut around each section, loosening fruit from membrane. Sprinkle lightly with sugar to taste; chill. Beat egg whites with salt until foamy. Add 6 tablespoons sugar, beating until stiff and glossy. Add vanilla. Place 1 scoop ice cream in center of each grapefruit half. Cover with meringue, sealing well around edges. Place on baking sheet. Bake at 500 degrees for 1 minute or until lightly browned. Serve at once. Yield: 6 servings.

M. Lee Smith, California

GRAPEFRUIT-APRICOT ICE CREAM

1¾ c. grapefruit juice
6 oz. dried apricots
1 c. sugar
4 egg whites
¼ tsp. salt
1 c. mashed bananas
2 c. whipping cream, whipped

C ombine 1 cup grapefruit juice and apricots in saucepan. Bring to a boil. Remove from heat. Let stand, covered, for 1 hour. Purée in blender. Combine remaining ¾ cup juice and sugar in saucepan. Boil for 5 minutes or until syrupy. Beat egg whites with salt in mixer bowl until soft peaks form. Add hot syrup gradually, beating until very stiff peaks form. Fold gently into mixture of apricot purée and bananas. Fold in half the whipped cream gently, blending well. Pour into 9x13-inch metal dish. Freeze for 1 hour or until partially frozen. Spoon into chilled mixer bowl. Beat until smooth. Fold in remaining whipped cream. Pour into dish. Freeze, covered, for 4 hours or until firm, stirring several times. Yield: 6 servings.

GRAPEFRUIT PARFAIT

4 *red grapefruit*
1 *env. unflavored gelatin*
½ *c. packed brown sugar*
2 *c. light cream*
1 *tsp. lemon juice*
2 *egg whites*
2 *tbsp. sugar*

S lice grapefruit into halves. Remove grapefruit sections; reserve. Squeeze enough juice from shells to measure ½ cup. Combine grapefruit juice and gelatin in saucepan. Let stand for 1 minute. Heat until gelatin is dissolved, stirring constantly. Stir in brown sugar until dissolved. Mix with cream and lemon juice in bowl. Chill until partially set. Beat egg whites until soft peaks form. Add sugar gradually, beating until stiff peaks form. Fold gently into chilled mixture. Alternate layers of mousse and grapefruit sections in chilled parfait glasses. Chill until serving time.
Yield: 8 servings.

GRAPEFRUIT BREAD PUDDING

15 *thin slices French bread*
2½ *tbsp. butter, softened*
⅓ *c. raisins*
2 *c. milk*
1 *c. grapefruit juice*
4 *eggs, beaten*
⅓ *c. plus 2 tbsp. brown sugar*
½ *tsp. grated grapefruit rind*
¼ *tsp. cinnamon*
2 *grapefruit, sectioned*

S pread 1 side of each bread slice with butter. Arrange buttered side down in 9x13-inch baking dish. Sprinkle with raisins. Combine milk, grapefruit juice, eggs, ⅓ cup brown sugar, grapefruit rind and cinnamon in bowl; mix well. Pour over bread. Let stand for 30 minutes. Place dish in pan of hot water. Bake at 350 degrees for 1 hour or until set. Arrange grapefruit sections over top. Sprinkle with remaining 2 tablespoons brown sugar. Broil for 2 minutes or until brown sugar melts.
Yield: 8 servings.

GRAPEFRUIT PUDDING

1 *tbsp. butter*
⅔ *c. sugar*
2 *eggs, separated*
2 *tbsp. potato starch*
¾ *c. frozen grapefruit juice*
   concentrate, thawed
1 *c. milk*
¾ *c. sugar*

B eat butter and ⅔ cup sugar in bowl until light and fluffy. Add egg yolks 1 at a time, beating well after each addition. Blend in 1 tablespoon potato starch, ¼ cup grapefruit juice concentrate and milk. Fold in stiffly beaten egg whites gently. Spoon into greased 1-quart baking dish. Place in larger pan filled with 1-inch hot water. Bake at 350 degrees for 45 to 50 minutes or until set. Cool. Chill until serving time. Combine ¾ cup sugar and remaining 1 tablespoon potato starch in saucepan. Stir in remaining ½ cup grapefruit juice concentrate and ½ cup water. Cook over medium heat until thickened, stirring constantly. Cool. Serve with pudding.
Yield: 4 servings.

RUBY RED GRAPEFRUIT CAKE

1 *2-layer pkg. white cake mix*
1 *env. unflavored gelatin*
¾ *c. oil*
¾ *c. ruby red grapefruit juice*
4 *eggs*
1 *c. ruby red grapefruit sections*

C ombine cake mix, gelatin, oil and grapefruit juice in mixer bowl; mix well. Add eggs 1 at a time, beating well after each addition. Add grapefruit sections. Beat for 30 seconds longer. Tint with red food coloring if desired. Pour into greased and floured tube pan. Bake at 300 degrees for 1 hour. Cool in pan on wire rack for 10 minutes. Invert onto cake plate. Cool completely. Frost as desired or garnish with light sifting of confectioners' sugar.
Yield: 12 to 16 servings.

Kay Lynn Van Winkle, Texas

GRAPEFRUIT JUICE PIE

1¼ c. grapefruit juice
1¼ c. sugar
3 tbsp. cornstarch
2 eggs, separated
1 baked 9-in. pie shell
¼ tsp. salt

Mix 1 cup grapefruit juice, ½ cup water and 1 cup sugar in saucepan. Bring to a boil. Combine cornstarch and remaining ¼ cup grapefruit juice. Stir into hot mixture. Cook until thick, stirring constantly. Stir a small amount of hot mixture into beaten egg yolks; stir egg yolks into hot mixture. Pour into pie shell. Beat egg whites with salt and remaining ¼ cup sugar until stiff. Spread over filling; seal to edge. Bake at 350 degrees for 15 minutes or until brown. Yield: 6 servings.

Jenny Brewer, Nevada

PINK GRAPEFRUIT PARFAIT PIE

1 env. unflavored gelatin
½ c. pink grapefruit juice
1 pt. vanilla ice cream, softened
2 egg whites
1 tbsp. sugar
2 c. pink grapefruit sections, chopped
1 baked 9-in. pie shell

Soften gelatin in juice in small saucepan for 1 minute. Cook over low heat until gelatin dissolves, stirring constantly. Remove from heat. Stir in ice cream. Chill until thick, stirring occasionally. Beat egg whites in medium bowl until soft peaks form. Add sugar gradually, beating until stiff. Fold gently into gelatin mixture. Fold in grapefruit. Pour into pie shell. Chill until firm. Garnish with whipped cream and additional grapefruit sections. Yield: 6 to 8 servings.

Julie Wilkes, Indiana

Store lemon, orange and grapefruit rinds in the freezer. Grate for use in baking or candy for a holiday treat.

HONEY

HONEY CUSTARD

3 eggs, beaten
¼ c. honey
¼ tsp. salt
2 c. milk
Nutmeg

Beat eggs, honey and salt in bowl. Scald milk. Stir slowly into egg mixture. Pour into custard cups. Sprinkle with nutmeg. Set cups in pan of hot water. Bake at 325 degrees for 30 minutes or until knife inserted in mixture comes out clean. Yield: 6 servings.

HONEY-RICE PUDDING

2 c. cooked rice
3 c. milk
¾ c. honey
3 eggs
1 c. raisins
½ tsp. cinnamon

Combine rice, milk and honey in bowl. Add eggs; mix well. Stir in raisins. Place in greased casserole. Sprinkle with cinnamon. Bake at 300 degrees for about 1 hour. Serve with whipped cream. Yield: 6 to 8 servings.

HONEY CAKE

½ c. shortening
1 c. honey
2 eggs
2 c. flour
½ tsp. salt
2 tsp. baking powder
½ c. milk
1 tsp. vanilla extract

Cream shortening in mixer bowl until fluffy. Add honey in a fine stream, beating constantly. Add eggs, 1 at a time, beating well after each addition. Sift dry ingredients together. Add sifted ingredients to the creamed mixture alternately with milk, beating well after each addition. Add vanilla. Pour into 2 greased and floured 9-inch cake pans. Bake at 350 degrees for 25 to 35 minutes or until cake tests done. Frost with favorite frosting if desired. Yield: 12 servings.

HONEY GINGERBREAD

2¾ c. sifted flour
1 tsp. soda
1 tsp. salt
2 tsp. baking powder
1 tsp. ginger
1 tsp. cinnamon
1 egg, beaten
1 c. oil
¾ c. honey
¾ c. molasses
1 c. buttermilk

Sift flour, soda, salt, baking powder and spices together. Cream egg and oil together in bowl until light. Add honey in a fine stream, beating constantly. Add molasses in a fine stream, beating constantly. Add sifted flour alternately with buttermilk, beating until smooth after each addition. Pour into greased 9x13-inch baking pan. Bake at 325 degrees for 40 minutes or until gingerbread tests done. Cool in pan for 5 minutes. Invert onto wire rack to cool completely. Serve with whipped cream. Yield: 12 servings.

Patricia Malone, Missouri

HONEY-CAROB BROWNIES

½ c. melted butter
½ c. carob powder
1 c. honey
2 eggs, beaten
1 c. whole wheat flour
1 tsp. baking powder
¼ tsp. salt
1 tsp. vanilla extract
½ c. chopped walnuts

Combine butter, carob powder, honey and eggs in bowl; mix well. Sift in flour, baking powder and salt; mix well. Stir in vanilla and walnuts. Pour into greased 8-inch square baking dish. Bake at 350 degrees for 40 minutes. Cool. Cut into squares. Yield: 1½ dozen.

Deborah Peek, Arkansas

Use shiny cookie sheets and baking pans. Dark pans absorb more heat and cause overbrowning.

HONEY DROPS

1 c. sugar
2 eggs
1 c. flour
1 tsp. soda
1 c. chopped nuts
¼ c. honey

Mix first 5 ingredients in bowl; mix well. Add honey in a fine stream, stirring constantly. Drop by spoonfuls onto greased cookie sheet. Bake at 350 degrees until light brown. Cool on wire rack. Yield: 3 dozen.

Falisia Williams, Texas

HONEY FUDGE

⅔ c. evaporated milk
½ c. honey
¼ tsp. salt
¼ c. butter
1 c. peanut butter
2 c. chocolate chips
1 7-oz. jar marshmallow creme

Mix evaporated milk and next 3 ingredients in saucepan. Bring to a boil. Boil for 5 minutes. Stir in peanut butter, chocolate chips and marshmallow creme. Pour into buttered 9x13-inch dish. Chill for 1 hour. Cut into squares. Yield: 2½ pounds.

Teri Douglas, California

HEALTHY HONEY BALLS

½ c. peanut butter
¼ c. honey
½ c. nonfat dry milk powder
1 tbsp. sunflower seed
1 tbsp. chopped walnuts
1 tbsp. chopped raisins
3 tbsp. sesame seed

Combine peanut butter and honey in bowl, mix well. Add milk powder gradually, mixing until of bread dough consistency. Stir in next 3 ingredients. Shape into small balls. Roll in sesame seed. Chill in refrigerator. Yield: 1½ dozen.

KIWIFRUIT

KIWI EMERALD ICE

1 *lb. kiwifruit*
1 *c. sugar*
¼ *c. lemon juice*

Peel and quarter kiwifruit. Beat with electric mixer until coarsely mashed. Measure 1½ cups mashed fruit; stir in sugar. Let stand for 10 to 15 minutes to dissolve sugar. Stir in 1 cup water and lemon juice. Pour mixture into 8-inch cake pan. Freeze just until mixture is firm but not hard. Spoon into mixing bowl. Beat at high speed until smooth. Freeze until firm. Let stand for 10 to 15 minutes to soften slightly. Scoop or spoon into individual serving dishes. Yield: 3½ cups.

KIWIFRUIT FIESTA CUPS

6 *flour tortillas*
Oil for deep frying
6 *scoops lime sherbet*
1 *c. sliced banana*
1 *c. fresh strawberries*
2 *c. sliced kiwifruit*
1 *c. fresh orange sections*

Place tortillas 1 at a time in several inches deep hot oil in skillet. Form cup by pressing down in center with empty can with holes punched in bottom. Fry until crisp and golden; drain on paper towels. Store in airtight container. Place on serving plates. Fill with sherbet and fruit. Yield: 6 servings.

Donita Massey, New Mexico

KIWIFRUIT PAVLOVA

1 *c. whipping cream*
1 *tbsp. sugar*
6 *meringue shells*
3 *kiwifruit*

Whip cream in mixer bowl until soft peaks form. Fold in sugar. Mound in meringue shells. Peel and slice kiwifruit; cut slices into halves. Arrange over whipped cream. Serve immediately. Yield: 6 servings.

KIWIFRUIT TANGO

2 *c. sour cream*
1½ *c. packed brown sugar*
½ *c. ginger ale*
2 *tsp. almond extract*
6 *c. sliced fresh kiwifruit*

Combine sour cream, brown sugar, ginger ale and almond extract in bowl; mix well. Fold in 5½ cups sliced kiwifruit. Spoon into serving dishes. Garnish with remaining ½ cup kiwifruit. Yield: 6 servings.

Marilyn Wilkinson, Ontario, Canada

KIWIFRUIT AND YOGURT

2 *c. sliced kiwifruit*
3 *tbsp. sugar*
3 *egg yolks*
⅓ *c. sugar*
1 *tsp. vanilla extract*
Dash of nutmeg
2 *c. yogurt*
2 *tbsp. sliced almonds*
Shaved chocolate

Mix kiwifruit with 3 tablespoons sugar in bowl. Let stand, covered, for 5 minutes. Combine egg yolks, ⅓ cup sugar, vanilla and nutmeg in bowl; beat until smooth. Fold in yogurt. Spoon kiwifruit into 4 dessert dishes. Top with yogurt mixture. Sprinkle with almonds. Garnish with shaved chocolate. Yield: 4 servings.

Mary Harvey, California

KIWIFRUIT PIE

1   *7-oz. jar marshmallow creme*
2 *tbsp. nonalcoholic Crème de Menthe*
1 *c. whipping cream, whipped*
1   *9-in. chocolate crumb pie shell*
2 *kiwifruit, peeled, sliced*

Blend marshmallow creme and Crème de Menthe in bowl. Fold in whipped cream. Spread in pie shell. Arrange kiwifruit slices over top. Chill until serving time. Yield: 6 servings.

Martine Gabler, Oregon

LEMON

LUSCIOUS LEMON DESSERT

½ c. margarine, softened
1 c. flour
½ c. chopped pecans
1 c. confectioners' sugar
1   8-oz. package cream cheese,
    softened
1   16-oz. carton whipped
    topping
2   4-oz. packages lemon
    instant pudding mix
3 c. milk

Combine margarine, flour and pecans in bowl; mix well. Pat into 9x13-inch baking pan. Bake at 375 degrees for 15 minutes. Cool. Cream confectioners' sugar, cream cheese and 1 cup whipped topping in bowl until fluffy. Spread over baked layer. Prepare pudding mix using package directions, with 3 cups milk. Spread over creamed layer. Top with remaining whipped topping. Chill until serving time.
Yield: 12 servings.

Mary Alice Fritts, Tennessee

LEMON-FRUIT FREEZE

⅔ c. butter, melted
⅓ c. sugar
3 c. crushed Rice Chex
1 can sweetened
    condensed milk
½ c. lemon juice
1   21-oz. can lemon pie filling
1   17-oz. can fruit cocktail,
    drained
Whipped cream

Combine butter, sugar and 2⅔ cups crushed cereal, mixing well. Press mixture into 9x13-inch baking dish. Bake at 300 degrees for 12 minutes. Mix sweetened condensed milk, lemon juice and pie filling in bowl. Fold in fruit cocktail. Pour over prepared crust. Freeze for 4 hours. Remove from freezer 20 minutes before serving. Top with whipped cream and remaining ⅓ cup crushed Rice Chex.

Mrs. Noah R. Blosser, Ohio

WHITE HOUSE SHERBET

Grated rind of 2 lemons
½ c. lemon juice
2½ c. sugar
4 c. cold milk

Combine lemon rind with ½ cup cold water in small bowl. Let stand for 20 minutes. Pour lemon juice over sugar in bowl. Add lemon rind mixture and milk; mix well. Pour into 9x13-inch dish. Freeze until partially set. Remove to bowl. Beat until smooth. Repeat process several times. Freeze until firm.
Yield: 12 servings.

Irene Sommers, Wisconsin

SCHAUM TORTE

3 egg whites
¼ tsp. cream of tartar
Pinch of salt
½ tsp. vinegar
2 c. sugar
3 tbsp. cornstarch
3 egg yolks, beaten
6 tbsp. lemon juice
2 tsp. grated lemon rind
1 c. whipping cream, whipped

Beat egg whites, cream of tartar, salt and vinegar in mixer bowl until soft peaks form. Add 1 cup sugar 1 tablespoon at a time, beating until sugar is dissolved after each addition. Beat until very stiff and glossy peaks form. Spread in pie plate, shaping into shell. Bake at 325 degrees for 50 minutes. Cool. Combine cornstarch and remaining 1 cup sugar in saucepan. Add mixture of beaten egg yolks and 1 tablespoon lemon juice; mix well. Add 1 cup water; mix well. Bring to a boil, stirring constantly. Add lemon rind and remaining 5 tablespoons lemon juice. Cook for 5 minutes or until thick. Cool. Spread half the whipped cream, all the lemon filling and remaining whipped cream in meringue shell. Chill overnight.
Yield: 5 servings.

Rosalind Popkey, Washington

To reduce cleanup time, measure dry ingredients before liquids.

LEMON SAUCE

1 egg
1 c. sugar
Juice of 2 lemons
Grated rind of 1 lemon
1 tbsp. melted butter

Beat egg and sugar in saucepan. Add lemon juice, lemon rind and butter, mixing well after each addition. Cook over low heat until mixture is smooth and thickened, stirring constantly.

Clara Richardson, Oklahoma

LEMON CHIFFON CAKE

2¼ c. sifted cake flour
1½ c. sugar
1 tbsp. baking powder
½ tsp. salt
6 egg yolks
½ c. corn oil
1 tbsp. grated lemon rind
¼ c. plus 1 tbsp. lemon juice
6 egg whites
½ tsp. cream of tartar
1 c. confectioners' sugar
½ tsp. grated lemon rind

Sift flour, sugar, baking powder and salt into large mixer bowl. Make well in center. Add egg yolks, corn oil, 1 tablespoon lemon rind, ¼ cup lemon juice and ½ cup water. Beat at medium speed until smooth. Beat egg whites with cream of tartar until very stiff peaks form. Fold into batter gently. Pour into ungreased 10-inch tube pan. Bake at 325 degrees for 65 to 70 minutes or until cake springs back when touched lightly. Cool in inverted pan. Loosen cake from sides of pan. Invert onto cake plate. Blend confectioners' sugar with ½ teaspoon lemon rind and enough remaining lemon juice to make of desired consistency. Drizzle over cake.
Yield: 14 to 16 servings.

LEMON-POPPY SEED CAKE

4 eggs, beaten
1 4-oz. package lemon instant
    pudding mix
1 2-layer pkg. lemon cake mix
⅓ c. oil
3 tbsp. poppy seed

Combine all ingredients and 1 cup water in mixer bowl; mix well on low speed. Beat at high speed for 4 minutes. Pour into greased and floured 12-cup bundt pan. Bake at 350 degrees for 35 minutes or until cake tests done. Cool in pan for 10 minutes. Invert onto serving plate. Serve warm with whipped topping. Yield: 12 servings.

Mandy Fine, Oregon

MICROWAVE LEMON BUNDT CAKE

1 2-layer pkg. lemon supreme
    cake mix
1 4-oz. package lemon instant
    pudding mix
2 tbsp. oil
4 eggs
1 6-oz. can frozen lemonade
    concentrate, thawed
1 c. confectioners' sugar

Mix first 4 ingredients with ¾ cup water in bowl. Pour into greased glass bundt pan. Let stand for 15 minutes. Microwave on Medium for 12 to 14 minutes or until completely risen, turning pan every 4 minutes. Microwave on High for 1 to 2 minutes or until cake tests done. Let stand for 5 to 10 minutes. Invert onto plate. Combine lemonade concentrate and confectioners' sugar in glass bowl; blend well. Microwave on High for 2 minutes or until heated through. Pour mixture over hot cake. Yield: 16 servings.

Lucina B. Helton, Florida

LEMON ANGEL ROLL

1 16-oz. package angel food
    cake mix
1 14-ounce can sweetened
    condensed milk
⅓ c. lemon juice
2 tsp. grated lemon rind
1 4-ounce container frozen
    nondairy whipped topping,
    thawed
½ c. flaked coconut

Prepare 15x10-inch jellyroll pan with aluminum foil liner, extending foil 1 inch over ends of pan. Prepare cake mix using package directions. Spread batter evenly into prepared pan. Bake at 350 degrees for 30 minutes or until top springs back when lightly touched. Invert onto towel sprinkled with confectioners' sugar. Remove foil. Roll up cake with towel as for jelly roll, beginning at narrow end. Cool thoroughly. Combine sweetened condensed milk, lemon juice and rind in medium mixer bowl; mix well. Fold in whipped topping. Unroll cake; trim edges. Spread with half the lemon filling; reroll. Place on serving plate, seam-side down; spread remaining filling over roll. Garnish with coconut. Chill thoroughly before serving. Store in refrigerator.
Yield: 8 to 10 servings.

Phoebe Jensen, Utah

LEMON RIBBON ALASKA PIE

6 tbsp. butter
Grated rind of 1 lemon
1/3 c. lemon juice
1/8 tsp. salt
1 c. plus 6 tbsp. sugar
2 eggs
2 egg yolks
1 qt. vanilla ice cream, softened
1 baked 9-in. pie shell
2 egg whites

Blend butter, lemon rind and juice with salt and 1 cup sugar in double boiler. Add eggs and egg yolks; mix well. Cook over boiling water until thickened and smooth, beating constantly. Cool. Layer half the ice cream and half the sauce in pie shell. Freeze until firm. Repeat layers with remaining ice cream and sauce. Freeze until firm. Beat egg whites until soft peaks form. Add 6 tablespoons sugar gradually, beating until stiff peaks form. Spread over pie, sealing to edge. Bake at 375 degrees until light brown. Serve immediately.
Yield: 6 to 8 servings.

Catherine Eburg, Maryland

FROZEN LEMON PIE

3 eggs, separated
8 tbsp. sugar
3 tbsp. lemon juice
1 tsp. grated lemon rind
1 c. whipping cream, whipped
1 c. vanilla wafer crumbs

Combine egg yolks and 7 tablespoons sugar in double boiler; mix well. Cook for 2 minutes or until thick, beating constantly with rotary beater; remove from heat. Beat in lemon juice and rind; cool. Beat egg whites in bowl with 1 tablespoon sugar until stiff peaks form. Fold egg whites and whipped cream gently into lemon mixture. Sprinkle half the cookie crumbs over bottom of buttered freezer container. Spread lemon filling over crumbs. Top with remaining crumbs. Freeze until firm. Yield: 6 servings.

Marie Mattox, Ohio

DOUBLE CRUST LEMON PIE

1 1/4 c. sugar
2 tbsp. flour
1/8 tsp. salt
1/4 c. butter, softened
3 eggs
1 tsp. grated lemon rind
1 lemon, peeled, thinly sliced
1 recipe 2-crust pie pastry

Mix sugar, flour and salt in bowl. Blend in butter. Reserve 1 teaspoon egg white. Beat remaining eggs together. Add to flour mixture with lemon rind and 1/2 cup water; mix well. Stir in lemon. Pour into pastry-lined 8-inch pie plate. Top with remaining pastry; seal edge and cut vents. Brush top with reserved egg white. Bake at 400 degrees for 30 to 35 minutes or until golden brown. Yield: 6 to 8 servings.

Naomi Peters, Kentucky

To put the top crust onto your pie easily, roll it out, cut the air vents, then pick up one edge of the crust on your rolling pin and roll to wrap the entire crust loosely around the pin. "Roll" the top crust over your pie.

MARVELOUS LEMON MERINGUE PIE

1½ c. sugar
⅓ c. cornstarch
¼ tsp. salt
4 eggs, separated
2 tbsp. butter
1   6-oz. can frozen lemonade
    concentrate, thawed
1 baked 9-in. pie shell
¼ tsp. cream of tartar

Combine 1 cup sugar, cornstarch and salt in saucepan; mix well. Stir in 1½ cups hot water gradually. Mix in slightly beaten egg yolks, butter and lemonade. Bring to a boil over low heat, stirring constantly. Boil for 1 minute, stirring constantly. Cool to lukewarm. Spread in pie shell. Beat egg whites with cream of tartar until soft peaks form. Add remaining ½ cup sugar, 1 tablespoon at a time, beating until stiff peaks form. Spread over filling; seal to edge. Bake at 325 degrees for 20 to 25 minutes or until lightly browned.

Ann Dever, North Carolina

LEMON SQUARES

1 c. margarine, softened
½ c. confectioners' sugar
½ tsp. salt
2 c. plus 6 tbsp. flour
4 eggs
½ tsp. vanilla extract
2 c. sugar
2 tbsp. lemon juice

Combine margarine, confectioners' sugar and salt with 2 cups flour in bowl; mix until crumbly. Pat into buttered 8x8-inch baking dish. Bake at 350 degrees for 25 minutes. Combine eggs, vanilla, sugar, lemon juice and remaining 6 tablespoons flour in bowl. Beat for 1 minute. Pour over baked layer. Bake for 30 minutes longer. Cut into squares. Sprinkle with additional confectioners' sugar. Yield: 16 squares.

Marleen Thomas, Massachusetts

Place unpeeled lemon or lime in hot water for 15 minutes before squeezing to yield more juice.

LIME

FLOATING ISLAND LIME DESSERTS

2 eggs, separated
2 tbsp. sugar
1   14-oz. can sweetened
    condensed milk
½ c. lime juice
2 tbsp. flaked coconut, toasted

Beat 2 egg whites in small mixer bowl until soft peaks form. Add 2 tablespoons sugar, beating until stiff but not dry. Drop ¼ of the mixture onto simmering water in large skillet; repeat to make 4 islands. Simmer, uncovered, for 5 minutes or until meringues are set. Remove with slotted spoon; drain on paper towels. Beat sweetened condensed milk and egg yolks in medium mixer bowl. Stir in lime juice and green food coloring if desired. Spoon into four 6-ounce dessert dishes. Top each with meringue. Chill for 2 hours or until set. Garnish with coconut. Yield: 4 servings.

LIME FREEZE

3 eggs, separated
½ c. sugar
Grated rind and juice of 1 lime
2 tbsp. lemon juice
1 c. whipping cream, whipped
Green gumdrop slivers

Mix egg yolks, sugar, lime rind, lime juice and lemon juice in double boiler. Cook over hot water until slightly thickened, stirring constantly. Cool. Add green food coloring, if desired. Beat egg whites until stiff peaks form. Fold egg whites, whipped cream and gumdrop slivers gently into lime mixture. Pour into refrigerator tray. Freeze until firm. Yield: 4 servings.

LIME MOUSSE

1 env. unflavored gelatin
3 eggs, separated
¾ c. light corn syrup
1 tsp. grated lime rind
½ c. lime juice
¼ c. sugar
1 c. whipping cream, whipped

Soften gelatin in ¼ cup cold water in 2-quart saucepan. Stir in egg yolks, corn syrup, lime rind and juice. Cook over low heat for 5 minutes or until gelatin is dissolved, stirring constantly. Stir in green food coloring if desired. Pour into large bowl. Chill for 1 hour or until thick, stirring occasionally. Beat egg whites in small mixer bowl until soft peaks form. Add sugar gradually. Beat until stiff peaks form. Fold gently into lime mixture. Fold in whipped cream. Spoon into 2-quart serving dish. Chill until firm. Garnish with additional whipped cream and lime slices. Yield: 8 servings.

LIME PARFAIT

1 *6-oz. package lime gelatin*
1 *tsp. grated lime rind*
⅓ *c. lime juice*
1 *qt. vanilla ice cream*
Whipped cream
Maraschino cherries

Dissolve gelatin in 2 cups boiling water; stir in lime rind and juice. Add ice cream by spoonfuls, stirring until melted. Chill mixture until partially thickened. Spoon into parfait glasses. Chill until firm. Top with whipped cream; garnish with cherries. Yield: 4 servings.

KEY LIME CAKE

2 *tbsp. plus ⅓ c. Key lime juice*
1 *2-layer pkg. lemon cake mix*
1 *4-oz. pkg. lemon instant pudding mix*
4 *eggs, beaten*
1 *c. oil*
2 *c. confectioners' sugar*

Combine 2 tablespoons lime juice, cake mix, pudding mix, eggs, oil and 1 cup water in mixer bowl; beat until smooth. Pour into greased 9x13-inch baking pan. Bake at 325 degrees for 45 minutes or until cake tests done. Cool for 10 minutes. Pierce with fork. Mix confectioners' sugar and remaining ⅓ cup lime juice in small bowl. Pour over warm cake. Yield: 16 servings.

Hazel Benson, Kansas

LIME GELATIN CAKE

1 *2-layer pkg. white cake mix*
1 *3-oz. package lime gelatin*
4 *tsp. mint flavoring*
⅓ *c. oil*
4 *eggs, separated*
1 *c. confectioners' sugar*
¼ *c. milk*

Combine cake mix, gelatin, mint flavoring and oil with 1 cup water in bowl. Add egg yolks; beat well. Beat egg whites until stiff peaks form. Fold egg whites gently into batter. Pour into greased and floured tube pan. Bake at 325 degrees for 1 hour. Combine confectioners' sugar with milk in small bowl. Pour over hot cake. Yield: 12 servings.

Karen Hammond, Alabama

GRASSHOPPER CHIFFON PIE

3 *tbsp. green Crème de Menthe*
3 *tbsp. Crème de Cacao*
1 *3-oz. package lime gelatin*
3 *tbsp. sugar*
Pinch of salt
½ *tsp. vanilla extract*
1 *egg white*
1 *env. whipped topping mix*
1 *baked 9-in. chocolate crumb pie shell*

Bring 1 cup water and liqueurs to a boil in saucepan. Stir in gelatin, 1 tablespoon sugar and salt until dissolved. Add ½ cup cold water and vanilla. Chill for 1½ hours. Beat egg white in bowl until frothy. Add 2 tablespoons sugar gradually, beating until stiff. Prepare whipped topping according to package directions. Reserve ½ cup gelatin. Fold egg white and 1 cup whipped topping gently into remaining gelatin. Layer gelatin mixtures ½ at a time in pie shell. Cut through with knife to marbleize. Chill until firm. Garnish with remaining whipped topping. Yield: 8 servings.

Sue Gephart, Florida

To prepare whipped cream in advance, pipe onto waxed paper-lined baking sheet and freeze. About 20 minutes before serving, remove from freezer and place on dessert.

KEY LIME PIE

1 c. vanilla wafer crumbs
¼ c. butter, softened
½ c. chopped pecans
3 eggs, separated
½ c. lime juice
1 tsp. grated lime rind
1 can sweetened condensed
  milk
3 drops of green food coloring
¼ tsp. cream of tartar
2 tbsp. sugar

Combine wafer crumbs, butter and pecans in bowl; mix well. Reserve a small amount of crumbs for topping. Press remaining mixture over bottom and side of 8-inch pie plate. Chill for 20 minutes. Beat egg yolks, lime juice, rind, condensed milk and food coloring in bowl. Pour into pie shell. Beat egg whites and cream of tartar until soft peaks form. Add sugar gradually, beating until stiff peaks form. Spoon over filling, sealing to edge. Sprinkle with reserved crumbs. Bake at 425 degrees for 4 minutes. Yield: 6 servings.

Sallie Minton, Georgia

LIME SQUARES

1 c. plus 2 tbsp. flour
¼ c. butter, softened
½ c. chopped pecans
1¼ c. sugar
2 eggs
2 tbsp. lime juice
1 to 1½ tbsp. grated lime rind
½ tsp. baking powder
Confectioners' sugar

Combine 1 cup flour, butter, pecans and ¼ cup sugar in bowl; mix until crumbly, using a pastry blender. Press into greased and floured 8x12-inch baking pan. Bake at 350 degrees for 15 minutes. Beat eggs with fork in bowl; add lime juice, rind, remaining 1 cup sugar and 2 tablespoons flour and baking powder. Pour mixture over crust. Bake an additional 25 minutes. Cool. Sprinkle with confectioners' sugar.
Yield: 3½ dozen.

Alma Saunders, Virginia

LIME CHIFFON SQUARES

¼ c. margarine, melted
1 c. graham cracker crumbs
1 3-oz. package lime gelatin
1 14-oz. can sweetened
  condensed milk
1 8-oz. can crushed
  pineapple, undrained
2 tbsp. lime juice
4 c. miniature marshmallows
1 c. whipping cream, whipped

Mix margarine and crumbs in bowl; press firmly on bottom of 9-inch square baking dish. Dissolve gelatin in 1 cup boiling water in large mixer bowl. Stir in sweetened condensed milk, pineapple and lime juice. Fold in marshmallows and whipped cream. Pour into prepared dish. Chill for 2 hours or until set. Yield: 10 to 12 servings.

LIME BUTTER COOKIES

10 tbsp. butter, softened
1 c. sugar
1 egg
Grated rind of 1 lime
3 tbsp. fresh lime juice
2½ c. sifted flour
¼ tsp. soda
½ tsp. salt
2 c. sifted confectioners' sugar
1 egg yolk
½ tsp. vanilla extract

Beat ½ cup butter and sugar in bowl until light and fluffy. Add egg; beat well. Add half the lime rind and 2 tablespoons lime juice; mix well. Sift in flour, soda and salt; mix well. Shape into 2-inch diameter roll. Wrap in plastic wrap. Chill in refrigerator. Cut into ⅛-inch slices. Arrange on greased cookie sheet. Bake at 400 degrees for 10 minutes or until firm. Cool on wire rack. Cream remaining 2 tablespoons butter, confectioners' sugar, egg yolk, remaining lime rind and vanilla in bowl until light and fluffy. Add enough remaining lime juice and food coloring to make of desired consistency and color. Frost cooled cookies. Yield: 4 dozen.

Louanne Heinricks, Ohio

MALT CHEWS

¾ c. packed brown sugar
6 tbsp. melted butter
2 eggs, beaten
½ tsp. vanilla extract
¾ c. sifted flour
½ c. chocolate malted milk
  powder
½ tsp. baking powder
1 c. chopped dates
½ c. chopped walnuts
½ c. flaked coconut
2 tbsp. confectioners' sugar

Beat brown sugar and butter in mixer bowl until light and fluffy. Add eggs and vanilla; mix well. Add flour, malted milk powder and baking powder; mix well. Fold in dates, walnuts and coconut. Spread in greased and floured 9-inch square baking pan. Bake at 350 degrees for 25 minutes or until brown. Cool. Sprinkle confectioners' sugar over top. Cut into squares. Yield: 3 dozen.

Robert Long, Texas

MALT DROPS

2 c. flour
1 pkg. coconut-pecan frosting
  mix
1 c. crushed malted milk balls
1 c. butter, softened
½ tsp. soda
2 eggs, beaten

Combine first 5 ingredients in bowl; mix well. Add eggs; mix well. Drop by teaspoonfuls onto greased cookie sheet. Bake at 375 degrees for 8 minutes or until golden brown. Cool on wire rack. Yield: 4 to 5 dozen.

Barbara Roader, California

MAPLE

MAPLE PARFAITS

¾ c. maple syrup
4 egg yolks, beaten
⅛ tsp. salt
1 tsp. vanilla extract
1 pt. whipping cream
4 egg whites

Bring maple syrup to a simmer in double boiler pan. Stir a small amount of hot syrup into beaten egg yolks; stir egg yolks into hot syrup. Cook until thickened, stirring constantly. Stir in salt and vanilla. Spoon into small mixer bowl; beat until cool. Chill in refrigerator. Whip cream in mixer bowl until soft peaks form. Beat maple custard until smooth. Add to whipped cream; mix well. Beat egg whites in bowl until stiff peaks form. Fold gently into whipped cream mixture. Spoon into parfait glasses. Freeze until firm. Yield: 6 servings.

VERMONT MAPLE CAKE

½ c. butter, softened
1 c. packed brown sugar
2 eggs
1 c. maple syrup
2 c. flour
1 tbsp. baking powder
½ tsp. salt
2 tsp. ginger
1 tsp. cinnamon
½ tsp. cloves
½ tsp. nutmeg
¼ c. milk
3 c. whipped cream

Cream butter and ¾ cup brown sugar in mixer bowl until light and fluffy. Add eggs; mix well. Add syrup gradually, beating constantly. Add sifted dry ingredients and milk alternately, beating well after each addition. Pour into 2 greased and floured 8-inch cake pans. Bake at 350 degrees for 25 to 30 minutes or until cake tests done. Cool in pans for 10 minutes. Remove to wire rack to cool completely. Flavor whipped cream with remaining ¼ cup brown sugar. Spread between layers and over top of cake. Chill until serving time.
Yield: 16 servings.

Stella Myers, Florida

Allow for the variation in oven temperatures by setting the timer for the minimum time indicated in the recipe. Test by inserting a cake tester or toothpick into the center of the cake. If the tester comes out clean, cake is done.

MAPLE SYRUP SNACK CAKE

2 eggs
1 c. packed brown sugar
1 c. maple syrup
1 tsp. baking powder
1 tsp. soda
1 c. sour cream
1 tsp. vanilla extract
2 c. flour

Combine eggs and brown sugar in mixer bowl; mix well. Stir in maple syrup, baking powder, soda and sour cream. Add vanilla and flour; mix well. Pour into greased 9x13-inch cake pan. Bake at 325 degrees for 40 minutes or until cake tests done. Cut into squares. Serve warm or cool. Yield: 16 servings.

Martha Warner, Michigan

MAPLE COCONUT PIE

1 c. flaked coconut
1 unbaked 9-in. pie shell
⅓ c. butter, softened
½ c. sugar
3 eggs, well beaten
1 c. maple syrup
½ tsp. vanilla extract

Sprinkle coconut over pie shell. Cream butter and sugar in bowl until fluffy. Add remaining ingredients; mix well. Pour into prepared pie shell. Bake at 425 degrees for 10 minutes. Reduce temperature to 350 degrees. Bake for 15 to 20 minutes longer or until set. Yield: 6 to 8 servings.

Monica Howard, Michigan

MAPLE CREAM PIE

1½ c. milk, scalded
¾ c. maple syrup
2 tbsp. cornstarch
1 egg
¼ c. sugar
Dash of salt
1 baked 9-in. pie shell
1 c. whipping cream, whipped

Mix first 6 ingredients in double boiler. Cook until thick, stirring constantly. Pour into pie shell. Chill until serving time. Top with whipped cream. Yield: 6 to 8 servings.

MAPLE-PECAN BARS

1½ c. plus 2 tbsp. sifted flour
¼ c. plus ⅔ c. packed brown sugar
½ c. butter, softened
1 c. maple syrup
2 eggs, slightly beaten
½ tsp. vanilla extract
¼ tsp. salt
1 c. chopped pecans

Combine 1½ cups flour and ¼ cup brown sugar in bowl. Cut in butter until crumbly. Press into greased 9x13-inch baking pan. Bake at 350 degrees for 15 minutes. Combine ⅔ cup brown sugar and maple syrup in small saucepan. Simmer for 5 minutes. Pour over eggs very gradually, stirring constantly with wire whisk. Stir in vanilla, 2 tablespoons flour and salt. Pour into prepared pan. Sprinkle pecans on top. Bake at 350 degrees for 20 to 25 minutes or until set. Cool in pan on wire rack. Cut into bars. Yield: 2½ dozen.

Cheryle Harte, California

MAPLE WALNUT BRITTLE

2 c. packed light brown sugar
½ c. maple syrup
¼ c. butter
½ tsp. maple flavoring
1½ c. chopped walnuts
¼ tsp. soda

Bring brown sugar, maple syrup and ½ cup water to a boil in heavy saucepan. Cook, covered, over medium heat for 2 to 3 minutes or until steam washes sugar crystals from side of pan. Cook, uncovered, over high heat to 300 to 310 degrees on candy thermometer, hardcrack stage. Add butter, flavoring and walnuts. Stir in soda. Pour onto buttered baking sheet. Let stand until firm. Break into pieces. Yield: 1½ pounds.

Yvonne Selnick, Iowa

The hard-crack stage of candy making is reached when a drop of the mixture in cold water separates into hard threads that crack when pressed.

MELON

AUSTRIAN CANTALOUPE

½ c. Brandy
1 c. confectioners' sugar
Juice of 1 lemon
1 cantaloupe, peeled and cubed
½ pt. whipping cream
1 tsp. sugar

Mix Brandy, confectioners' sugar and lemon juice in saucepan. Simmer for 5 minutes. Add cantaloupe; mix lightly. Chill, covered, for 2 hours or longer. Whip cream with sugar in bowl until soft peaks form. Spoon cantaloupe into dessert glasses. Top with whipped cream. Garnish with maraschino cherries and mint sprigs. Yield: 6 servings.

Helga Blitz, Massachusetts

CANTALOUPE WITH BLUEBERRY SAUCE

½ c. sugar
1 tbsp. cornstarch
3 thin slices lemon
¾ c. Port
1½ to 2 c. blueberries
8 peeled cantaloupe rings
8 vanilla ice cream scoops

Combine sugar, cornstarch, lemon slices and wine in small saucepan. Simmer for 5 minutes or until clear. Remove lemon slices. Add blueberries. Chill well. Place cantaloupe rings on serving plates. Place scoop of ice cream in each ring. Top with chilled blueberry sauce. Yield: 8 servings.

Nonnie Coombs, California

FROZEN CANTALOUPE DELIGHT

⅓ c. milk
20 marshmallows
1½ c. cantaloupe pulp
⅛ tsp. salt
¼ c. chopped maraschino
*   cherries*
1 c. whipping cream

Place milk and marshmallows in saucepan. Cook, covered, over low heat for 10 minutes or until marshmallows are melted. Cool. Add cantaloupe pulp, salt and cherries. Chill in freezer until mixture begins to thicken. Whip cream in bowl until soft peaks form. Fold into cantaloupe mixture. Pour into refrigerator tray. Freeze, covered, until firm. Yield: 6 servings.

CANTALOUPE PIE

4 eggs, separated
1 c. sugar
1 tbsp. lemon juice
1 tbsp. grated lemon rind
½ c. orange juice
1 sm. package orange gelatin
¼ tsp. cream of tartar
1½ c. chopped cantaloupe
1   10-in. baked pie shell
1 c. whipping cream, whipped

Beat egg yolks in double boiler. Add ½ cup sugar, lemon juice and lemon rind. Cook until mixture coats spoon, stirring frequently; remove from heat. Bring orange juice to a boil in saucepan. Stir in gelatin until dissolved. Stir gradually into egg yolk mixture; cool. Beat egg whites and cream of tartar until soft peaks form. Beat in remaining ½ cup sugar gradually. Fold in gelatin mixture. Add well-drained cantaloupe. Spoon into pie shell. Top with whipped cream. Chill for 4 hours or longer.
Yield: 8 servings.

CANTALOUPE SUPREME

2 c. strawberries
1 c. sugar
2 tsp. cornstarch
2 tbsp. butter
3 drops of red food coloring
2 tsp. lemon juice
4 c. small cantaloupe balls

Mix first 5 ingredients in heavy saucepan. Cook until thickened, stirring constantly. Add lemon juice. Place cantaloupe balls in mold. Pour strawberry mixture over cantaloupe. Chill for 4 hours or until set. Unmold onto serving plate. Garnish with whipped cream. Yield: 6 servings.

GINGERED HONEYDEW

1 *honeydew melon*
2 *kiwifruit*
Juice of 1 lemon
1 *tsp. grated gingerroot*

Cut melon into bite-sized pieces. Peel and slice kiwifruit. Combine fruit, lemon juice and ginger in bowl; toss lightly. Chill until serving time. Spoon into sherbet glasses. Garnish with lime wedges and sprinkle of flaked coconut. Yield: 4 servings.

Gordon Hines, Tennessee

MELON-MINT MOLD

1 *lg. package lemon gelatin*
2 *sprigs of fresh mint*
2 *tbsp. lemon juice*
½ *c. mayonnaise*
½ *tsp. salt*
2 *c. chopped honeydew melon*
¼ *c. toasted blanched almonds,*
   slivered

Dissolve gelatin in 1 cup hot water in bowl; add mint sprigs. Let stand for 5 minutes. Remove mint. Add ½ cup cold water, lemon juice, mayonnaise and salt; mix well. Chill until partially set. Beat until fluffy. Fold in remaining ingredients. Pour into mold. Chill until firm. Unmold onto serving plate. Yield: 6 servings.

Hazel Jones, Arkansas

HONEYDEW CHIFFON PIE

1 *sm. package lemon gelatin*
2 *tbsp. lemon juice*
1 *c. whipping cream*
¼ *c. sifted confectioners' sugar*
¼ *tsp. pumpkin pie spice*
2 *c. chopped honeydew melon*
1   *9-in. baked crumb crust*

Dissolve gelatin in 1 cup boiling water in bowl. Stir in lemon juice. Chill until partially congealed. Whip cream in bowl until soft peaks form. Beat in confectioners' sugar and spice. Whip gelatin until fluffy. Fold in whipped cream and honeydew. Spoon into crumb crust. Chill until set. Yield: 6 servings.

PATIO WATERMELON ICE

½ *lg. watermelon*
Juice of 4 oranges
Juice of 2 lemons
1 *c. sugar*
1 *egg white, stiffly beaten*

Scoop pulp from watermelon; reserve rind. Place pulp in cloth bag. Squeeze juice into bowl. Add citrus juices and sugar; mix well. Pour into 1-gallon freezer container. Freeze until partially set. Fold in egg white. Freeze until firm. Spoon into watermelon rind. Garnish with melon balls. Yield: 24 servings.

Alice Brooks, Georgia

MINTED MELON BALLS

1 *c. sugar*
4 *mint leaves*
¼ *c. lemon juice*
1 *c. cantaloupe balls*
4 *c. watermelon balls*
1 *c. honeydew melon balls*

Bring 2 cups water, sugar and mint leaves to a boil in saucepan; mix well. Cook for 2 minutes. Remove from heat; strain. Mix with lemon juice in bowl. Chill syrup. Arrange melon balls in chilled dessert cups. Pour syrup over melon. Yield: 8 servings.

Nadine Collins, Illinois

ZABAGLIONE WITH MELON

4 *egg yolks*
¼ *c. sugar*
¾ *c. Marsala*
6 *c. watermelon balls*

Mix egg yolks and sugar in double boiler. Cook over simmering water until light and fluffy, beating constantly. Add wine gradually, beating constantly at high speed for 10 minutes or until mixture is very thick. Place melon balls in dessert glasses. Spoon warm zabaglione over melon. Yield: 8 servings.

Andrea Mineschi, Tennessee

SPICED WATERMELON RIND PIE

1½ c. cubed peeled watermelon
  rind
1 c. sugar
1 tsp. cinnamon
⅓ tsp. nutmeg
¼ tsp. cloves
⅛ tsp. salt
2 tbsp. flour
¼ c. vinegar
½ c. raisins
1 recipe 2-crust pie pastry

Combine watermelon rind cubes with water to cover in saucepan. Simmer until tender; drain. Add sugar, cinnamon, nutmeg, cloves, salt, flour, vinegar and raisins to watermelon cubes; mix well. Pour into pastry-lined pie plate; top with remaining pastry. Seal edge; cut vents. Bake at 450 degrees until crust begins to brown. Reduce temperature to 350 degrees. Bake until set. Yield: 6 to 8 servings.

MOCHA

MOCHA BAVARIAN

1 env. unflavored gelatin
3 oz. semisweet chocolate
  chips
2 tbsp. strong coffee
3 egg yolks
¼ c. sugar
1 c. milk, scalded
1 c. whipping cream
2 egg whites

Soften gelatin in ¼ cup water. Melt chocolate chips with coffee in heavy saucepan, stirring to blend well. Beat egg yolks and sugar in double boiler until thick and lemon-colored. Stir in hot milk very gradually. Cook until thickened, stirring constantly. Stir in gelatin until dissolved. Add chocolate mixture; mix well. Chill until partially set. Whip cream in bowl until soft peaks form. Beat egg whites until stiff peaks form. Fold whipped cream and beaten egg whites into partially congealed mixture. Spoon into small mold. Chill until set. Unmold on serving plate. Yield: 6 servings.

PATIO COFFEE ICE CREAM

6 tbsp. ground coffee
3 c. milk
2 eggs
1½ c. sugar
2 tbsp. arrowroot
2 c. whipping cream, whipped

Scald coffee and milk in saucepan. Strain through cheesecloth. Beat eggs, sugar and arrowroot in double boiler. Stir in milk gradually. Cook until mixture thickens, stirring constantly. Remove from heat; cool. Fold in whipped cream. Pour into freezer container. Freeze according to manufacturer's instructions. Yield: 2 quarts.

Mrs. Arzo Carson, Tennessee

MOCHA MOUSSE

8 oz. semisweet chocolate
2 tsp. instant coffee powder
½ c. sugar
1 tsp. vanilla extract
6 eggs, separated
2 c. whipping cream, whipped,
  sweetened
2 pkg. ladyfingers

Blend chocolate, instant coffee, ¼ cup water and sugar in saucepan. Cook until chocolate is melted, stirring constantly. Cool. Add vanilla and beaten egg yolks; mix well. Fold in stiffly beaten egg whites and half the whipped cream. Arrange half the ladyfingers in bottom of 9-inch springform pan. Spoon half the chocolate mixture over ladyfingers. Repeat layers. Spread remaining whipped cream on top. Garnish with chocolate curls. Place on serving plate. Remove side of pan.
Yield: 12 to 14 servings.

Anne M. Pridgen, Virginia

To unmold gelatin desserts, run a thin hot knife around the edge and wrap mold with a kitchen towel dipped in hot water and squeezed dry.

CAFE AU LAIT PETITS PUFFS

⅓ c. sugar
1 c. whipping cream
2 tbsp. instant coffee powder
3 doz. Miniature Cream Puffs
1 c. confectioners' sugar

Blend sugar gradually into whipping cream in bowl, beating until soft peaks form. Dissolve coffee in 2 tablespoons boiling water. Fold half the coffee mixture into whipped cream. Spoon into puffs. Blend remaining coffee mixture with confectioners' sugar in bowl. Spoon over puffs.

Miniature Cream Puffs

½ c. butter
¼ tsp. salt
1 c. sifted flour
4 eggs

Mix 1 cup water, butter and salt in saucepan. Bring to a full rolling boil. Reduce heat. Stir in flour quickly, mixing vigorously with wooden spoon until mixture leaves side of pan. Remove from heat. Add eggs 1 at a time, beating after each addition until smooth. Drop by heaping teaspoonfuls onto greased baking sheet. Bake at 400 degrees for 20 minutes. Yield: 3 dozen.

MOCHA VELVET PUDDING

1 env. whipped topping mix
1 sm. package chocolate instant
    pudding mix
1 tbsp. instant coffee powder
2 c. cold milk

Combine all ingredients in mixer bowl. Beat for 5 minutes at high speed or until thick. Spoon into dessert dishes. Garnish with chopped nuts. Chill in refrigerator. Yield: 6 servings.

June Graf, Ohio

CHOCOLATE MOCHA ROLL

6 oz. semisweet chocolate
3 tbsp. strong coffee
5 eggs, separated
1 c. sugar
Cocoa
1¼ c. whipping cream

Line greased 12x18-inch baking pan with buttered waxed paper. Melt chocolate with coffee in double boiler; blend well. Cool slightly. Beat egg yolks and ⅔ cup sugar in mixer bowl until thick and lemon-colored. Blend in chocolate mixture. Beat egg whites until stiff peaks form. Fold gently into chocolate mixture. Spread evenly in prepared pan. Bake at 350 degrees for 15 minutes or until wooden pick inserted in middle comes out clean; do not overbake. Let stand, covered with damp cloth, for 30 minutes or until cool; cake will fall. Invert onto cloth sprinkled with cocoa; remove waxed paper. Whip cream in mixer bowl until soft peaks form. Add remaining ⅓ cup sugar; mix well. Spread on baked layer. Roll as for jelly roll from long side, lifting cloth to roll and place on serving platter. Garnish with additional cocoa. Yield: 8 servings.

Elise Newman, Texas

MOCHA CAKE

1½ c. sugar
½ c. shortening
1 egg
½ c. baking cocoa
2 tsp. vanilla extract
2 c. flour
1 tsp. soda
1 tsp. baking powder
½ tsp. salt
1½ c. coffee

Cream sugar and shortening in mixer bowl until light and fluffy. Blend in egg, cocoa and vanilla. Add sifted dry ingredients alternately with coffee, mixing well after each addition. Pour into greased tube pan. Bake at 350 degrees for 45 minutes. Remove to wire rack to cool. Frost as desired. Yield: 16 servings.

Billie Warfield, Tennessee

COFFEE-YOGURT CHIFFON PIE

1 env. unflavored gelatin
⅔ c. sugar
3 eggs, separated
¾ c. milk
8 oz. coffee-flavored yogurt
1 chocolate crumb pie shell

Mix gelatin, ⅓ cup sugar, beaten egg yolks and milk in saucepan. Cook over low heat until gelatin dissolves and mixture is thickened, stirring constantly. Cool. Blend in yogurt. Chill until partially set. Add remaining ⅓ cup sugar gradually to softly beaten egg whites, beating until stiff. Fold into gelatin mixture. Spoon into pie shell. Chill until firm. Yield: 8 servings.

Judy Evans, Iowa

CHOCOLATE MOCHA CREAM PIE

2 tbsp. gelatin
2 eggs
2 egg yolks
6 tbsp. sugar
6 tbsp. flour
12 oz. semisweet chocolate, chopped
10 tbsp. strong coffee
1½ c. hot milk
1 c. whipping cream
4 egg whites
1 tbsp. rum extract
1 baked 9-in. pie shell

Soften gelatin in ¼ cup cold water. Combine eggs, egg yolks, sugar and flour in bowl. Beat until light and fluffy. Melt chocolate in coffee in saucepan over low heat; blend well. Blend in hot milk. Stir a small amount of hot mixture into egg mixture; stir egg mixture into hot mixture. Cook over low heat until thickened; remove from heat. Stir in gelatin until dissolved. Chill until partially set. Whip cream in bowl until soft peaks form. Whip egg whites until stiff peaks form. Fold whipped cream, beaten egg whites and rum into custard. Spoon into pie shell. Chill until set. Yield: 8 servings.

PECAN MOCHA ANGEL PIE

2 egg whites
⅛ tsp. cream of tartar
½ c. sugar
½ c. chopped pecans
6 oz. semisweet chocolate chips
3 tbsp. strong coffee
1 tsp. vanilla extract
1 c. whipping cream

Beat egg whites and cream of tartar in mixer bowl until foamy. Add sugar 1 tablespoon at a time, beating until stiff peaks form. Spread over bottom and side of greased 9-inch pie plate, shaping high edge. Sprinkle with pecans. Bake at 275 degrees for 50 minutes or until light brown and crisp. Cool. Melt chocolate chips in double boiler over hot water. Blend in coffee. Cook for 5 minutes, stirring constantly. Stir in vanilla. Cool. Whip cream in bowl until soft peaks form. Fold in chocolate mixture. Spoon into meringue shell. Chill for 2 hours or until set. Yield: 9 servings.

Yolanda Sawyer, Oregon

MOCHA FUDGE PIES

½ c. butter, softened
1½ c. packed dark brown sugar
6 eggs
24 oz. semisweet chocolate
4 tsp. instant coffee powder
2 tsp. almond extract
½ c. flour
1 c. chopped walnuts
2 unbaked 9-in. pie shells
2 c. whipping cream
2 tbsp. sugar
¼ c. chopped maraschino cherries

Cream butter and brown sugar in mixer bowl until light and fluffy. Blend in eggs 1 at a time. Melt chocolate in double boiler over hot water. Add to creamed mixture gradually, stirring constantly. Add coffee powder, flavoring, flour and walnuts; mix well. Spoon into pie shells. Bake at 375 degrees for 25 minutes. Cool on wire racks. Whip cream in bowl until soft peaks form. Add sugar gradually, beating constantly. Fold in cherries. Spread over pies. Garnish with chocolate sprinkles. Chill. Yield: 12 servings.

Maggie Thomas, California

Pies with cream or custard filling should be cooled to room temperature and then stored in the refrigerator to prevent spoilage.

MOLASSES

MOLASSES POUND CAKE

1 c. molasses
1 c. oil
1 c. buttermilk
2 eggs, slightly beaten
1 c. packed dark brown sugar
4 tsp. mixed spices
1   18-ounce jar mincemeat
½ c. chopped pecans
4 c. whole wheat flour
1 tsp. soda
1 tsp. salt
1 tbsp. baking powder

Beat first 5 ingredients in bowl. Stir in spices, mincemeat and pecans. Add flour, soda, salt and baking powder; mix well. Pour into greased and floured bundt pan. Bake at 325 degrees for 1 hour or until cake tests done.
Yield: 16 servings.

Virginia Rolen, Tennessee

MOLASSES SNACK CAKE

1 tsp. soda
⅔ c. molasses
½ c. sugar
½ c. shortening
1 egg
2 c. flour, sifted
2 tsp. cinnamon
½ tsp. salt

Dissolve soda in ⅔ cup boiling water. Mix remaining ingredients in bowl in order listed. Add soda mixture; mix well. Pour into greased 9-inch square pan. Bake at 350 degrees for 40 minutes. Serve warm with whipped cream, if desired. Yield: 9 servings.

Hope A. Knight, New York

MOLASSES CRUMB PIES

3 c. flour
1 c. sugar
1 c. margarine
1 tsp. soda
1 c. molasses
3 baked 8-in. pie shells

Combine flour and sugar in bowl. Cut in margarine until crumbly. Dissolve soda in 1 cup hot water. Mix with molasses until foamy. Reserve 1 cup flour mixture. Stir molasses mixture into remaining flour mixture. Pour into pie shells. Bake at 325 degrees for 8 minutes. Sprinkle with reserved flour mixture. Bake for 15 to 20 minutes longer or until crumbs are browned. Yield: 3 pies.

Ilona Tatum, Colorado

OLD-FASHIONED MOLASSES PIE

1¼ c. molasses
2 tbsp. butter
4 eggs, beaten
2 tbsp. flour
⅔ c. sugar
1 unbaked pie shell

Bring molasses and butter to a boil in saucepan. Beat eggs until light and fluffy in bowl. Mix flour and sugar with eggs. Add to molasses mixture; mix well. Pour into pie shell. Bake at 350 degrees for 30 minutes or until set.
Yield: 6 servings.

Ann Potts, Pennsylvania

MOLASSES SQUARES

1¾ c. sugar
1 c. shortening, melted, cooled
½ c. molasses
1 tsp. cloves
1 tsp. cinnamon
1 tsp. ginger
1 tsp. soda
1 tsp. baking powder
4 c. flour
½ c. sifted confectioners' sugar

Combine first 6 ingredients in large bowl. Dissolve soda in 1 cup hot water. Add to sugar mixture, blending well. Combine baking powder and flour. Stir into sugar mixture gradually, mixing well. Pour batter into greased and floured 10x15-inch pan. Bake at 375 degrees for 15 minutes or until toothpick inserted in center comes out clean. Combine confectioners' sugar with 3 teaspoons water in bowl; spread thinly over top while hot. Cool. Cut into small squares. Yield: 3 dozen.

Marilyn Markell, Colorado

OLD-FASHIONED MOLASSES COOKIES

1 c. molasses
1 c. sugar
¾ c. shortening
⅔ c. milk
6 c. (about) flour
1 tsp. salt
1 tsp. cream of tartar
1 tbsp. (about) soda
¼ tsp. nutmeg

Beat first 3 ingredients in bowl. Add milk alternately with dry ingredients, mixing well. Roll to ¼-inch thickness on floured surface. Cut with cookie cutter. Place on cookie sheet. Bake at 400 degrees for 6 minutes or until brown. Yield: 6 dozen.

Marion Brown, North Carolina

CRISP MOLASSES COOKIES

10 tbsp. butter
1 c. sugar
½ c. molasses
2 eggs
½ tsp. vanilla extract
1¾ c. flour
¼ tsp. soda
¼ tsp. salt
¼ tsp. mace
2 c. chopped pecans

Cream butter, sugar and molasses in large mixer bowl. Blend in eggs and vanilla. Sift flour, soda, salt and mace together. Add to butter mixture, ½ cup at a time, mixing well after each addition. Stir in pecans. Drop by heaping teaspoonfuls 2 inches apart onto greased and floured cookie sheet. Bake at 350 degrees for 8 minutes. Remove to wire racks to cool. Yield: 5 dozen.

CREAMY NECTARINE CHEESECAKE

1⅓ c. graham cracker crumbs
1¼ c. sugar
¼ c. melted butter
1½ tbsp. cornstarch
1 c. chopped peeled nectarines
1½ c. cream-style cottage cheese
3 eggs
1 tsp. vanilla extract
1 c. sour cream

Mix cracker crumbs, ¼ cup sugar and butter in bowl. Press over bottom and 1½ inches up side of buttered 9-inch springform pan. Sprinkle cornstarch over nectarines; toss lightly. Beat cottage cheese in mixer bowl until smooth and creamy. Add remaining 1 cup sugar, eggs and vanilla; beat until smooth. Layer nectarines and cottage cheese mixture over crust. Bake at 350 degrees for 1 hour. Cool completely. Chill until serving time. Spread sour cream over top. Garnish with fresh nectarine slices. Place on serving plate; remove side of pan. Yield: 8 servings.

Morgan Jones, Tennessee

NUT

CASHEW BARS

1 c. flour
¼ c. packed brown sugar
½ tsp. baking powder
¼ tsp. soda
½ c. margarine, chilled, sliced
1 tbsp. vanilla extract
3 c. miniature marshmallows
1 can sweetened condensed milk
1 c. peanut butter chips
1 3-ounce can chow mein noodles
1 c. coarsely chopped cashews

Combine flour, sugar, baking powder and soda in bowl. Cut in margarine and 1 teaspoon vanilla until crumbly. Press over bottom of 9x13-inch baking pan. Bake at 350 degrees for 15 minutes or until lightly brown. Top with marshmallows. Bake for 2 minutes longer or until marshmallows begin to puff. Remove from oven; cool. Combine sweetened condensed milk and peanut butter chips in heavy saucepan. Cook for 6 to 8 minutes or until slightly thickened. Remove from heat. Stir in remaining 2 teaspoons vanilla, chow mein noodles and cashews. Spread evenly over marshmallows. Chill. Cut into bars.
Yield: 3 dozen.

Mary M. Rodgers, Alabama

CASHEW DROPS

½ c. plus 3 tbsp. butter,
  softened
1 c. packed brown sugar
1 egg
1½ tsp. vanilla extract
2 c. flour
¾ tsp. soda
¾ baking powder
½ tsp. cinnamon
¼ tsp. nutmeg
¼ tsp. salt
⅓ c. sour cream
1 c. chopped cashews
3 tbsp. butter
2 tbsp. milk
2 c. sifted confectioners' sugar

Cream ½ cup butter and brown sugar in bowl until light and fluffy. Add egg and ½ teaspoon vanilla; beat well. Combine flour, soda, baking powder, cinnamon, nutmeg and salt. Add to creamed mixture alternately with sour cream, mixing well after each addition. Stir in cashews. Drop by teaspoonfuls onto greased cookie sheet. Bake at 400 degrees for 8 minutes. Cool on wire rack. Brown remaining 3 tablespoons butter in saucepan. Add remaining 1 teaspoon vanilla, milk and confectioners' sugar; beat until smooth. Spread over cooled cookies. Yield: 4 dozen.

Gayla Carson, Virginia

CHESTNUT-COCONUT TART

1 recipe 1-crust pie pastry
3 eggs
1   8¾-oz. can chestnut purée
1 c. packed brown sugar
¼ c. melted margarine
¼ c. orange marmalade
⅔ c. flaked coconut
Unsweetened whipped cream
Glacéed orange slices, cut into
  wedges (optional)

Fit pastry into 11-inch tart pan. Prick bottom. Cover with foil, pressing foil gently onto surface of pastry. Bake at 450 degrees for 5 minutes. Remove foil. Bake for 5 to 7 minutes longer or until golden. Combine eggs, chestnut purée, brown sugar, margarine and marmalade in mixer bowl. Beat until smooth. Stir in coconut. Pour into tart shell. Bake at 350

degrees for 30 to 35 minutes or until knife inserted near center comes out clean. Cool on wire rack. Garnish with whipped cream and orange slices. Yield: 8 to 10 servings.

HAZELNUT PIE

3 eggs
½ c. packed dark brown sugar
1 c. light corn syrup
¼ tsp. salt
1 tsp. vanilla extract
½ c. melted butter
1½ c. coarsely chopped toasted
  hazelnuts
1 unbaked 9-in. pie shell

Place first 5 ingredients in mixer bowl; beat until smooth. Stir in butter and hazelnuts. Pour into pie shell. Bake at 375 degrees for 45 minutes or until set. Yield: 6 to 8 servings.

HAZELNUT COOKIES

1 c. sifted flour
½ c. butter, softened
1 c. finely chopped hazelnuts
⅛ tsp. salt
2 tbsp. sugar
1 tsp. vanilla extract
Confectioners' sugar

Combine flour, butter, hazelnuts, salt, sugar and vanilla in bowl; mix well with hands. Chill for 30 minutes. Shape into 1¼-inch balls. Place 1 inch apart on cookie sheet. Bake at 375 degrees for 15 to 20 minutes or until set but not brown. Let stand for 1 minute. Remove to wire rack to cool for several minutes. Roll warm cookies in confectioners' sugar. Cool completely. Roll in confectioners' sugar again. Yield: 1½ to 2 dozen.

Virginia Luethe, Oregon

HAZELNUT SHORTBREAD

1¼ c. butter, softened
½ c. sugar
2 c. flour
1 c. cornstarch
⅓ c. ground hazelnuts

Beat butter and sugar in mixer bowl until light. Add mixture of flour, cornstarch and nuts; mix well. Divide into 6 portions. Roll each portion into 6-inch circle on ungreased cookie sheet. Smooth edges with fingers. Score each circle into 8 wedges with spatula. Press edges with fork. Bake at 325 degrees for 35 minutes or until light brown. Cool on cookie sheet on wire rack. Break into wedges. Store in airtight container.

HAZELNUT SWIRLS

1 c. butter, softened
1 c. sugar
1 egg
1 tsp. vanilla extract
2½ c. flour
½ tsp. baking powder
¼ tsp. nutmeg
¾ c. ground hazelnuts

Cream butter and sugar in bowl until light and fluffy. Add egg and vanilla; mix well. Sift in flour, baking powder and nutmeg; mix well. Stir in hazelnuts. Spoon into pastry bag fitted with ½-inch plain tip. Pipe into spirals on greased cookie sheet. Bake at 350 degrees for 10 minutes or just until firm and golden brown. Cool on cookie sheet for 5 minutes. Remove to wire rack to cool completely. Yield: 3 dozen.

Clara Schwintz, Nebraska

HICKORY NUT CAKE

2 c. sugar
¾ c. plus 1 tbsp. margarine, softened
3 eggs, separated
1 c. milk
2 tsp. vanilla extract
2½ c. flour
½ tsp. salt
1 tbsp. baking powder
2¼ c. chopped hickory nuts
1½ c. packed light brown sugar
1 c. light cream

Cream sugar and ¾ cup margarine in mixer bowl until light. Add egg yolks; mix well. Add milk and 1 teaspoon vanilla. Add flour, salt and baking powder; beat well. Fold in beaten egg whites. Add 1¼ cups nuts. Pour into 2 greased and floured 9-inch cake pans. Bake at 350 degrees for 30 to 35 minutes or until cake tests done. Cool on wire rack. Cook brown sugar and cream in saucepan until mixture reaches spreading consistency. Remove from heat. Add remaining 1 tablespoon margarine and 1 teaspoon vanilla; mix well. Add remaining 1 cup nuts. Spread between layers and over top and side of cake. Yield: 16 servings.

Naomi Lauchnor, Pennsylvania

HICKORY NUT CAKE
WITH BUTTERMILK FROSTING

3¾ c. sifted cake flour
4 tsp. baking powder
½ tsp. salt
4¼ c. sugar
¾ c. butter, softened
3 tsp. vanilla extract
3 eggs, separated
¾ c. milk
1½ c. ground hickory nuts
⅓ c. oil
½ c. packed brown sugar
1 c. buttermilk
½ c. margarine
1 tsp. soda

Sift first 3 ingredients together 3 times. Cream 2¼ cups sugar, butter and 2 teaspoons vanilla in mixer bowl until light. Add egg yolks; beat well. Add sifted ingredients and milk alternately, beating well after each addition. Fold in hickory nuts and stiffly beaten egg whites gently. Blend in oil. Pour into 2 greased and floured 9-inch cake pans. Bake at 350 degrees for 35 minutes or just until cake pulls from side of pan. Cool in cake pans for 5 minutes. Remove to wire rack to cool. Combine remaining 2 cups sugar and last 4 ingredients in saucepan. Cook over low heat to 240 to 248 degrees on candy thermometer, firm soft-ball stage, stirring mixture occasionally. Cool to lukewarm. Add remaining 1 teaspoon vanilla. Beat until mixture thickens and loses its gloss. Spread between layers and over top and side of cake.

Martha E. Roush, Ohio

HICKORY NUT MERINGUE PIE

2 *c. maple syrup*
1 *tsp. salt*
⅔ *c. cornstarch*
3 *eggs, separated*
2 *tbsp. butter*
1 *tsp. vanilla extract*
Dash of cinnamon
½ *c. chopped hickory nuts*
1 *baked 9-in. pie shell*
6 *tbsp. sugar*

Bring syrup, salt and 1 cup water to a boil in saucepan. Add cornstarch blended with ½ cup water. Cook, covered, over low heat for 5 minutes or until mixture comes to a boil. Stir a small amount of hot mixture into beaten egg yolks; stir egg yolks into hot mixture. Cook for 1 minute, stirring constantly; remove from heat. Stir in butter, vanilla, cinnamon and nuts. Pour into pie shell. Beat egg whites with sugar until stiff peaks form. Spread over pie, sealing to edge. Bake at 375 degrees for 10 minutes or until light brown.

Mrs. John Logan, Ohio

HICKORY NUT PUDDING

2 *c. packed brown sugar*
1 *c. flour*
1 *tsp. baking powder*
1 *c. sugar*
1 *c. milk*
½ *c. chopped hickory nuts*

Dissolve brown sugar in 1 cup hot water in small bowl. Combine remaining ingredients in bowl; mix well. Pour into 9x9-inch greased baking dish. Pour brown sugar mixture over top. Bake at 300 degrees for 40 minutes. Serve with whipped cream.

Carol Leak, Texas

MACADAMIA-MOCHA PIE

½ *c. chopped macadamia nuts*
1   *9-in. chocolate crumb pie shell*
¼ *c. coffee*
1   *7-oz. jar marshmallow creme*
12 *oz. whipped topping*

Sprinkle nuts into pie shell, reserving 1 tablespoon. Mix coffee, marshmallow creme and 2 tablespoons water in bowl. Fold in whipped topping. Pour into pie shell. Freeze. Sprinkle with reserved nuts. Yield: 6 to 8 servings.

Violet S. Voges, Texas

MACADAMIA-COCONUT PIE

1 *env. unflavored gelatin*
½ *c. sugar*
⅛ *tsp. salt*
1¼ *c. milk*
3 *eggs, separated*
1 *tsp. vanilla extract*
½ *c. coconut*
½ *c. finely chopped macadamia nuts*
1 *baked 9-in. pie shell*
1 *c. whipping cream, whipped*

Mix first 3 ingredients in double boiler. Beat in milk and egg yolks. Cook over simmering water until thick, stirring constantly. Cool slightly. Stir in vanilla. Fold in stiffly beaten egg whites, coconut and nuts. Spoon into pie shell. Spread whipped cream over top. Garnish with additional coconut and nuts. Chill until serving time.
Yield: 6 to 8 servings.

Christine Cross, New York

MAPLE-MACADAMIA PIE

1 *c. chopped macadamia nuts*
1 *c. shredded coconut*
1 *unbaked pie shell*
1 *c. maple syrup*
3 *eggs, lightly beaten*
¼ *c. sugar*
¼ *tsp. salt*
6 *tbsp. melted butter*

Sprinkle nuts and coconut in pie shell. Chill for 15 minutes. Combine remaining ingredients in bowl; mix well. Pour into prepared pie shell. Bake at 400 degrees for 15 minutes. Reduce temperature to 350 degrees. Bake for 20 to 25 minutes or until set. Serve warm with whipped cream. Yield: 6 servings.

Hazel Newton, Pennsylvania

MACADAMIA BARS

⅓ c. butter, softened
1 c. flour
⅓ c. packed brown sugar
½ c. chopped macadamia nuts
1 egg
¼ c. sugar
8 oz. cream cheese, softened
2 tbsp. milk
2 tbsp. lemon juice
½ tsp. vanilla extract

Mix butter, flour and brown sugar in bowl. Add nuts. Reserve 1 cup mixture. Pat remaining mixture into ungreased 8-inch square baking dish. Bake at 350 degrees for 12 minutes or until light brown. Combine egg, sugar, cream cheese, milk, lemon juice and vanilla in bowl. Spread over baked layer. Sprinkle reserved crumb mixture over top. Bake at 350 degrees for 25 minutes or until set. Cool. Cut into bars. Yield: 2 dozen.

Carol Hall, California

MACADAMIA TEA COOKIES

1 c. butter, softened
½ c. confectioners' sugar
1 tsp. vanilla extract
¼ tsp. salt
2½ c. flour
¾ c. finely chopped macadamia
nuts

Beat butter, confectioners' sugar and vanilla in bowl until light and fluffy. Add salt and flour; mix well. Stir in macadamia nuts. Shape into 1-inch balls. Place on ungreased cookie sheet. Bake at 400 degrees for 10 minutes or until golden brown. Roll warm cookies in additional confectioners' sugar. Cool on wire rack. Yield: 3½ dozen.

Janice K. Ballard, Michigan

When chopping nuts for desserts in a blender or food processor, add 2 teaspoons sugar to each ½ cup nuts to prevent nuts from forming a paste.

OATMEAL

OATMEAL PIE

½ c. sugar
½ c. packed light brown sugar
½ c. margarine
2 eggs
¾ c. dark corn syrup
¾ c. quick-cooking oats
1 c. coconut
1 c. milk
1 unbaked 9-in. pie shell

Combine sugar, brown sugar, margarine and eggs in mixer bowl. Beat at medium speed until smooth. Add next 4 ingredients; mix well. Pour into unbaked pie shell. Bake at 350 degrees for 45 minutes or until set. Yield: 6 servings.

Mrs. Ernest W. Hofman, Pennsylvania

DUTCH OATMEAL CAKE

1 c. quick-cooking oats
1 c. packed brown sugar
1 c. sugar
½ c. shortening
2 eggs, beaten
1½ c. flour
1 tsp. soda
1 tsp. cinnamon
½ tsp. salt

Pour 1½ cups boiling water over oats in bowl; cool. Cream brown sugar, sugar, shortening and eggs in bowl until fluffy. Add flour, soda, cinnamon and salt. Add oats mixture. Pour into 9x13-inch cake pan. Spoon Frosting over cake. Bake at 350 degrees for 40 to 45 minutes. Yield: 16 servings.

Brown Sugar-Coconut Frosting

6 tbsp. margarine
½ c. packed brown sugar
½ tsp. vanilla extract
1 c. shredded coconut
½ c. chopped nuts

Melt margarine in skillet. Add remaining ingredients; mix well.

OATMEAL-ORANGE CAKE

½ c. butter, softened
1 c. sugar
2 eggs
1½ c. flour
2 tsp. baking powder
½ tsp. cinnamon
½ tsp. salt
1 c. quick-cooking oats
1 c. milk
¼ c. butter
½ c. packed brown sugar
½ c. chopped nuts
3 tbsp. orange juice

Cream ½ cup butter and sugar in mixer bowl. Add eggs 1 at a time, beating well after each addition. Sift flour, baking powder, cinnamon and salt together. Add sifted dry ingredients, oats and milk to creamed mixture alternately, mixing well after each addition. Spoon into 9-inch square baking pan. Bake at 350 degrees for 35 to 40 minutes. Melt remaining ¼ cup butter in saucepan. Add brown sugar, nuts and orange juice; mix well. Spread glaze over warm cake. Place under broiler until bubbly. Yield: 8 servings.

OATMEAL COOKIES

2½ c. flour
1 c. sugar
1 c. packed brown sugar
2 tsp. baking powder
1½ tsp. soda
1 tsp. salt
1 c. margarine
2 eggs
2 c. coconut
2 c. quick-cooking oats
1 c. chopped nuts
2 tsp. vanilla extract

Stir flour, sugar, brown sugar, baking powder, soda and salt together in large bowl. Melt margarine in saucepan. Pour over dry ingredients; mix well. Beat in eggs. Stir in coconut, oats, nuts and vanilla. Drop by teaspoonfuls onto lightly greased cookie sheet. Bake at 350 degrees for 10 to 12 minutes or until browned. Cool on wire rack. Yield: 4 dozen.

Michelle Emmrich, Indiana

APPLE-FILLED OATMEAL COOKIES

1 c. butter, softened
1 c. packed brown sugar
2 eggs
2 c. flour
2 tsp. baking powder
½ tsp. salt
1 tsp. cinnamon
½ tsp. cloves
½ c. milk
2 c. quick-cooking oats

Beat butter and sugar in mixer bowl until light and fluffy. Beat in eggs. Sift next 5 ingredients together. Add to creamed mixture alternately with milk. Stir in oats. Reserve about ¾ cup dough. Drop remaining dough by teaspoonfuls onto greased cookie sheet. Make small depression in center of each cookie; fill with Apple Filling. Cover filling with small amount of reserved dough. Bake at 375 degrees for 10 to 12 minutes. Yield: 3 dozen.

Apple Filling

1 c. chopped unpeeled apples
¼ c. raisins
¼ c. chopped pecans
½ c. sugar

Mix all ingredients with 2 tablespoons water in saucepan. Cook for 10 minutes or until mixture is thickened and apples are tender, stirring constantly. Cool.

OATMEAL AND PEANUT COOKIES

2 eggs, beaten
2 c. packed brown sugar
1½ c. melted butter
1½ c. chopped salted peanuts
2½ c. sifted flour
1 tsp. baking powder
1 tsp. soda
½ tsp. salt
3 c. quick-cooking oats
1 c. cornflakes

Beat eggs with brown sugar in bowl. Stir in butter and peanuts. Add sifted dry ingredients mixed with oats and cornflakes; mix well. Drop by spoonfuls onto greased baking sheet. Bake at 400 degrees for 8 to 10 minutes or until brown. Cool on wire rack. Yield: 6 dozen.

OATMEAL-CHOCOLATE DROP COOKIES

½ c. butter, softened
½ c. shortening
1 c. sugar
1 c. packed brown sugar
2 eggs
2 c. flour
1 tsp. soda
1 tsp. salt
2 c. quick-cooking oats
1 c. chopped nuts
1 c. chocolate chips

Cream butter, shortening, sugar and brown sugar in mixer bowl until light and fluffy. Blend in eggs. Add flour, soda and salt; beat until smooth. Stir in oats, nuts and chocolate chips. Drop by teaspoonfuls onto ungreased cookie sheet. Bake at 375 degrees for 10 minutes or until light brown. Remove to wire rack to cool. Yield: 8 dozen.

Gerda Mullins, Maryland

CINNAMON OATMEAL COOKIES

1 c. flour
½ c. sugar
½ c. packed brown sugar
½ tsp. baking powder
½ tsp. soda
¼ tsp. salt
1 tsp. cinnamon
½ c. shortening
1 egg
¼ tsp. vanilla extract
¾ c. quick-cooking oats

Combine flour, sugar, brown sugar, baking powder, soda, salt and cinnamon in bowl. Beat in shortening, egg and vanilla until well mixed. Stir in oats. Shape into small balls. Dip tops in additional sugar. Place on cookie sheet. Bake at 350 degrees for 12 to 15 minutes or until browned. Cool on wire rack. Yield: 3 dozen.

Sarah Spangler, Indiana

OATMEAL CARAMELITAS

1 14-oz. package caramels
½ c. evaporated milk
2 c. flour
2 c. quick-cooking oats
1½ c. packed brown sugar
1 tsp. soda
½ tsp. salt
1 c. melted margarine
6 oz. semisweet chocolate chips
1 c. chopped pecans

Melt caramels in evaporated milk in heavy saucepan over low heat. Cool slightly. Combine next 6 ingredients in large bowl; mix well. Press half the crumb mixture over bottom of greased 9x13-inch baking pan. Bake at 350 degrees for 10 minutes. Sprinkle with chocolate chips and pecans. Spread with caramel mixture. Sprinkle remaining crumb mixture on top. Chill until firm. Cut into bars. Yield: 3 dozen.

Frances Tharpe, North Carolina

OATMEAL NIBBLES

1 c. butter
1⅓ c. packed dark brown sugar
⅔ c. honey
3 c. quick-cooking oats
2 c. chopped raisins
1 c. shredded coconut
1 c. chopped almonds
1 c. wheat germ

Microwave butter in 2-quart glass baking dish on High for 1 minute or until melted. Blend in brown sugar and honey. Add remaining ingredients; mix well. Spread evenly in dish. Microwave on High for 6 minutes or until firm but moist, stirring once. Cool slightly. Shape into bite-sized balls; place in paper bonbon cups. Store in airtight container. Yield: 8 dozen.

Donae Parker, Texas

ORANGE

ORANGE BONNE BELLE

1½ c. graham cracker crumbs
¼ c. plus ⅓ c. sugar
⅓ c. melted butter
11 oz. cream cheese, softened
⅛ tsp. salt
6 oz. frozen orange juice
  concentrate
2 tsp. vanilla extract
1½ c. whipping cream,
  whipped
1 orange, sectioned

Combine crumbs, ¼ cup sugar and butter in bowl; mix well. Press over bottom of 9-inch springform pan. Bake at 375 degrees for 8 minutes. Cool. Cream ⅓ cup sugar, cream cheese and salt in bowl until light and fluffy. Add orange juice concentrate and vanilla; mix well. Fold in whipped cream gently. Spoon into prepared pan. Chill overnight. Place on serving plate; remove side of pan. Garnish with orange sections and candied violets. Yield: 6 to 8 servings.

Nancy Ricketts, North Carolina

ORANGE CHEESECAKE

1 c. plus 3 tbsp. sifted flour
2 c. sugar
2 tbsp. grated orange rind
½ c. butter
3 egg yolks
¾ tsp. vanilla extract
40 oz. cream cheese, softened
¼ tsp. salt
5 eggs
¼ c. frozen orange juice
  concentrate, thawed

Mix 1 cup flour, ¼ cup sugar and 1 tablespoon orange rind in bowl. Cut in butter until crumbly. Add 1 egg yolk and ½ teaspoon vanilla; mix well. Pat ⅓ of the dough over bottom of 9-inch springform pan. Bake at 400 degrees for 5 minutes. Cool. Pat remaining dough over side of pan to ½ inch from top, sealing to bottom. Combine cream cheese, remaining 1¾ cups sugar, 3 tablespoons flour, 1 tablespoon orange rind, ¼ teaspoon vanilla and salt in mixer bowl. Beat at low speed until smooth. Add whole eggs and remaining 2 egg yolks 1 at a time, beating well after each addition. Stir in orange juice. Pour into prepared pan. Place on foil on oven rack. Bake for 8 to 10 minutes. Reduce temperature to 225 degrees. Bake for 1 hour and 20 minutes longer. Let stand at room temperature until completely cool. Chill in refrigerator until serving time. Place on serving plate; remove side of pan. Garnish with orange sections and mint sprigs. Yield: 16 servings.

Bobbie Sanders, Michigan

ORANGE PARADISE

1 env. unflavored gelatin
1 6-oz. can frozen Florida
  orange juice concentrate
¾ c. sugar
2 egg whites
½ c. nonfat dry milk powder

Soften gelatin in ½ cup cold water in saucepan. Heat until gelatin is dissolved, stirring constantly. Remove from heat. Do not thaw orange juice concentrate. Reserve 1 tablespoon concentrate. Add remaining concentrate and ½ cup sugar to gelatin; stir until dissolved. Chill until partially set, stirring occasionally. Beat egg whites until soft peaks form. Add remaining ¼ cup sugar, beating until stiff peaks form. Combine dry milk powder and ½ cup ice water in mixer bowl; beat until stiff peaks form. Add reserved orange juice concentrate; beat until stiff peaks form. Fold egg whites and whipped milk powder into partially congealed mixture. Spoon into dessert dishes. Chill until set. Garnish with mint sprigs and orange sections. Yield: 8 servings.

Frozen orange juice concentrate is made from oranges at the peak of the season and has a better flavor than out-of-season fresh fruit. Store concentrate quickly in the freezer to prevent loss of color and quality.

ORANGE PUDDING

2 tbsp. butter, softened
1½ c. sugar
1 egg, beaten
1 c. raisins, ground
1 orange, ground
2 c. flour
1 tsp. soda
⅛ tsp. salt
1 c. sour milk
½ c. orange juice

Beat butter, 1 cup sugar and egg in bowl. Combine raisins, orange and sifted dry ingredients in bowl; mix well. Add to creamed mixture alternately with sour milk, mixing well after each addition. Pour into casserole. Bake at 375 degrees for 1 hour. Combine orange juice and remaining ½ cup sugar in bowl. Pour over warm pudding. Serve with whipped cream. Yield: 15 servings.

Nellie Boundy, West Virginia

ORANGE SHERBET COOLER

6 cans orange soda
1 can sweetened condensed
   milk
1 sm. can evaporated milk
1   7-oz. can crushed pineapple

Mix soda, condensed milk, evaporated milk and pineapple in ice cream freezer container. Chill for 20 minutes. Freeze using manufacturer's instructions. Yield: 2 quarts.

Kathy Graham, Tennessee

WHIPPED ORANGE SURPRISE

1 env. unflavored gelatin
½ c. sugar
½ c. nonfat dry milk powder
2 c. milk
1 tbsp. grated orange rind
6 tbsp. frozen Florida orange
   juice concentrate, thawed
2 egg whites

Blend gelatin, sugar, dry milk powder and milk in saucepan. Let stand until gelatin is softened. Heat until gelatin is dissolved, stirring constantly. Pour into shallow pan. Freeze until firm. Spoon into mixer bowl. Add remaining ingredients. Beat until smooth. Freeze until firm. Let stand at room temperature for 5 minutes. Scoop into dessert dishes. Yield: 8 servings.

Photograph for this recipe on page 35.

GOOD MORNING ORANGE CAKE

¼ c. plus 1 tbsp. butter,
   softened
1⅓ c. plus 3 tbsp. sugar
2 eggs
1½ c. sifted flour
1 tsp. soda
1 tsp. baking powder
½ tsp. salt
1 c. sour cream
2 tsp. vanilla extract
1 tbsp. cinnamon
½ c. chopped walnuts
2   11-oz. cans mandarin
   oranges
2 tbsp. cornstarch
¼ tsp. almond extract

Cream ¼ cup butter and 1 cup sugar in mixer bowl until light and fluffy. Blend in eggs. Sift flour, soda, baking powder and salt into bowl. Add sifted ingredients to batter alternately with sour cream, mixing well after each addition. Stir in vanilla. Combine ⅓ cup sugar, cinnamon and walnuts in small bowl. Layer cake batter and walnut mixture ½ at a time in greased 8-inch springform pan. Bake at 350 degrees for 35 to 40 minutes or until cake tests done. Cool in pan on wire rack. Drain oranges, reserving juice. Blend reserved orange juice, remaining 3 tablespoons sugar, and cornstarch in saucepan. Cook over low heat until thickened, stirring constantly. Stir in almond flavoring and remaining 1 tablespoon butter. Cool for 10 minutes. Fold in oranges. Place cake on serving plate; remove side of pan. Spoon orange sauce over top. Yield: 8 servings.

Drucie Brown, Kentucky

ORANGE SLICE CAKE

1 lb. candy orange slices
1 8-oz. package chopped dates
1 c. chopped nuts
3½ c. sifted flour
1 c. margarine, softened
2 c. sugar
4 eggs
½ c. buttermilk
1 tsp. soda
1 c. shredded coconut
2 c. confectioners' sugar
1 c. orange juice

Cut candy slices into small pieces. Coat candy, dates and nuts in ½ cup flour; set aside. Cream margarine and sugar in mixer bowl until light. Add eggs 1 at a time, mixing well. Add buttermilk. Sift in remaining 3 cups flour and soda; mix well. Fold in candy mixture and coconut. Spoon into greased and floured 9-inch tube pan. Bake at 250 degrees for 3 hours. Combine confectioners' sugar and orange juice in bowl; mix well. Pour on hot cake. Cool cake in tube pan. Remove to serving plate. Yield: 16 servings.

Mary Bayley, Illinois

ORANGE PARTY ROLL

4 eggs
1 c. sugar
¾ c. plus 1½ tbsp. flour
¾ tsp. baking powder
½ tsp. salt
1 tsp. vanilla extract
Confectioners' sugar
½ c. orange juice
1 tsp. grated orange rind
1 egg yolk, beaten
½ c. whipping cream, whipped

Beat eggs in mixer bowl at high speed until foamy. Add ¾ cup sugar gradually, beating until very thick. Sift ¾ cup flour, baking powder and ¼ teaspoon salt together; fold into egg mixture. Stir in vanilla. Pour into greased, waxed paper-lined 10x15-inch baking pan. Bake at 400 degrees for 13 minutes or until light brown. Invert onto towel dusted with confectioners' sugar. Roll cake in towel from narrow end. Cool for 10 minutes. Mix remaining ¼ cup sugar, 1½ tablespoons flour and ¼ teaspoon salt in saucepan. Add orange juice, orange rind and egg yolk. Bring to a boil over medium heat, stirring constantly. Cook for 1 minute. Cool thoroughly. Fold in whipped cream. Chill for ½ hour. Unroll cake. Spread with filling; reroll as for jelly roll. Let stand, wrapped in towel, for 1 hour. Chill until serving time. Yield: 12 servings.

ORANGE MARMALADE PIE

3 tbsp. cornstarch
3 tbsp. flour
Pinch of salt
½ c. plus 6 tbsp. sugar
½ c. orange juice
½ c. orange marmalade
3 eggs, separated
2 tbsp. lemon juice
2 tbsp. butter
⅛ tsp. orange extract
1 baked 8-in. pie shell

Mix first 3 ingredients and ½ cup sugar in double boiler. Stir in 1 cup water gradually. Cook over boiling water until very thick, stirring frequently. Add orange juice and marmalade. Add 1 tablespoon hot mixture to egg yolks; beat until smooth. Stir 2 tablespoons hot mixture into egg yolks; stir egg yolks into hot mixture. Cook until thickened, beating constantly. Remove from heat. Stir in lemon juice, butter and orange extract. Cool. Pour into pie shell. Beat egg whites and remaining 6 tablespoons sugar until stiff peaks form. Spread over pie, sealing to edge. Bake at 350 degrees for 15 minutes.
Yield: 6 servings.

Alma Irey, Oregon

ORANGE DROP COOKIES

⅔ c. shortening
1 c. sugar
1 egg
½ c. orange juice
2 tbsp. grated orange rind
2 c. flour
½ tsp. baking powder
½ tsp. soda
½ tsp. salt

Cream shortening, sugar and egg in bowl. Blend in orange juice and rind. Add mixture of flour, baking powder, soda and salt; mix well. Drop by rounded teaspoonfuls 2 inches apart onto ungreased cookie sheet. Bake at 400 degrees for 8 to 10 minutes or until edges are light brown. Cool on wire rack. Yield: 4 dozen.

Andrea Lyn Mummey, Oregon

FROZEN PAPAYA SOUFFLÉ

½ c. sugar
7 egg yolks
¾ c. coconut rum
1 c. whipping cream, whipped
1¼ c. papaya purée
¾ c. finely chopped walnuts
Papaya slices

Blend sugar and ½ cup water in double boiler. Cook over direct heat for 5 minutes or until syrupy. Cool for 5 minutes. Beat egg yolks until thick. Add sugar syrup and rum gradually, beating constantly. Cook over hot water until thickened, stirring constantly. Place pan in bowl of ice water. Beat with electric mixer until chilled and thickened. Fold in whipped cream and papaya purée. Pour into 1-quart soufflé dish with collar. Freeze until firm. Remove collar. Press walnuts around side of soufflé. Garnish with papaya slices. Yield: 8 servings.

PEACH

CREAMY PEACH CHEESECAKE

¾ c. flour
1 tsp. baking powder
½ tsp. salt
1 sm. package vanilla pudding and pie filling mix
3 tbsp. butter, softened
1 egg
½ c. milk
1 20-oz. can sliced peaches
½ c. sugar
8 oz. cream cheese, softened
1 tbsp. sugar
½ tsp. cinnamon

Mix first 7 ingredients in mixer bowl. Beat at medium speed for 2 minutes. Pour into greased 9-inch cake pan. Drain peaches, reserving 3 tablespoons juice. Arrange peaches over batter. Combine ½ cup sugar, cream cheese and reserved peach juice in bowl. Beat for 2 minutes. Spoon over batter, leaving 1-inch border. Combine 1 tablespoon sugar and cinnamon. Sprinkle over top. Bake at 350 degrees for 30 minutes or until golden brown. Cool.

Shirlene Nugene, Mississippi

PEACH COBBLER

1 c. flour
1 c. sugar
1 tbsp. baking powder
¼ tsp. cinnamon
½ c. milk
1 16-oz. can sliced peaches
3 tbsp. butter

Stir first 4 ingredients together in bowl. Add milk; mix well. Spread in baking dish. Combine peaches and butter in saucepan. Heat until butter melts; mix well. Pour over batter. Bake at 350 degrees for 45 minutes.

Ruby Surber, Maryland

PEACHES AND CREAM DESSERT

1 16-oz. can sliced peaches
¾ c. flour
1 sm. package vanilla instant pudding mix
1 tsp. baking powder
1 egg, beaten
½ c. milk
3 tbsp. butter, melted
8 oz. cream cheese, softened
½ c. plus 1 tbsp. sugar
½ tsp. cinnamon

Drain peaches, reserving ⅓ cup juice. Chop peaches. Combine next 3 ingredients in bowl. Stir in mixture of egg, milk and butter. Spread in greased 8-inch baking pan. Spoon peaches into prepared pan. Combine cream cheese, ½ cup sugar and peach juice in bowl; mix well. Pour over peaches. Sprinkle mixture of 1 tablespoon sugar and cinnamon over top. Bake at 350 degrees for 30 minutes. Cool. Yield: 9 servings.

GRANOLA PEACHES

1   *28-oz. can peach halves,
    drained*
1 *c. (about) packed brown sugar*
⅔ *c. granola*
¼ *c. packed brown sugar*
3 *tbsp. melted margarine*
¼ *c. chopped pecans*

Place peach halves cut sides up in ungreased 8-inch square baking pan.
Sprinkle 2 tablespoons brown sugar on
each peach half. Broil 5 inches from heat
source for 2 to 3 minutes or until bubbly.
Combine granola, ¼ cup brown sugar,
margarine and pecans in bowl; mix well.
Spoon onto peach halves. Broil for 1
minute longer. Place on heated serving
plate. Yield: 4 servings.

Laura Henderson, Missouri

PERSIAN PEACHES

4 *c. sliced peaches*
1 *c. orange juice*
6 *tbsp. honey*
1 *tbsp. finely chopped candied
    ginger*
Dash of salt

Mix all ingredients gently in bowl.
Chill mixture, covered, in refriger-
ator. Spoon into chilled sherbet glasses.
Yield: 5 servings.

POACHED PEACHES
WITH CUSTARD

1½ *c. sugar*
3 *tsp. rum extract*
8 *med. peaches, peeled*
¼ *tsp. salt*
1 *tbsp. cornstarch*
2 *egg yolks, beaten*
2 *c. milk*

Dissolve 1¼ cups sugar in 6 cups
water in skillet. Bring to a boil. Add
2 teaspoons rum flavoring and peaches.
Simmer, covered, for 10 minutes, turning peaches and basting occasionally.
Remove peaches to dessert dishes. Chill
until serving time. Mix ¼ cup sugar, salt
and cornstarch in saucepan. Add egg
yolks; mix well. Stir in milk gradually.

Cook over medium heat until thickened, stirring constantly; remove from
heat. Add 1 teaspoon rum flavoring.
Cover surface with plastic wrap. Cool to
room temperature. Serve custard over
peaches. Yield: 8 servings.

Joan Stockman, Colorado

PEACH PUDDING

6 *peaches, chopped*
Sugar
1¾ *c. milk*
2 *tbsp. (heaping) flour*
2 *eggs, beaten*
1 *tsp. vanilla extract*

Combine peaches with sugar to taste
in bowl; let stand for several minutes. Heat milk in saucepan over low
heat. Blend mixture of flour and ⅔ cup
sugar into eggs in bowl. Stir small
amount of hot milk into egg mixture;
stir egg mixture into hot milk. Cook
until thickened, stirring constantly; let
cool. Stir in vanilla and peaches. Spoon
into dessert dishes. Yield: 6 servings.

Cecil Stuart, Ohio

FRESH PEACH CAKE

2 *c. flour*
1 *tsp. soda*
1 *tsp. salt*
1 *tsp. cinnamon*
3 *eggs, well beaten*
1¾ *c. sugar*
1 *c. oil*
2 *c. sliced fresh peaches*
½ *c. chopped pecans*

Sift 1½ cups flour, soda, salt and cinnamon together. Combine eggs,
sugar and oil in mixer bowl. Beat until
smooth. Add flour mixture. Beat at low
speed just until blended. Toss peaches
and pecans with remaining ½ cup flour
in bowl. Fold gently into batter. Spoon
into greased and floured 9x13-inch cake
pan. Bake at 375 degrees for 50 minutes
or until cake tests done. Cool completely. Garnish with whipped cream.
Yield: 12 servings.

Audrey McElhany, Massachusetts

PEACH UPSIDE-DOWN CAKE

¼ c. melted butter
¾ c. packed brown sugar
18 blanched almonds
9 maraschino cherries
9 peach halves
2 eggs
2 egg yolks
1 c. sugar
¼ c. peach juice
1 c. flour, sifted
1 tsp. baking powder
¼ tsp. salt
2 egg whites, stiffly beaten

Combine butter and brown sugar in bowl; mix well. Spread in 8x8-inch baking pan. Insert 9 almonds in cherries. Arrange cherries in prepared pan. Place peaches cut side down over cherries. Place remaining almonds between peach halves. Beat eggs and egg yolks in bowl until light. Add sugar gradually, beating well after each addition. Add peach juice gradually, beating well after each addition. Add sifted dry ingredients; mix well. Fold stiffly beaten egg whites gently into batter. Pour over fruit. Bake at 350 degrees for 50 minutes or until cake tests done. Cool on wire rack for 10 minutes. Invert onto cake plate. Yield: 9 servings.

Sophie Newman, Rhode Island

FRESH PEACH PIE

¾ c. sugar
¼ c. peach gelatin
2 tbsp. cornstarch
¼ tsp. salt
Sliced fresh peaches
1 baked pie shell
Whipped topping

Mix sugar, gelatin, cornstarch and salt in saucepan. Blend in 1 cup water. Bring to a boil, stirring until gelatin dissolves. Cook for 2 minutes, stirring constantly. Cool. Place sliced peaches in pie shell. Spoon gelatin mixture over peaches. Chill until set. Spread whipped topping over pie. Garnish with additional sliced peaches and sprig of mint. Yield: 6 servings.

Betty Morris, Maryland

SOUR CREAM PEACH PIE

5 lg. ripe peaches, peeled,
   sliced
1 unbaked deep-dish pie shell
3 tbsp. plus ⅓ c. flour
1 c. sour cream
¾ c. sugar
1 egg
⅛ tsp. nutmeg
1 to 2 tbsp. Amaretto
¼ tsp. vanilla extract
¼ c. melted butter
¼ c. packed light brown sugar

Place peaches in pie shell. Combine 3 tablespoons flour, sour cream, sugar, egg, nutmeg, Amaretto and vanilla in bowl; mix well. Pour over peaches. Bake at 400 degrees for 25 minutes. Mix butter, remaining ⅓ cup flour and brown sugar in bowl until crumbly. Sprinkle over pie. Bake for 20 minutes longer. Cool. Yield: 6 servings.

Mim Kary, Maryland

PEANUT

PEANUT BUTTER PARFAIT

1 c. packed brown sugar
⅓ c. milk
¼ c. white corn syrup
1 tbsp. butter
¼ c. peanut butter
Vanilla ice cream
Peanuts

Combine brown sugar, milk, corn syrup and butter in saucepan. Cook over medium heat until sugar dissolves and butter melts, stirring constantly; remove from heat. Add peanut butter; beat until smooth. Cool. Alternate layers of peanut butter sauce and ice cream in parfait glasses, beginning and ending with ice cream. Top with peanuts. Serve immediately. Yield: 4 servings.

If brown sugar becomes too hard to use, place it in a tightly sealed container with a small piece of lettuce. Let stand for 2 days to soften.

OLD-FASHIONED PEANUT BUTTER PUDDING

¼ c. cornstarch
1 tbsp. sugar
3 tbsp. honey
¼ c. peanut butter
3 c. milk, scalded

Mix cornstarch, sugar and ½ cup cold water in bowl until dissolved. Mix honey and peanut butter in small bowl. Combine with scalded milk and cornstarch mixture in double boiler. Cook for 10 to 15 minutes or until thickened and clear, stirring constantly. Cook, covered, for 15 minutes longer. Cool slightly. Spoon into serving dishes. Chill in refrigerator. Yield: 4 servings.

Jean Vitelli, Maryland

MICROWAVE PEANUT BUTTER SAUCE

1 can sweetened condensed milk
⅓ c. peanut butter
Chopped peanuts

Blend sweetened condensed milk and peanut butter in 1-quart glass dish. Microwave on High for 2½ to 3½ minutes or to desired consistency, stirring occasionally. Stir in peanuts. Serve over ice cream. Store in refrigerator. Yield: 1½ cups.

PEANUT BUTTER CAKE

1 c. plus 6 tbsp. margarine
1 c. baking cocoa
½ c. buttermilk
2 eggs, beaten
2 tsp. vanilla extract
2 c. sugar
2 c. flour
1 tsp. soda
1 c. peanut butter
2⅔ c. confectioners' sugar
½ c. milk
1 c. chopped peanuts

Combine 1 cup margarine, ¼ cup cocoa, buttermilk, eggs, 1 teaspoon vanilla and 1 cup water in saucepan; mix well. Bring to a boil. Stir in sugar, flour and soda. Pour into 2 greased 9-inch cake pans. Bake at 350 degrees for

25 minutes. Cool in pans for 10 minutes. Cool on wire rack. Spread peanut butter on layers. Cream remaining 6 tablespoons margarine, ¾ cup cocoa, confectioners' sugar, milk and 1 teaspoon vanilla in bowl until light. Stir in nuts. Spread between layers and over top and side of cake.

Jerry Gibson, Washington

PEANUT BUTTER REFRIGERATOR PIE

¾ c. chunky peanut butter
3 oz. cream cheese, softened
1 c. confectioners' sugar, sifted
8 oz. whipped topping ·
1 baked pie shell

Whip peanut butter, cream cheese and confectioners' sugar in mixer bowl until light and fluffy. Mix in whipped topping. Spoon into pie shell. Chill. Yield: 6 to 8 servings.

OLD-FASHIONED PEANUT BUTTER PIE

1 c. corn syrup
¾ c. sugar
3 eggs, well beaten
½ c. peanut butter
1 unbaked 9-in. pie shell

Combine corn syrup, sugar, eggs and peanut butter in bowl; mix well. Pour into pie shell. Bake at 450 degrees for 15 minutes. Reduce temperature to 350 degrees. Bake for 30 minutes longer. Yield: 6 to 8 servings.

Jean Sullenbarger, Ohio

PEANUT BUTTER-CHOCOLATE CHIP BROWNIES

⅓ c. butter, softened
½ c. peanut butter
1 c. sugar
¼ c. packed brown sugar
2 eggs
1 c. flour
1 tsp. baking powder
¼ tsp. salt
1 tsp. vanilla extract
½ c. semisweet chocolate chips

Cream butter and peanut butter in bowl until fluffy. Add sugars gradually, beating constantly. Add eggs 1 at a time, beating well after each addition. Blend in dry ingredients and vanilla. Fold in chocolate chips. Pour into greased 9-inch square baking dish. Bake at 350 degrees for 30 minutes or until brownies test done. Cool. Cut into squares. Yield: 1 dozen.

Janice Sechrist, Oklahoma

PEANUT BUTTER-GLAZED CHOCOLATE BARS

¾ *c. melted butter*
½ *c. baking cocoa*
1¾ *c. sugar*
1½ *tsp. vanilla extract*
3 *eggs*
1¼ *c. flour*
¼ *tsp. baking powder*
1 *c. peanut butter chips*
⅓ *c. semisweet chocolate chips*
1 *tsp. shortening*

Blend butter and cocoa in bowl. Add 1½ cups sugar and vanilla; mix well. Add eggs 1 at a time, mixing well after each addition. Stir in flour and baking powder. Spread in 10x15-inch baking pan lined with greased foil. Bake at 350 degrees for 14 minutes. Cool for 2 minutes. Invert onto wire rack. Peel off foil. Cool completely. Combine remaining ¼ cup sugar and ¼ cup water in saucepan. Bring to a boil. Remove from heat. Add peanut butter chips. Stir until chips melt. Cool slightly. Cut baked layer in half. Spread peanut butter mixture between and on top of layers. Let stand until set. Melt chocolate chips and shortening in double boiler over hot water; mix well. Drizzle over layers. Let stand until set. Cut into bars. Yield: 3½ dozen.

PEANUT BUTTER AND JELLY BARS

3 *c. flour*
1 *c. sugar*
1½ *tsp. baking powder*
½ *c. butter, softened*
½ *c. peanut butter*
2 *eggs, slightly beaten*
1 *c. grape jelly*

Stir flour, sugar and baking powder together in bowl. Cut in butter and peanut butter until crumbly. Stir in eggs. Press half the mixture into 9x13-inch baking pan. Spread jelly over top. Crumble remaining dough over jelly. Bake at 375 degrees for 30 minutes or until light brown. Cool. Cut into bars. Yield: 2 dozen.

Irene Reppard, West Virginia

PEANUT BUTTER STARS

⅔ *c. shortening*
½ *c. peanut butter*
1 *c. packed brown sugar*
1 *egg*
½ *tsp. vanilla extract*
1½ *c. sifted flour*
½ *tsp. baking powder*
½ *tsp. salt*
36 *chocolate stars*

Cream first 3 ingredients in bowl until light and fluffy. Add egg and vanilla; mix well. Sift in dry ingredients; mix well. Shape by rounded teaspoonfuls into balls. Place on ungreased cookie sheet. Press chocolate star into each cookie. Bake at 375 degrees for 10 minutes or until brown. Cool on wire rack. Yield: 3 dozen.

Amber Asher, Indiana

CREAMY PEANUT BUTTER SQUARES

1 *c. melted margarine*
⅔ *c. graham cracker crumbs*
1 *12-oz. jar creamy peanut butter*
1 *16-oz. package confectioners' sugar*
12 *oz. chocolate chips, melted*

Mix margarine and graham cracker crumbs in bowl. Add peanut butter; mix well. Add confectioners' sugar; mix well. Spread in 9x13-inch dish. Chill until firm. Spread chocolate over peanut butter layer. Chill until firm. Cut into squares. Yield: 5 dozen.

Gayle Bosman, Illinois

BUCKEYES

2 c. chunky peanut butter
½ c. margarine, softened
2 c. confectioners' sugar
3 c. crispy rice cereal
6 oz. chocolate chips
1 to 1½ tbsp. melted paraffin

Combine first 4 ingredients in large bowl; mix well. Chill until firm. Shape into walnut-sized balls. Melt chocolate chips in saucepan over low heat. Blend in paraffin. Dip each ball into chocolate, leaving small portion uncoated to represent eye. Place in paper bonbon cups. Store in airtight container in freezer. Yield: 2 pounds.

Cindy Fischer, South Dakota

QUICK PEANUT BUTTER FUDGE

2 c. sugar
1 c. evaporated milk
3 tbsp. butter
1   12-oz. jar peanut butter
1 c. miniature marshmallows
1 tsp. vanilla extract

Combine sugar, evaporated milk and butter in electric skillet. Bring to a boil at 280 degrees. Boil for 5 minutes, stirring constantly. Turn off heat. Add remaining ingredients; mix well. Pour into buttered 9-inch square dish. Let stand until firm. Cut into squares. Yield: 2½ pounds.

Norma P. Dabney, Florida

PEANUT PATTIES

1½ c. sugar
½ c. sweetened condensed milk
½ c. light corn syrup
½ c. margarine
1 tsp. red food coloring
3 c. raw peanuts
1 tsp. vanilla extract

Mix first 6 ingredients in saucepan. Cook to 234 to 240 degrees, softball stage, on candy thermometer, stirring constantly. Stir in vanilla. Let stand for 10 minutes. Beat until glossy. Drop by spoonfuls onto buttered foil. Let stand until firm. Store in airtight container. Yield: 1½ pounds.

PEANUT BUTTER PENUCHE

2 c. sugar
2 c. packed brown sugar
1 c. milk
1 tbsp. light corn syrup
¼ tsp. salt
½ c. creamy peanut butter
2 tsp. vanilla extract

Butter bottom and side of heavy 4-quart saucepan. Combine sugar, brown sugar, milk, corn syrup and salt in saucepan. Bring to a boil over medium heat, stirring constantly. Cook over medium heat to 234 to 240 degrees on candy thermometer, soft-ball stage, stirring occasionally. Add peanut butter; do not stir. Let cool to 115 degrees. Add vanilla. Beat by hand for 10 minutes or until mixture thickens and loses its luster. Pour into buttered 8x8-inch dish. Let stand until cool. Cut into squares. Yield: 2½ pounds.

Ruth Ann Runyan, Pennsylvania

PEANUT BUTTER ROLL

1   12-oz. jar peanut butter
2 tbsp. margarine, softened
3 lb. confectioners' sugar
4 c. sugar
½ c. light corn syrup
5 egg whites, stiffly beaten
1 tsp. vanilla extract

Cream peanut butter, margarine and ½ cup confectioners' sugar in bowl; set aside. Bring 1½ cups water to the boiling point in saucepan; remove from heat. Add sugar and corn syrup; stir until completely dissolved. Cook, covered, over high heat for 2 to 3 minutes or until steam washes sugar crystals from side of pan. Cook, uncovered, to 240 to 248 degrees on candy thermometer, firm-ball stage; do not stir. Pour over mixture of egg whites and vanilla; beating constantly. Pour over 2 pounds confectioners' sugar spread on flat surface. Knead until no longer sticky, adding confectioners' sugar as necessary. Roll into 3 rectangles; spread each with peanut butter mixture. Roll to enclose filling; shape into logs. Chill, wrapped in plastic wrap, until firm. Slice as desired. Yield: 6 pounds.

Diane Matthey, West Virginia

PEANUT SPONGE

3 c. sugar
1 c. corn syrup
3 c. salted peanuts
2 tsp. soda

Combine sugar, corn syrup and ½ cup water in heavy saucepan. Bring to a boil over medium heat, stirring constantly. Cook, covered, for 2 to 3 minutes or until steam washes sugar crystals from side of pan. Cook, uncovered, to 280 degrees on candy thermometer, soft-crack stage; do not stir. Stir in peanuts gradually, maintaining boiling point. Cook to 300 degrees, hard-crack stage, stirring frequently. Remove from heat. Stir in soda quickly but gently. Pour onto 2 greased cookie sheets. Let stand until firm. Break into pieces. Yield: 2½ pounds.

PEAR

BRANDIED PEARS

6 pears, peeled, cored
2 c. red wine
2 whole cloves
1 sm. stick cinnamon, broken
½ c. sugar
2 oz. Brandy

Place whole pears and wine in saucepan. Add cloves, cinnamon and sugar. Simmer until pears are tender. Place pears in serving bowl. Remove cloves and cinnamon from hot syrup. Stir in Brandy. Heat gently for 1 minute. Pour over pears. Yield: 6 servings.

Marie Faulkner, New Mexico

SPICY COCONUT PEARS

5 winter pears, peeled
1¼ c. sugar
¼ c. lemon juice
2 tbsp. butter
2 tbsp. cornstarch
¼ tsp. cinnamon
¼ tsp. nutmeg
⅛ tsp. cloves
½ c. (or more) coconut

Cut pears into halves or quarters; remove core. Arrange in saucepan. Add ¾ cup sugar dissolved in 1½ cups boiling water. Simmer, covered, for 10 minutes or until pears are tender, turning occasionally. Drain, reserving syrup. Arrange pears in baking dish. Combine ¾ cup reserved liquid, remaining ½ cup sugar, lemon juice and butter in saucepan. Bring to a boil. Add mixture of ¼ cup reserved liquid, cornstarch and spices. Cook until thickened, stirring constantly. Pour over pears. Sprinkle with coconut. Bake at 350 degrees for 15 minutes. Serve warm.
Yield: 4 to 6 servings.

Francis Redmon, Tennessee

FRESH PEAR CRUNCH

6 med. pears
½ c. sugar
1 tsp. cinnamon
1 c. flour
½ c. packed brown sugar
1 tsp. baking powder
½ tsp. salt
6 tbsp. shortening

Peel pears; cut into halves. Arrange in baking dish. Mix sugar, 1 cup water and cinnamon in bowl. Pour over pears. Mix flour, brown sugar, baking powder, salt and shortening in bowl until crumbly. Sprinkle over pears. Bake at 350 degrees for 30 minutes or until pears are tender and top is golden brown. Serve with ice cream or whipped cream.
Yield: 6 servings.

Maddie Barnes, Kansas

Store pears in refrigerator and wash only at serving time to retard spoilage.

PEAR AND CHEESE CAKE

1 pkg. quick nut bread mix
1 c. chopped canned pears
½ c. pear juice
1 c. shredded Cheddar cheese
4 eggs
1 pkg. oatmeal or spice cake mix
⅓ c. oil

Combine nut bread mix, pears, pear juice, cheese and 1 egg in bowl; mix gently until blended. Combine cake mix, remaining 3 eggs, oil and 1 cup water in mixer bowl. Beat at high speed for 2 minutes. Combine with pear mixture; mix gently. Pour into 3 greased and floured cake pans. Bake at 350 degrees for 35 minutes. Cool. Frost with Cream Cheese Frosting. Yield: 16 servings.

Cream Cheese Frosting

3 oz. cream cheese, softened
6 tbsp. butter, softened
1 tbsp. milk
1½ tsp. vanilla extract
3 c. sifted confectioners' sugar
½ can vanilla frosting

Blend cream cheese and butter in bowl. Add milk, vanilla, confectioners' sugar and frosting. Beat until light and fluffy.

Maggie Burgess, Maryland

FRESH PEAR CAKE

2 c. sugar
3 eggs, beaten
1½ c. oil
3 c. flour
1 tsp. soda
1 tsp. salt
1 tsp. vanilla extract
2 tsp. cinnamon
3 c. thinly sliced pears
1¼ c. sifted confectioners'
   sugar
2 to 4 tbsp. milk

Combine sugar, eggs and oil in bowl. Mix flour, soda and salt in bowl. Add to egg mixture 1 cup at a time, mixing well after each addition. Stir in vanilla, cinnamon and pears. Pour into greased and floured bundt pan. Bake at 350 degrees for 1½ hours. Cool in pan for 5 minutes. Invert onto cake plate.

Blend confectioners' sugar with enough milk to make glaze. Drizzle over cooled cake. Yield: 16 servings.

PEAR UPSIDE-DOWN CAKE

3 tbsp. melted butter
3 tbsp. brown sugar
1 tsp. grated orange rind
3 pears, peeled, cut into halves
⅓ c. butter, softened
1 c. sugar
1 egg
1 tsp. vanilla extract
1⅔ c. flour
2 tsp. baking powder
½ tsp. salt
½ c. milk

Mix 3 tablespoons butter, brown sugar and orange rind in 6x10-inch baking dish. Arrange pears cut side down in prepared pan. Cream ⅓ cup butter and sugar in bowl until light and fluffy. Add egg and vanilla; mix well. Add combined dry ingredients and milk; mix well. Spread over pears. Bake at 350 degrees for 45 minutes. Cool in pan for 5 minutes. Invert onto serving plate. Yield: 8 servings.

Valerie Lloyd, Tennessee

PEAR PIE

2 eggs
1 c. sour cream
¼ tsp. salt
1 tsp. vanilla extract
2 tbsp. plus 1 cup flour
1 c. sugar
1 unbaked 9-in. pie shell
3 c. sliced pears
¼ c. melted butter

Beat first 4 ingredients with 2 tablespoons flour and ½ cup sugar in mixer bowl until smooth. Pour half the mixture into pie shell. Arrange pears in pie shell. Pour remaining sour cream mixture over pears. Combine remaining 1 cup flour, ½ cup sugar and butter in bowl; mix until crumbly. Sprinkle over pie. Bake at 350 degrees for 1 hour. Yield: 6 servings.

Pauline Tipton, Oregon

PEAR TART

¾ c. flour
3 tbsp. sugar
¼ tsp. allspice
6 tbsp. butter
1 env. unflavored gelatin
½ c. orange juice
3 ripe pears, puréed
3 tbsp. brown sugar
¼ tsp. salt
½ c. orange marmalade
3 ripe pears, thinly sliced

Mix flour, sugar and allspice in bowl. Cut in butter until crumbly. Knead until mixture forms ball. Press over bottom and side of 9-inch tart pan; prick with fork. Bake at 400 degrees for 10 minutes or until golden. Cool on wire rack. Soften gelatin in orange juice in saucepan. Cook over low heat until gelatin dissolves, stirring constantly. Remove from heat. Add pear purée, brown sugar, salt and ¼ cup marmalade to gelatin mixture; blend well. Chill for 45 minutes, stirring occasionally. Pour into prepared tart pan. Chill, covered, until set. Arrange sliced pears over top. Brush with remaining ¼ cup melted marmalade. Chill until serving time. Yield: 12 servings.

D'Lyn Loessin, Texas

PEAR TART ELEGANTE

½ c. butter, softened
5 tbsp. sugar
1 tsp. grated lemon rind
½ tsp. vanilla extract
1 egg yolk
1¼ c. flour
¼ c. ground blanched almonds
¼ c. red currant jelly, melted
1 egg
½ tsp. almond extract
3 oz. cream cheese, softened
6 canned pear halves
18 strawberry halves

Cream ¼ cup butter and 2 tablespoons sugar in bowl until light and fluffy. Add ½ teaspoon lemon rind, vanilla and egg yolk; beat until smooth. Stir in ¾ cup flour and almonds. Roll on floured surface. Fit into 9-inch springform pan. Bake at 375 degrees for 10 minutes. Brush with 2 tablespoons jelly.

Combine remaining ½ cup flour, 3 tablespoons sugar, ¼ cup butter, ½ teaspoon lemon rind, 1 egg, almond flavoring and cream cheese in mixer bowl. Beat at medium speed for 1 minute. Pour over pastry. Arrange pear halves cut sides down over filling; score pears. Bake at 375 degrees for 15 to 17 minutes or until filling is set. Arrange strawberries between pears. Spoon remaining 2 tablespoons melted jelly over fruit. Cut into wedges. Yield: 8 servings.

Jamie Kile, Oregon

PEAR DROPS

½ c. butter
¾ c. packed brown sugar
½ c. sour cream
1 egg
½ tsp. peppermint flavoring
1⅓ c. sifted flour
1 tsp. soda
½ tsp. salt
1 c. chopped canned pears
1 c. walnuts
¼ c. chopped maraschino cherries

Beat butter and brown sugar in bowl. Blend in sour cream, egg and flavoring. Add sifted dry ingredients; mix well. Stir in pears, walnuts and cherries. Drop by teaspoonfuls onto greased cookie sheet. Bake at 375 degrees for 15 to 18 minutes. Cool on wire rack. Yield: 2½ dozen.

PECAN

CREAMY PECAN SAUCE

¼ c. margarine
1 can sweetened condensed milk
½ tsp. rum flavoring
¼ c. chopped pecans

Melt margarine in saucepan over medium heat. Add remaining ingredients. Cook for 10 minutes or until slightly thickened, stirring constantly. Cool for 10 minutes. Sauce thickens as it cools. Serve warm over baked apples, fruit or ice cream. Yield: 1½ cups.

HEAVENLY PECAN TORTE

6 eggs, separated
1½ c. sugar
1½ tsp. vanilla extract
2 tbsp. flour
3 c. finely chopped pecans
2 tsp. baking powder
¼ tsp. salt
½ c. confectioners' sugar
2 c. whipping cream
½ c. grated sweet baking
  chocolate

Grease bottoms of three 9-inch cake pans. Line pans with waxed paper; grease waxed paper. Beat egg yolks and 1 cup sugar in mixer bowl until thick and lemon-colored. Blend in vanilla. Stir in flour, pecans and baking powder. Beat egg whites and salt at high speed until stiff but not dry. Add ½ cup sugar gradually, beating constantly. Fold into pecan mixture. Spoon into prepared pans. Bake at 325 degrees for 15 minutes. Cool in cake pans for 15 minutes. Loosen edge with knife. Remove to wire rack to cool; remove waxed paper. Combine confectioners' sugar and whipping cream in mixer bowl; beat until soft peaks form. Chill. Spread over layers. Sprinkle with chocolate. Stack layers. Garnish with pecan halves. Yield: 12 servings.

Dot Ogden, Maryland

PECAN FUDGE CAKE

½ c. shortening
1 c. sugar
2 tsp. vanilla extract
2 eggs, beaten
3 sq. baking chocolate, melted
2 c. cake flour
2 tsp. baking powder
1 tsp. salt
1½ c. milk
1 c. chopped pecans

Beat shortening, sugar and vanilla in mixer bowl until light and fluffy. Blend in eggs. Add melted chocolate; mix well. Add sifted dry ingredients alternately with milk, mixing well after each addition. Stir in pecans. Pour into 10x15-inch cake pan. Bake at 375 degrees for 30 minutes. Cool in pan. Frost as desired. Yield: 28 servings.

PECAN FUDGE PIE

4 oz. sweet cooking chocolate
¼ c. butter
1 can sweetened condensed
  milk
2 eggs, well beaten
1 tsp. vanilla extract
⅛ tsp. salt
1¼ c. pecan halves
1 unbaked 9-in. pie shell

Melt chocolate and butter in medium saucepan over low heat. Add condensed milk, ½ cup hot water and eggs; mix well. Remove from heat. Stir in vanilla, salt and pecans. Pour into pie shell. Bake at 350 degrees for 50 to 60 minutes or until center is set. Chill for 3 hours. Yield: 6 to 8 servings.

Zonell Cook, Texas

SOUTHERN PECAN PIE

3 eggs
⅔ c. sugar
1 c. dark corn syrup
⅓ c. melted butter
Pinch of salt
1 c. pecan halves
1 unbaked 9-in. pie shell

Combine eggs, sugar, corn syrup, butter and salt in mixer bowl; mix well. Stir in pecans. Pour into pie shell. Bake at 350 degrees for 50 minutes. Cool before cutting. Yield: 6 to 8 servings.

Beulah Dourm, Ohio

PECAN-FILLED GOODIES

1 c. margarine, softened
1 c. cream-style cottage cheese
2 c. sifted flour
1 c. finely ground pecans
½ c. dark corn syrup
36 pecan halves

Cream margarine and cottage cheese in bowl until light and fluffy. Add flour; mix well. Chill for 1 hour to overnight. Divide into 3 portions. Roll each portion ⅛ inch thick on lightly floured surface. Cut into 3-inch squares. Mix ground pecans and corn syrup in bowl. Place 1 teaspoon pecan mixture on each

surface. Fold corners to center; press to seal. Top each with pecan half dipped in additional corn syrup. Place on ungreased cookie sheet. Bake at 350 degrees for 25 minutes or until light brown. Cool on wire rack.
Yield: 3 dozen.

Patsy Reynolds, Kentucky

TEATIME TASSIES

9 tbsp. margarine, softened
3 oz. cream cheese, softened
1 c. flour
1 egg
¾ c. packed brown sugar
1 tsp. vanilla extract
Dash of salt
⅔ c. chopped pecans

Cream 8 tablespoons margarine and cream cheese in mixer bowl until fluffy. Add flour; mix well. Chill for 1 hour. Shape into 1-inch balls. Press into miniature muffin cups. Combine next 4 ingredients and remaining 1 tablespoon margarine in bowl; mix well. Sprinkle half the pecans into pastry-lined muffin cups. Spoon brown sugar mixture over pecans. Sprinkle with remaining pecans. Bake at 325 degrees for 25 minutes or until set. Cool completely in pan.
Yield: 2 dozen.

Dona M. McCloud, Virginia

PECAN DIVINITY ROLLS

2½ c. sugar
⅔ c. light corn syrup
2 egg whites, stiffly beaten
½ tsp. vanilla extract
4 c. coarsely chopped nuts

Bring ½ cup water to the boiling point in saucepan. Remove from heat. Add sugar and corn syrup. Stir until sugar is completely dissolved. Cook, covered, over high heat for 2 to 3 minutes or until steam washes sugar crystals from side of pan. Cook, uncovered, to 300 to 310 degrees on candy thermometer, hard-crack stage; do not stir. Add hot syrup to egg whites gradually, beating constantly. Add vanilla. Beat until very stiff and cool enough to handle. Shape into 5 or 6 rolls. Dip in

Caramel Coating. Coat with nuts. Chill until firm. Slice as desired.
Yield: 3 pounds.

Caramel Coating

1 c. sugar
½ c. packed brown sugar
½ c. light corn syrup
½ c. cream
1 c. milk
¼ c. butter

Mix all ingredients in heavy saucepan. Cook over medium heat until all sugar is dissolved, stirring constantly. Cook, covered, for 2 to 3 minutes or until sugar crystals are dissolved from side of pan. Cook, uncovered, to 240 to 248 degrees on candy thermometer, firm-ball stage, stirring frequently. Cool slightly.

Joy Roberts, Illinois

MILLIONAIRES

1 c. sugar
1 c. packed brown sugar
1 c. margarine
1 tsp. vanilla extract
2 c. evaporated milk
1 lb. pecan halves
12 oz. sweet chocolate, melted
2 tbsp. melted paraffin

Combine sugar, brown sugar, margarine, vanilla and 1 cup evaporated milk in saucepan; mix well. Bring to a boil, stirring constantly. Add remaining milk gradually. Cook to 234 to 240 degrees on candy thermometer, soft-ball stage. Stir in pecans. Pour into large buttered pan. Chill overnight. Cut into squares. Place on waxed paper. Blend melted chocolate and paraffin in bowl. Spoon carefully over squares.
Yield: 5 pounds.

Annelle Salyer, Iowa

To determine if pecans bought in the shell are fresh, always shake them. If the kernels inside rattle, they are old and dried out.

CREAM PRALINES

1 c. evaporated milk
1 c. sugar
1 c. packed brown sugar
⅛ tsp. soda
⅛ tsp. salt
¼ c. margarine
2 c. pecans
2 tsp. vanilla extract

Heat evaporated milk to the boiling point in saucepan. Remove from heat. Add sugars, soda and salt; stir until sugars are completely dissolved. Cook, covered, over medium heat for 2 to 3 minutes or until steam dissolves sugar crystals from side of pan. Cook, uncovered, to 234 to 240 degrees on candy thermometer, soft-ball stage; do not stir. Remove from heat. Add margarine, pecans and vanilla. Cool to luke-warm, 110 degrees; do not stir. Beat with spoon until mixture thickens and loses its luster. Drop by spoonfuls onto waxed paper. Let stand until firm. Yield: 2 pounds.

Dee Dee Guess, Texas

PEPPERMINT

FROZEN PEPPERMINT SPECIAL

2 c. confectioners' sugar
⅔ c. butter, softened
3 eggs, separated
2 sq. baking chocolate, melted
1 tsp. vanilla extract
½ c. crushed pecans
1½ c. crushed vanilla wafers
1 qt. peppermint stick ice
    cream, softened

Cream confectioners' sugar and but-ter in mixer bowl until light. Blend in beaten egg yolks, chocolate and vanil-la. Fold in pecans and stiffly beaten egg whites. Place 1 cup cookie crumbs in 9x9-inch dish. Spoon chocolate mixture into prepared dish. Freeze for 3 hours. Spread ice cream over chocolate layer. Sprinkle with remaining ½ cup crumbs. Freeze until serving time. Garnish with whipped cream. Yield: 8 servings.

PEPPERMINT MERINGUES

2 egg whites, at room
    temperature
½ tsp. peppermint extract
½ c. sugar
6 drops of red food coloring
    (optional)
6 oz. semisweet chocolate chips

Beat egg whites and peppermint ex-tract until foamy. Add sugar, 2 table-spoons at a time, beating until stiff peaks form. Do not underbeat. Fold in food coloring and chocolate chips. Drop by rounded teaspoonfuls 2 inches apart onto greased cookie sheet. Bake at 200 degrees for 1 hour or until dry and set but not brown. Remove to wire rack to cool. Yield: 2½ dozen.

Lynette Halprin, Nevada

MINT CHOCOLATE DESSERT

1½ c. vanilla wafer crumbs
2 sq. baking chocolate
½ c. butter, softened
1 c. confectioners' sugar
3 eggs, separated
½ c. chopped walnuts
4 oz. peppermint candy,
    crushed
10 marshmallows, chopped
½ c. chopped pecans
¾ c. whipping cream

Spread ½ cup vanilla wafer crumbs in 9x13-inch dish. Melt chocolate in double boiler over hot water. Cream but-ter and confectioners' sugar in mixer bowl until light and fluffy. Blend in chocolate and beaten egg yolks. Stir in walnuts. Beat egg whites until stiff peaks form. Fold gently into chocolate mixture. Spoon into prepared dish. Chill until firm. Combine peppermint candy, marshmallows and pecans in bowl. Whip cream in bowl until soft peaks form. Fold in ½ cup vanilla wafer crumbs gently. Spread over chocolate mixture. Sprinkle with remaining ½ cup vanilla wafer crumbs. Chill for 24 hours or longer. Yield: 18 servings.

Charlotte Fuqua, Texas

MINTY NUT FUDGE CAKE

2 sq. baking chocolate
½ c. butter, softened
1½ c. sugar
4 eggs, separated
1 tsp. vanilla extract
1¾ c. cake flour
1 tbsp. baking powder
¾ c. milk
½ c. chopped nuts

Dissolve chocolate in 5 tablespoons boiling water; cool. Cream butter and sugar in mixer bowl until light and fluffy. Blend in beaten egg yolks, chocolate and vanilla. Add sifted flour and baking powder alternately with milk, mixing well after each addition. Beat egg whites until stiff peaks form. Fold gently into batter. Fold in nuts. Pour into 2 greased and floured 9-inch cake pans. Bake at 350 degrees for 25 minutes. Remove to wire rack to cool. Spread Peppermint Frosting between layers and over top and side of cake. Garnish with additional nuts. Yield: 16 servings.

Peppermint Frosting

1 sq. baking chocolate
2 tbsp. butter
¼ c. cream
3 drops oil of peppermint
1 lb. confectioners' sugar

Melt chocolate and butter with cream in double boiler; mix well. Remove from heat. Beat in oil of peppermint and enough confectioners' sugar to make of desired consistency.

CHOCOLATE-PEPPERMINT PIE

2 sq. baking chocolate
2 oz. semisweet chocolate
⅔ c. butter, softened
1 c. sugar
3 eggs, lightly beaten
¼ tsp. peppermint extract
1 9-in. graham cracker pie shell
1 c. whipping cream
1 tbsp. confectioners' sugar

Melt chocolates in double boiler over boiling water; cool to lukewarm. Cream butter and sugar in mixer bowl until light. Blend in chocolate, eggs and flavoring. Pour into pie shell. Chill for 8 hours. Whip cream with confectioners' sugar in bowl until soft peaks form. Spoon on pie. Yield: 6 to 8 servings.

PEPPERMINT STICK PIE

1 env. unflavored gelatin
2 eggs, separated
½ c. sugar
¼ c. crushed peppermint candy
¼ tsp. salt
1½ c. milk, scalded
1 baked 9-in. pie shell

Soften gelatin in ¼ cup cold water. Beat egg yolks, ¼ cup sugar, candy, salt and a small amount of hot milk. Stir into hot milk in double boiler. Cook over simmering water until thickened, stirring constantly. Stir in gelatin until dissolved. Chill until partially set. Beat egg whites until foamy. Add remaining ¼ cup sugar gradually, beating until stiff peaks form. Fold into chilled mixture. Pour into pie shell. Chill until firm. Yield: 6 servings.

MINT CHOCOLATE BARS

3 oz. baking chocolate
¾ c. butter
2 eggs
1 c. sugar
1 tsp. peppermint extract
½ c. sifted flour
½ c. chopped almonds
1 c. sifted confectioners' sugar
1 tbsp. cream

Melt 2 squares chocolate and ½ cup butter in double boiler over hot water. Beat eggs in mixer bowl until foamy. Add sugar, chocolate mixture and ¼ teaspoon peppermint extract; mix well. Mix in flour and almonds. Pour into greased 9x9-inch baking pan. Bake at 350 degrees for 20 minutes or until layer tests done. Cool. Cream 2 tablespoons softened butter and confectioners' sugar in mixer bowl until light. Blend in cream and ¾ teaspoon peppermint extract. Tint with food coloring, if desired. Spread over baked layer. Chill in refrigerator. Melt 1 square chocolate and remaining 2 tablespoons butter in double boiler over hot water. Drizzle over top. Cut into bars. Yield: 1½ dozen.

PEPPERMINT CHOCOLATE COOKIES

1 c. margarine, softened
1 c. sugar
1 c. packed brown sugar
2 eggs
2 tsp. vanilla extract
3 c. flour
1 tsp. soda
½ tsp. salt
4 oz. baking chocolate, melted
1 c. crushed peppermint candy

Beat margarine and sugars in mixer bowl until light. Blend in eggs and vanilla. Add mixture of flour, soda and salt; mix well. Fold in chocolate and candy. Drop by tablespoonfuls 2 inches apart onto ungreased cookie sheet. Bake at 350 degrees for 12 to 15 minutes or just until set in center. Cool on wire rack. Yield: 3 dozen.

Holly Schmorl, Oregon

BUTTER MINTS

3 tbsp. butter, softened
¼ c. cream
¼ tsp. salt
1 tsp. vanilla extract
2 tsp. peppermint flavoring
1 16-oz. package
   confectioners' sugar

Combine butter and cream in bowl. Stir in salt, vanilla and flavoring. Knead in confectioners' sugar until mixture is smooth. Tint with food coloring as desired. Shape into small balls. Place on cookie sheet; press to flatten. Let stand for 24 hours to dry. Store in airtight container. Yield: 1½ pounds.

Rachel Wagner, Washington

CRYSTAL CANDY

2 c. sugar
½ c. light corn syrup
Dash of salt
Red or green food coloring
4 to 5 drops of oil of cinnamon,
   peppermint or wintergreen

Mix sugar, corn syrup and salt in heavy saucepan. Cook to 270 to 290 degrees on candy thermometer, soft-crack stage. Stir in food coloring and flavoring. Drop by teaspoonfuls onto buttered foil. Let stand until firm. Yield: 1 pound.

Donis Eiseminger, Missouri

PERSIMMON

STEAMED PERSIMMON PUDDING

2 tbsp. plus ⅓ cup butter
1⅔ c. sugar
1 c. persimmon pulp
1 c. flour
1 tsp. soda
½ tsp. salt
½ tsp. cinnamon
¼ tsp. nutmeg
⅛ tsp. allspice
⅔ c. chopped pecans
½ c. pickled peach juice
1 egg, beaten

Cream 2 tablespoons butter and 1 cup sugar in mixer bowl until light and fluffy. Blend in persimmon pulp. Sift in dry ingredients; mix well. Stir in pecans. Pour into buttered 1-pound mold; cover tightly. Place in deep saucepan. Add enough boiling water to cover half the mold. Steam for 2½ hours. Invert onto serving plate. Combine remaining ⅔ cup sugar, ⅓ cup butter and peach juice in double boiler. Bring to a simmer over hot water, stirring to dissolve sugar. Stir a small amount of hot mixture into egg; stir egg into hot mixture. Cook until thick, stirring constantly. Serve warm on warm pudding. Yield: 8 servings.

Carolyn Braud, Iowa

It is usually more successful to make 2 recipes of candy rather than double the recipe.

PERSIMMON CAKE

½ c. plus 2 tbsp. butter
2½ c. sugar
2 eggs, beaten
2 tsp. vanilla extract
2 c. persimmon pulp
2 c. flour
2 tsp. cinnamon
2 tsp. baking powder
2 tsp. soda
1 tsp. salt
½ c. milk
2 c. raisins
2 c. chopped nuts
1 tbsp. cornstarch
1 tbsp. grated lemon rind

Cream ½ cup butter and 2 cups sugar in mixer bowl. Stir in eggs, vanilla and persimmon pulp. Sift flour, cinnamon, baking powder, soda and salt. Add to creamed mixture alternately with milk, blending well. Stir in raisins and nuts. Bake in greased 9x13-inch pan at 350 degrees for 40 to 45 minutes. Dissolve remaining ½ cup sugar and cornstarch in 1 cup boiling water in saucepan. Cook over low heat until mixture is thickened and clear, stirring constantly; remove from heat. Add 2 tablespoons butter and lemon rind. Serve over warm cake. Yield: 16 servings.

Louise Marino, California

PERSIMMON COOKIES

¾ c. sugar
¾ c. packed brown sugar
½ c. shortening
1 egg
2 c. flour
1 tsp. soda
1 c. persimmon pulp
1 c. raisins
1 tsp. cinnamon
½ tsp. nutmeg
½ tsp. ginger

Cream sugars and shortening in mixer bowl until smooth. Add egg; mix well. Add flour and soda. Add persimmon, raisins and spices; mix well. Drop by teaspoonfuls onto greased cookie sheet. Bake at 350 degrees for 10 to 12 minutes. Yield: 3 dozen.

Janet Ridenour, California

LEMON-GLAZED PERSIMMON BARS

1 egg, beaten
1 c. sugar
1½ c. finely chopped dates
7½ tsp. lemon juice
1 tsp. soda
1¾ c. flour
½ tsp. salt
1 tsp. cinnamon
1 tsp. nutmeg
¼ tsp. cloves
1 c. persimmon pulp
1 c. chopped walnuts
1 c. confectioners' sugar

Mix egg, sugar and dates in bowl. Stir in 1½ teaspoons lemon juice and soda. Add mixture of flour, salt and spices alternately with persimmon pulp, mixing well after each addition. Stir in walnuts. Spread in greased and floured 10x15-inch baking pan. Bake at 350 degrees for 25 minutes or until light brown. Cool for 5 minutes. Glaze cake with mixture of confectioners' sugar and remaining 2 tablespoons lemon juice. Cool. Cut into bars. Yield: 4 dozen.

Clara Sampson Berryessa, California

PERSIMMON FUDGE

2½ c. milk
6 c. sugar
¼ c. light corn syrup
1 c. puréed persimmon
½ c. margarine
1 c. (or more) chopped nuts

Bring milk to the boiling point in saucepan. Remove from heat. Stir in sugar and corn syrup until sugar is completely dissolved. Add persimmon; mix well. Cook, covered, over medium heat for 2 to 3 minutes or until steam washes sugar crystals from side of pan. Cook mixture, uncovered, to 234 to 240 degrees on candy thermometer, soft-ball stage; do not stir. Cool to lukewarm, 110 degrees; do not stir. Add margarine. Beat until mixture is thickened and loses its luster. Stir in nuts. Pour into buttered 9x13-inch dish. Let stand until firm. Cut into squares. Yield: 2 pounds.

Pauline Roberts, California

PINEAPPLE

PINEAPPLE FLAN

3 c. pineapple juice
3 c. sugar
12 eggs
½ c. raisins

Bring pineapple juice and sugar to a boil in saucepan, stirring until sugar is dissolved. Cook until mixture is reduced to 2 cups. Reserve 1 cup syrup. Beat eggs in bowl until light and fluffy. Add to syrup. Stir in raisins. Pour into 2-quart mold. Place mold in pan of water. Bake at 350 degrees for 1 hour or until set. Cool. Unmold onto platter; pour reserved syrup over top. Garnish with pineapple slices. Yield: 6 to 8 servings.

Maria Young, Arizona

PINEAPPLE FLUFF

1½ c. graham cracker crumbs
1 c. sugar
1 c. crushed pineapple
3 eggs, well beaten
1 lg. package lemon gelatin
1   13-oz. can evaporated milk, chilled, whipped
½ c. chopped nuts

Spread 1 cup graham cracker crumbs in buttered 9x13-inch dish. Combine sugar, pineapple, eggs and gelatin in double boiler, mixing well. Cook until thickened, stirring constantly; cool. Fold in whipped evaporated milk. Pour over crumbs. Top with ½ cup remaining crumbs and nuts. Chill until set. Yield: 12 servings.

Zelda Ives, Ohio

PINEAPPLE-RICE PUDDING

1 c. rice
1   13-oz. can evaporated milk
½ c. sugar
1   16-oz. can crushed pineapple, drained
2 tsp. cinnamon
1 tsp. vanilla extract

Stir rice into 3 cups boiling water in saucepan. Cook, covered, over low heat for 20 to 25 minutes or until water is absorbed. Stir in remaining ingredients; mix well. Spoon into serving dish. Chill, covered, in refrigerator. Yield: 8 servings.

Virginia Howell, Ohio

PINEAPPLE TURNOVERS

1 c. butter, softened
8 oz. cream cheese, softened
2 c. flour
1 can pineapple pie filling

Combine butter, cream cheese and flour in bowl; mix well. Chill overnight. Roll ⅛ inch thick on lightly floured surface. Cut into rounds. Place 1 tablespoon pie filling on each round. Fold pastry over. Moisten edges with small amount of water; seal. Prick tops with fork. Place on baking sheet. Bake at 350 degrees for 30 minutes. Yield: 2 dozen.

PINEAPPLE-CARROT CAKE

1 c. oil
1½ c. sugar
4 eggs, beaten
2 c. grated carrots
1 c. well drained crushed pineapple
1 c. chopped walnuts
2 c. sifted flour
1½ tsp. soda
2 tsp. baking powder
1½ tsp. salt
2 c. confectioners' sugar
½ c. butter, softened
½ tsp. vanilla extract
3 oz. cream cheese, softened

Mix oil and sugar in mixer bowl. Add eggs; mix well. Add carrots, pineapple and walnuts. Add sifted flour, soda, baking powder and salt; mix well. Pour into greased and floured 9x13-inch baking pan. Bake at 350 degrees for 35 to 40 minutes. Cool. Combine confectioners' sugar, butter, vanilla and cream cheese in bowl. Beat until smooth. Spread on cooled cake. Yield: 16 servings.

PINEAPPLE POUND CAKE

1½ c. shortening
3 c. sugar
6 eggs
3 c. flour
Pinch of salt
1 c. crushed pineapple
1 tbsp. butter flavoring
1 tbsp. butternut flavoring
3 oz. cream cheese, softened
¼ c. melted margarine
1 tsp. vanilla extract
2 c. (about) confectioners' sugar

Beat shortening and sugar in mixer bowl until light. Blend in eggs 1 at a time. Add sifted flour and salt alternately with pineapple, mixing well after each addition. Mix in flavorings. Spoon into greased and floured tube pan. Bake at 325 degrees for 1 hour and 20 minutes. Cool in pan for 10 minutes. Remove to wire rack to cool completely. Combine cream cheese, margarine and vanilla in bowl; mix well. Add enough confectioners' sugar to make of spreading consistency. Spread over top and side of cake. Yield: 16 servings.

Sarah Edgar, Maryland

PINEAPPLE UPSIDE-DOWN CAKE

2 tbsp. plus ⅓ c. butter,
    softened
1 c. packed brown sugar
1   16-oz. can crushed
    pineapple, drained
1 c. sugar
2 eggs, well beaten
1¾ c. flour
2 tsp. baking powder
¼ tsp. salt
½ c. milk
1 tsp. vanilla extract

Melt 2 tablespoons butter in iron skillet. Blend in brown sugar. Add pineapple. Cream remaining ⅓ cup butter and sugar in mixer bowl until light and fluffy. Blend in eggs. Add sifted dry ingredients alternately with milk and vanilla, mixing well after each addition. Pour into prepared skillet. Bake at 350 degrees for 45 minutes. Invert onto serving plate. Yield: 6 to 8 servings.

Heidi Ahlschlager, Pennsylvania

PINEAPPLE-COTTAGE CHEESE PIE

1 c. flour
Pinch of salt
⅓ c. shortening
1¼ c. crushed pineapple
⅓ c. plus ½ c. sugar
1 tbsp. cornstarch
1½ c. cottage cheese
3 eggs, lightly beaten
¼ tsp. salt
½ tsp. vanilla extract
¼ c. cream
¼ tsp. cinnamon

Combine flour and pinch of salt in bowl. Cut in shortening until crumbly. Add 7 to 8 teaspoons ice water; mix well. Roll thin on floured surface; fit into 9-inch pie plate. Combine pineapple, ⅓ cup sugar and cornstarch in saucepan. Cook until thickened, stirring constantly. Cool. Pour into prepared pie plate. Beat cottage cheese until smooth. Add remaining ½ cup sugar, eggs, ¼ teaspoon salt, vanilla and cream; mix well. Pour over pineapple. Sprinkle with cinnamon. Bake at 450 degrees for 15 minutes. Reduce temperature to 325 degrees. Bake for 45 minutes.
Yield: 8 servings.

Miriam Stapleton, New York

HAWAIIAN PINEAPPLE PIE

3 eggs, well beaten
2 tbsp. (heaping) flour
1 c. sugar
1 c. crushed pineapple
1 c. coconut
1 c. light corn syrup
1 tsp. pineapple flavoring
1 unbaked 9-in. pie shell
¼ c. melted margarine

Combine eggs, flour and sugar in bowl; mix well. Add pineapple, coconut, corn syrup and flavoring; mix well. Pour into pie shell. Drizzle with margarine. Bake at 350 degrees until knife inserted in center comes out clean. Garnish with whipped cream and coconut. Yield: 6 servings.

Hazel Leiber, California

PINEAPPLE COOKIES

1 c. shortening
1 c. packed brown sugar
1 c. sugar
2 eggs
1 c. crushed pineapple
4 c. flour
2 tsp. baking powder
½ tsp. soda
½ tsp. salt
1 tsp. vanilla extract
1 c. chopped nuts

Cream shortening and sugars in bowl until light and fluffy. Add 1 egg, ½ cup pineapple and half the sifted dry ingredients, beating well after each addition. Add remaining egg, pineapple, dry ingredients, vanilla and nuts 1 at a time, beating well after each addition. Drop by teaspoonfuls onto greased cookie sheet. Bake at 400 degrees for 10 minutes or until brown. Cool on wire rack. Yield: 8 dozen.

Janet Francis, Texas

PINEAPPLE FUDGE

½ c. milk
2 c. sugar
1 c. packed brown sugar
1   8-oz. can crushed pineapple
1 tbsp. corn syrup
¼ tsp. salt
2 tbsp. butter
24 lg. marshmallows
1 tsp. vanilla extract
1 c. chopped pecans

Bring milk to the boiling point in saucepan. Remove from heat. Add sugars, stirring constantly until sugars are completely dissolved. Add pineapple, corn syrup, salt and butter; mix well. Cook, covered, for 2 to 3 minutes or until steam washes sugar crystals from side of pan. Cook, uncovered, to 234 to 240 degrees on candy thermometer, soft-ball stage; do not stir. Remove from heat. Add marshmallows and vanilla. Beat until thick and creamy. Stir in pecans. Pour into buttered 8-inch square dish. Let stand until firm. Cut into squares. Yield: 2½ pounds.

Dolores T. Bland, West Virginia

PISTACHIO

PISTACHIO-ALMOND TORTE

½ c. blanched almonds
½ c. blanched pistachio nuts
1¾ c. plus 6 tbsp. flour
5 eggs, separated
2 c. milk
⅓ c. sugar
Dash of salt
1 c. (about) butter, softened

Combine almonds and pistachio nuts in food processor container. Process into smooth paste. Mix 1¾ cups flour with egg whites in bowl until smooth. Shape into ball. Let stand, covered, for 2 hours. Blend 6 tablespoons flour with several teaspoons milk in saucepan. Blend in remaining milk. Cook over low heat for 10 minutes or until thick, stirring constantly; cool. Stir in sugar and salt. Add egg yolks 1 at a time, mixing well after each addition. Stir in nut paste. Divide dough into 12 portions. Layer 6 very thinly rolled portions alternately with 1 heaping tablespoon butter in generously buttered 9-inch baking pan. Spread with nut mixture. Repeat layers with remaining 6 portions dough and butter, ending with butter. Bake at 400 degrees for 35 minutes or until golden brown. Serve warm or cold. Yield: 8 servings.

Pauline Donnelly, Florida

PISTACHIO MARBLE CAKE

1 box white cake mix
1 pkg. pistachio pudding mix
4 eggs
½ c. oil
1 c. orange juice
¾ c. chocolate syrup

Mix first 5 ingredients in bowl. Pour ⅔ of the batter into greased bundt pan. Add chocolate syrup to remaining batter, mixing well. Spoon over white batter; swirl to marbleize. Bake at 350 degrees for 50 to 60 minutes or until cake tests done. Cool in pan. Invert onto serving plate. Garnish with confectioners' sugar. Yield: 16 servings.

Barbara Curtis, Alabama

MICROWAVE
PISTACHIO SWIRL CAKE

1 c. finely chopped pistachio
   nuts
¾ c. sugar
2 tbsp. cinnamon
1 2-layer pkg. yellow cake mix
1 sm. package pistachio instant
   pudding mix
4 eggs
1 c. sour cream
¾ c. orange juice
¼ c. oil
1 tsp. vanilla extract

Mix pistachio nuts, sugar and cinnamon in small bowl. Sprinkle ⅓ of the mixture into greased glass bundt pan. Combine remaining ingredients in large bowl; beat well. Alternate layers of batter and remaining cinnamon mixture in bundt pan. Swirl batter with fork. Microwave on High for 10 to 12 minutes or until cake tests done, turning dish once. Let stand for 10 minutes. Invert onto cake plate. Yield: 16 servings.

Mary Jane Laing, Texas

FROZEN PISTACHIO PIES

1 c. sugar
2 tsp. cornstarch
4 c. milk
3 eggs, separated
1 tsp. vanilla extract
½ tsp. almond extract
1 c. whipping cream, whipped
2 c. chopped pistachio nuts
2 chocolate crumb pie shells

Mix sugar and cornstarch in top of double boiler. Blend in milk and eggs. Beat until foamy. Cook over hot water for 15 minutes, stirring constantly. Cool. Stir in flavorings. Beat egg whites until stiff peaks form. Fold into cooled mixture. Spoon into bowl. Freeze until slushy. Beat until smooth. Fold in whipped cream and pistachio nuts gently. Tint green with food coloring if desired. Mound into pie shells. Freeze until firm. Yield: 2 pies.

Florence Hankins, Alabama

PISTACHIO CREAM TARTS

6 egg yolks
1 c. sugar
1 env. unflavored gelatin
2 c. heavy cream, whipped
1 c. chopped pistachio nuts
1½ tsp. rum extract
16 baked tart shells

Beat egg yolks until light. Beat in sugar. Soften gelatin in ½ cup cold water in saucepan. Heat until gelatin is dissolved, stirring constantly. Cool. Stir gelatin mixture into egg mixture. Fold in whipped cream and nuts. Blend in rum flavoring. Chill until partially set. Spoon into tart shells. Chill until firm. Garnish with additional pistachio nuts and chocolate curls. Yield: 16 servings.

Dorothy Malone, Louisiana

PISTACHIO SQUARES

1 c. butter, softened
½ c. sugar
1 egg
1 tsp. vanilla extract
1 c. flour
½ tsp. baking powder
¼ tsp. salt
½ c. milk
⅓ c. flaked coconut
6 tbsp. chopped pistachio nuts
1 c. confectioners' sugar
   frosting

Cream butter and sugar in bowl until light and fluffy. Add egg and vanilla; mix well. Add mixture of flour, baking powder and salt alternately with milk, mixing well after each addition. Add coconut and half the pistachio nuts. Spread in greased 9-inch square baking pan. Bake at 350 degrees for 20 minutes. Cool. Frost with confectioners' sugar frosting. Sprinkle with remaining nuts. Cut into squares. Yield: 2 dozen.

Susan Hodges, Texas

For a quick confectioners' sugar frosting, blend 2 tablespoons softened margarine, 2 cups confectioners' sugar and enough milk to make of spreading consistency. Flavor and tint as desired.

PLUM

PLUM CAKE

2 c. self-rising flour
2 c. sugar
1 tsp. ground cloves
1   7¾-oz. jar plum junior
    baby food
1 c. oil
3 eggs, beaten
1 c. chopped nuts

Combine flour, sugar, cloves, plums, oil, eggs and nuts in order given in large bowl; mix well. Pour into greased and floured 4x8-inch loaf pan. Bake at 350 degrees for 1 hour. Cool on wire rack. Yield: 12 servings.

Fran Smith, Florida

GERMAN PLUM TART

2¾ c. flour
4½ tsp. baking powder
1 c. sugar
½ tsp. salt
¼ c. margarine
1 egg, beaten
6 tbsp. milk
12 blue plums, halved
2 tbsp. butter
Cream

Sift 2 cups flour, 4 teaspoons baking powder, ¼ cup sugar and salt into bowl. Cut in margarine until crumbly. Combine egg and milk. Add to dry ingredients; mix well. Pat onto cookie sheet, crimping to make rim. Arrange plums over top. Combine remaining ¾ cup flour, ¾ cup sugar and ½ teaspoon baking powder in bowl; mix well. Cut in butter and enough cream to make coarse crumbs. Spread over plums. Bake at 375 degrees for 30 minutes. Yield: 12 servings.

Elsie White, Washington

FRESH DAMSON PLUM PIE

4 c. fresh damson plums,
    quartered
4 c. sugar
1 unbaked 9-in. pie shell

Combine plums and sugar in saucepan. Cook until plums are tender, stirring frequently. Spoon into pie shell. Bake at 450 degrees until crust is golden brown. Yield: 6 servings.

Diedre Somer, Utah

PLUM PRESERVE PIE

½ c. butter, softened
1½ c. sugar
5 eggs, separated
1 tbsp. flour
1 c. damson plum preserves
1 unbaked 9-in. pie shell

Beat butter with ¾ cup sugar in bowl until light and fluffy. Beat egg yolks with remaining ¾ cup sugar. Beat egg yolk mixture into creamed mixture. Add flour; mix well. Blend in preserves. Fold in stiffly beaten egg whites. Spoon into pie shell. Bake at 350 degrees until set. Garnish with whipped cream. Yield: 6 servings.

Tracy Regis, Arkansas

POPPY SEED CAKE

1   2-layer pkg. yellow cake mix
2   3-oz. packages butterscotch
    instant pudding mix
¾ c. oil
4 eggs
½ c. poppy seed

Mix first 4 ingredients and 1 cup water in bowl. Add poppy seed; mix well. Pour into greased and floured tube pan. Bake at 350 degrees for 1 hour. Cool in pan. Remove to serving plate. Yield: 16 servings.

Violet Duffy, Delaware

YOGURT POPPY SEED CAKE

1   2-oz. package poppy seed
8 oz. yogurt
1 c. butter, softened
1½ c. sugar
4 eggs, separated
2 c. plus 2 tbsp. sifted flour
2 tsp. soda
2 tsp. vanilla extract

often poppy seed in yogurt. Cream
butter and sugar in bowl. Beat in egg
yolks, yogurt, flour, soda and vanilla.
Fold in stiffly beaten egg whites. Pour
into greased and floured tube pan. Bake
at 375 degrees for 45 minutes. Top with
confectioners' sugar or lemon glaze.
Yield: 12 to 15 servings.

Sharon K. Kauffman, Colorado

PRUNE

PRUNE CAKE

1½ c. sugar
1 c. oil
3 eggs
1 tsp. cinnamon
1 tsp. nutmeg
1 tsp. allspice
2¼ c. flour
1 tsp. soda
1 c. buttermilk
1 tsp. vanilla extract
1 c. nuts, chopped
1 c. chopped cooked prunes

Blend sugar and oil in bowl. Add
eggs, 1 at a time, beating well after
each addition. Mix spices, flour and
soda together. Add to egg mixture alternately with buttermilk. Add vanilla,
nuts and prunes. Pour into greased and
floured 9x13-inch cake pan. Bake at 300
degrees for 50 minutes or until cake
tests done. Remove from oven. Frost hot
cake with Buttermilk Icing.

Buttermilk Icing

1 c. sugar
½ c. buttermilk
½ tsp. soda
1 tbsp. light corn syrup
¼ c. butter
1 tsp. vanilla extract

Combine first 5 ingredients in saucepan.
Bring to a boil. Cook to 234 degrees on
candy thermometer, soft-ball stage. Add
vanilla; do not beat. Pour icing over hot
cake. Yield: 16 servings.

Ann Kirk, Illinois

PRUNE DROPS

2 c. sugar
1 c. shortening
3 eggs
1 c. chopped cooked prunes
3 c. sifted flour
1 tsp. soda
½ tsp. salt
½ tsp. allspice
1 tsp. cinnamon
¼ tsp. nutmeg
¼ tsp. cloves
¾ c. chopped walnuts

Combine sugar, shortening, eggs and
prunes in bowl; mix well. Sift in dry
ingredients ⅓ at a time, mixing well
after each addition. Stir in walnuts.
Drop by teaspoonfuls 2 inches apart
onto greased cookie sheet. Bake at 375
degrees for 12 minutes or until light
brown. Cool on wire rack.
Yield: 6 dozen.

Sharon J. Barreto, California

PRUNE SQUARES

3 eggs, beaten
1 c. oil
2 c. flour
Pinch of cinnamon
2½ c. sugar
1½ tsp. vanilla extract
1 tsp. soda
1½ c. buttermilk
1 c. chopped cooked prunes
1 c. chopped nuts
1 tbsp. light corn syrup
½ c. butter

Beat eggs, oil, flour, cinnamon, 1½
cups sugar and 1 teaspoon vanilla in
bowl until smooth. Beat in mixture of
soda and 1 cup buttermilk. Stir in
prunes and nuts. Pour into greased and
floured 9x13-inch baking pan. Bake at
350 degrees until toothpick inserted in
center comes out clean. Combine remaining 1 cup sugar, remaining ½ cup
buttermilk, ½ teaspoon vanilla, corn
syrup and butter in saucepan. Bring to a
boil, stirring constantly. Pour over warm
layer. Cut into squares.
Yield: 16 servings.

Martha Scott, Tennessee

SUGARPLUMS

1 egg white
¼ tsp. cream of tartar
¼ tsp. salt
2 tsp. vanilla extract
6 c. confectioners' sugar
3 or 4 drops red food coloring
3 tbsp. unsalted butter,
  softened
1 c. coconut
2 lb. pitted, glacéed prunes
1 c. sugar

Beat egg white, cream of tartar, salt and vanilla in mixer bowl until soft peaks form. Beat in confectioners' sugar and 3 tablespoons water gradually. Tint pink with food coloring. Add butter and coconut; mix well. Chill for 4 hours or until firm. Press each prune into thin layer between palms of hands. Place a small amount of chilled mixture in center of each prune. Fold in half. Roll in sugar. Store between waxed paper in airtight container. Roll in sugar again before serving. Yield: 5 dozen.

PUMPKIN

PUMPKIN CHEESECAKE

2½ c. graham cracker crumbs
½ c. melted butter
2 tbsp. sugar
1½ tsp. cinnamon
1 env. unflavored gelatin
¾ c. pineapple juice
1 16-oz. can pumpkin
1 c. packed light brown sugar
3 eggs, beaten
½ tsp. ginger
16 oz. cream cheese, softened
1 tbsp. vanilla extract
1 20-oz. can crushed
  pineapple, drained
½ c. miniature marshmallows
1 c. whipping cream, whipped

Combine graham cracker crumbs, butter, sugar and ½ teaspoon cinnamon in bowl; mix well. Press mixture over bottom and 1½ inches up side of springform pan. Bake at 350 degrees for 10 minutes. Cool on wire rack. Soften gelatin in pineapple juice in saucepan. Add pumpkin, brown sugar, eggs, 1 teaspoon cinnamon and ginger; mix well.

Simmer, covered, for 30 minutes, stirring occasionally. Beat cream cheese with vanilla in mixer bowl until fluffy. Add to warm pumpkin mixture, stirring just until blended. Pour into prepared springform pan. Chill, covered, for 8 hours. Fold pineapple and marshmallows gently into whipped cream. Spoon over cheesecake. Chill until serving time. Place on serving plate. Remove side of pan. Yield: 16 servings.

PUMPKIN CRUMBLE

3½ c. pumpkin purée
1 lg. can evaporated milk
1 c. sugar
3 eggs
4 tsp. pumpkin pie spice
1 2-layer pkg. yellow cake mix
¾ c. melted butter
½ c. chopped pecans

Combine pumpkin, evaporated milk, sugar, eggs and spice in bowl; mix well. Pour into buttered 9x13-inch baking dish. Layer dry cake mix, butter and pecans on top. Bake at 350 degrees for 1 hour or until set. Yield: 12 servings.

Sharon Rocha, California

PUMPKIN DESSERT

4 eggs, lightly beaten
1 28-oz. can pumpkin
1½ c. sugar
1 tsp. salt
1 tsp. cinnamon
1 tsp. ginger
½ tsp. cloves
1 13-oz. can evaporated milk
1 2-layer pkg. yellow cake mix
2 c. chopped walnuts
1 c. melted butter

Mix first 8 ingredients in bowl. Pour into buttered 9x13-inch baking pan. Sprinkle dry cake mix over top. Top with chopped walnuts. Drizzle butter over all. Bake at 350 degrees for 1½ hours. Cool slightly. Cut into squares. Serve with whipped cream or ice cream. Yield: 16 servings.

Violet Miller, California

FROZEN PUMPKIN DELIGHT

16 *gingersnaps, crushed*
1 *c. pumpkin*
1 *qt. vanilla ice cream, softened*
½ *c. sugar*
½ *tsp. salt*
¼ *tsp. cinnamon*
⅛ *tsp. nutmeg*
½ *c. chopped nuts*

Reserve ¼ cup gingersnap crumbs. Place remaining crumbs in greased 8-inch pan. Combine remaining ingredients in bowl; mix well. Pour into prepared pan. Sprinkle reserved crumbs over top. Freeze until firm. Cut into squares to serve. Yield: 6 servings.

PUMPKIN SPICE CAKE

1 *2-layer pkg. spice cake mix*
1 *c. canned pumpkin*
½ *tsp. soda*
½ *c. chopped walnuts*
½ *c. chopped dates*
1 *c. whipping cream, whipped*
3 *tbsp. honey*
¼ *tsp. cinnamon*

Prepare cake mix according to package directions, using ½ cup less liquid. Stir in pumpkin, soda, walnuts and dates. Pour into 2 prepared 9-inch cake pans. Bake at 350 degrees for 35 minutes. Combine whipped cream, honey and cinnamon in bowl; mix well. Frost cooled cake. Yield: 8 servings.

Regina Lewis, Tennessee

PUMPKIN CAKE ROLL

3 *eggs*
1 *c. sugar*
⅔ *c. pumpkin*
1 *tsp. lemon juice*
¾ *c. flour*
1 *tsp. baking powder*
2 *tsp. cinnamon*
1 *tsp. ginger*
½ *tsp. nutmeg*
½ *tsp. salt*
¼ *c. margarine, softened*
6 *oz. cream cheese, softened*
1 *c. confectioners' sugar*
½ *tsp. vanilla extract*

Blend eggs, sugar, pumpkin, and lemon juice in mixer bowl. Add flour, baking powder, spices and salt; beat until smooth. Pour into greased and floured 10x15-inch cake pan. Bake at 375 degrees for 12 minutes. Invert onto towel sprinkled with confectioners' sugar. Roll as for jelly roll in towel. Cool. Cream margarine, cream cheese, 1 cup confectioners' sugar and vanilla in mixer bowl until light and fluffy. Unroll cake. Spread with creamed mixture. Roll as for jelly roll. Place on serving plate. Yield: 12 servings.

Diana Snyder, Pennsylvania

PUMPKIN PIE

¾ *c. packed brown sugar*
1 *tbsp. flour*
½ *tsp. salt*
¼ *tsp. nutmeg*
¼ *tsp. allspice*
¼ *tsp. ginger*
¼ *tsp. cloves*
1 *tsp. cinnamon*
1 *c. pumpkin*
1½ *c. half and half*
2 *eggs, well beaten*
1 *unbaked 9-in. pie shell*

Combine brown sugar, flour, salt and spices in mixer bowl. Mix in pumpkin, half and half and eggs. Pour into pie shell. Bake at 400 degrees for 10 minutes. Reduce temperature to 300 degrees. Bake at 400 degrees for 30 minutes. Yield: 6 to 8 servings.

Paul M. Dunkle, Ohio

PUMPKIN-PECAN PIE

4 *eggs, lightly beaten*
2 *c. mashed cooked pumpkin*
1 *c. sugar*
½ *c. dark corn syrup*
1 *tsp. vanilla extract*
½ *tsp. cinnamon*
¼ *tsp. salt*
1 *unbaked 9-in. pie shell*
1 *c. chopped pecans*

Mix eggs, pumpkin, sugar, corn syrup, vanilla, cinnamon and salt in bowl. Spoon into pie shell. Top with pecans. Bake at 350 degrees for 40 minutes or until set. Yield: 6 servings.

MICROWAVE PUMPKIN BARS

2 eggs
½ c. oil
1 c. sugar
1 c. pumpkin
1 c. flour
1 tsp. baking powder
½ tsp. soda
1 tsp. cinnamon
¼ tsp. cloves
¼ tsp. nutmeg
¼ tsp. ginger
¼ tsp. salt
½ c. chopped nuts
¼ c. chopped dates

Beat eggs, oil, sugar and pumpkin in mixer bowl until smooth. Add sifted dry ingredients; mix lightly. Stir in nuts and dates. Pour into 8x12-inch glass baking dish. Microwave on High for 8 to 10 minutes or until bars test done, turning pan occasionally. Let stand for 5 minutes. Cut into bars. Sprinkle with confectioners' sugar. Serve with whipped topping. Yield: 2 dozen.

Mrs. Lister Endsley, Ohio

PUMPKIN COOKIES

½ c. shortening
1¼ c. packed brown sugar
2 eggs
1 tsp. vanilla extract
1½ c. canned pumpkin
2½ c. flour
4 tsp. baking powder
½ tsp. salt
½ tsp. cinnamon
½ tsp. nutmeg
1 c. raisins
1 c. chopped nuts

Cream shortening and brown sugar in bowl until light and fluffy. Add eggs, vanilla and pumpkin; mix well. Sift in flour, baking powder, salt and spices; mix well. Stir in raisins and nuts. Drop by heaping teaspoonfuls 2 inches apart onto greased cookie sheet. Bake at 375 degrees for 15 minutes or until light brown. Cool on wire rack.
Yield: 5 dozen.

Beth Scott, Pennsylvania

PUMPKIN-CHOCOLATE CHIP COOKIES

½ c. shortening
1½ c. sugar
1 egg
1 c. canned pumpkin
1 tsp. vanilla extract
2½ c. flour
1 tsp. baking powder
1 tsp. soda
½ tsp. salt
1 tsp. nutmeg
1 tsp. cinnamon
½ c. chopped walnuts
1 c. chocolate chips

Cream shortening and sugar in bowl until light and fluffy. Add egg, pumpkin and vanilla; mix well. Add mixture of flour, baking powder, soda, salt and spices; mix well. Stir in walnuts and chocolate chips. Drop by teaspoonfuls onto greased cookie sheet. Bake at 350 degrees for 15 minutes or until light brown. Cool on wire rack.
Yield: 4 dozen.

Laura Mazzaferro, Pennsylvania

RAISIN

RAISIN PUDDING

2 c. packed brown sugar
¼ c. butter
1 c. sugar
1 tsp. cinnamon
1 tsp. nutmeg
2 c. flour
2 tsp. soda
2 c. sour milk
1 c. raisins
Whipped cream

Combine brown sugar, 4 cups hot water and 2 tablespoons butter in saucepan; bring to a boil. Pour into 9x13-inch baking pan. Cream sugar and remaining 2 tablespoons butter in bowl until light and fluffy. Add dry ingredients alternately with sour milk, mixing well after each addition. Fold in raisins. Drop by teaspoonfuls into brown sugar mixture. Bake at 375 degrees for 30 minutes or until firm to touch. Serve warm with whipped cream. Yield: 12 servings.

OLD-FASHIONED RAISIN CAKE

1 oz. package raisins
½ c. shortening
1 c. sugar
1 tsp. soda
2 tsp. baking powder
¼ tsp. salt
1 tsp. cinnamon
½ tsp. cloves
2 eggs, beaten
1 c. buttermilk
Flour

Combine raisins with water to cover in saucepan. Simmer until plump and tender. Drain, reserving ½ cup liquid. Cream shortening and sugar in bowl until light and fluffy. Add soda, baking powder, salt, spices, eggs and buttermilk; mix well. Add enough flour to make stiff batter. Stir in raisins and reserved raisin liquid. Pour into greased and floured 9x13-inch cake pan. Bake at 350 degrees for 40 minutes or until cake tests done. Yield: 12 to 16 servings.

Shari Klepfer, Pennsylvania

SWEDISH RAISIN CAKE

1 c. golden raisins
1 c. margarine, softened
1½ c. sugar
1½ tsp. vanilla extract
2 eggs
3 c. flour
1 tsp. soda
¼ tsp. salt
1 c. chopped nuts

Mix raisins with 1 cup water in saucepan. Cook for 20 minutes. Cool. Drain raisins, reserving liquid. Cream margarine and sugar in mixer bowl until light and fluffy. Add vanilla and eggs 1 at a time, mixing well after each addition. Add sifted dry ingredients alternately with reserved raisin liquid, mixing well after each addition. Stir in raisins and nuts. Pour into greased and floured 10x15-inch cake pan. Bake at 350 degrees for 25 to 30 minutes or until cake tests done. Drizzle favorite lemon-flavored glaze on warm cake. Yield: 16 servings.

Mary F. Smith, Oregon

RAISIN PIE

1½ c. sugar
¼ c. flour
1 egg, well beaten
3 tbsp. lemon juice
2 tsp. grated lemon rind
⅛ tsp. salt
1 c. raisins
1 recipe 2-crust pie pastry

Blend sugar, flour and egg in double boiler. Add lemon juice and rind, salt, raisins and 2 cups water; mix well. Cook for 15 minutes or until thick, stirring occasionally. Cool for 5 to 10 minutes. Pour into pastry-lined 9-inch pie plate. Top with lattice crust. Bake at 450 degrees for 10 minutes. Reduce temperature to 350 degrees. Bake for 20 minutes longer or until lightly browned. Yield: 6 servings.

Phyllis A. Stratton, Oklahoma

RAISIN-RICOTTA PIE

⅓ c. margarine, softened
1 c. ricotta cheese
½ c. sugar
½ c. packed brown sugar
4 eggs
½ tsp. salt
1 tsp. vanilla extract
1 c. raisins, chopped
1 unbaked 9-in. pie shell

Beat margarine and ricotta cheese in bowl until smooth. Beat in sugar and brown sugar. Add eggs 1 at a time, beating well after each addition. Stir in salt, vanilla and raisins. Pour into pie shell. Bake at 350 degrees for 45 minutes or until center is set. Cool completely. Garnish with whipped cream. Yield: 8 servings.

Mary E. Herron, West Virginia

Ricotta cheese is found in the dairy counter next to cottage cheese. It is made from the whey of either whole milk or low-fat milk.

SOUR CREAM-RAISIN PIE

1 c. raisins
1 tsp. soda
1 c. plus 2 tbsp. sugar
3 tbsp. cornstarch
1 c. milk
2 eggs, separated
1 c. sour cream
1 tbsp. butter
1 baked 9-in. pie shell

Pour 1 cup hot water over raisins and soda in saucepan. Add mixture of 1 cup sugar, cornstarch, milk and egg yolks. Cook over medium heat until thickened, stirring constantly. Stir in sour cream. Cook until heated through. Stir in butter. Pour into pie shell. Beat egg whites with remaining 2 tablespoons sugar until stiff peaks form. Spread over pie, sealing to edge. Bake at 375 degrees until golden brown. Yield: 6 servings.

Helen M. Frank, New York

RAISIN COOKIES

1   15-oz. package raisins
1/3 c. margarine
2 c. flour
1 tsp. baking powder
1 tsp. soda
1/2 tsp. salt
1/4 c. sugar
1/2 tsp. nutmeg
2 tbsp. cinnamon
2 eggs
1/2 c. coconut

Combine raisins, margarine and 1¼ cups water in saucepan. Bring to a boil. Boil for 3 minutes. Cool. Combine flour, baking powder, soda, salt, sugar and spices in bowl. Add eggs, coconut and raisin mixture; mix well. Drop by teaspoonfuls onto greased cookie sheet. Flatten with fork dipped in water. Bake at 350 degrees for 15 minutes. Cool on wire rack. Yield: 5 dozen.

Thelma Brammer, West Virginia

RASPBERRY

RED RASPBERRY PUDDING

2 c. sugar
1/3 c. margarine, softened
2 c. flour, sifted
2 tsp. baking powder
1 tsp. salt
1 c. milk
2 c. red raspberries

Cream 1 cup sugar and margarine in mixer bowl until light and fluffy. Add flour, baking powder, salt and milk; mix well. Pour into 9x13-inch baking pan. Sprinkle raspberries over top. Sprinkle with remaining 1 cup sugar. Pour 2 cups boiling water over pudding. Bake at 350 degrees until golden brown. Serve warm or cold. Yield: 10 servings.

Ruth Wallace, Tennessee

HOT RASPBERRY SOUFFLÉ

2 tbsp. plus 1/2 c. sugar
1   10-oz. package frozen
     raspberries in syrup, thawed
4 egg whites, at room
     temperature
1 c. chilled whipping cream
2 tbsp. or orange juice

Butter 6 individual soufflé dishes; sprinkle with 2 tablespoons sugar. Purée raspberries in food processor or blender. Beat egg whites until soft peaks form. Add remaining 1/2 cup sugar 1 tablespoon at a time, beating constantly until stiff peaks form. Fold egg whites gently into raspberry purée. Spoon into prepared dishes. Bake in preheated 375-degree oven for 12 to 15 minutes or until puffed and light golden. Whip cream with orange juice until soft peaks form. Serve soufflés hot with whipped cream. Yield: 6 servings.

Joan Dew, Tennessee

RASPBERRY SWIRL

1 c. graham cracker crumbs
3 tbsp. sugar
¼ c. melted butter
1   10-oz. package frozen
     raspberries
1   3-oz. package red raspberry
     gelatin
8 oz. marshmallows
½ c. milk
1 c. whipping cream, whipped

Mix graham cracker crumbs, 1 table-spoon sugar and butter in bowl. Press over bottom of 9-inch square dish. Chill until firm. Sprinkle raspberries with remaining 2 tablespoons sugar. Let stand for several minutes. Dissolve gelatin in 1 cup boiling water. Drain raspberries, reserving syrup. Add enough water to syrup to measure 1 cup liquid. Add to gelatin. Chill until partially set. Combine marshmallows and milk in saucepan. Heat until marshmallows are melted. Cool completely. Fold in whipped cream. Add raspberries to gelatin. Swirl in marshmallow mixture. Pour over crust. Chill until set. Yield: 9 servings.

BLACK RASPBERRY JAM CAKE

1 c. butter, softened
1 c. sugar
4 eggs, separated
1 tsp. soda
1 c. buttermilk
3 c. flour
1 tsp. cinnamon
1 tsp. nutmeg
1 tsp. cloves
1 tsp. allspice
1 c. raisins
1   4-oz. bottle of maraschino
     cherries
1 lb. walnuts, chopped
8 oz. dates, chopped
1 c. seedless black raspberry
     jam
1 tsp. vanilla extract

Cream butter, sugar and egg yolks in bowl until light and fluffy. Add mixture of soda and buttermilk; mix well. Add flour and spices; mix well. Stir in raisins, cherries, walnuts, dates and jam. Fold stiffly beaten egg whites and vanilla gently into batter. Spoon into greased and floured tube pan. Bake at 350 degrees for 1 hour and 20 minutes or until cake tests done. Cool on wire rack for 15 minutes. Loosen side; invert onto cake plate. Yield: 16 servings.

Thelma Boone, Missouri

FRESH RASPBERRY CAKE

¾ c. butter, softened
1½ c. sugar
3 eggs, separated
1½ tsp. vanilla extract
2¾ c. plus 1 tbsp. flour
2 tsp. baking powder
½ tsp. salt
½ c. milk
2 c. fresh raspberries
1½ c. confectioners' sugar
3 tbsp. raspberry juice

Beat butter and 1¼ cups sugar in mixer bowl until light and fluffy. Add egg yolks and vanilla; beat until smooth. Add mixture of 2¾ cups flour, baking powder and salt alternately with milk, mixing well after each addition. Sprinkle 1 tablespoon flour over raspberries; toss lightly. Stir into batter. Beat egg whites until soft peaks form. Add remaining ¼ cup sugar gradually, beating constantly until stiff peaks form. Fold gently into batter. Pour into greased and floured bundt pan. Bake at 350 degrees for 50 minutes or until cake tests done. Cool on wire rack. Invert onto cake plate. Blend confectioners' sugar and raspberry juice in bowl. Drizzle over cake. Yield: 16 servings.

Kirsten Bancroft, Michigan

BLACK RASPBERRY CUSTARD PIE

2 eggs, beaten
1 c. sugar
2 tbsp. flour
1 c. evaporated milk
2 c. black raspberries
1 unbaked 8-in. pie shell

Beat eggs, sugar, flour and milk in bowl. Spread raspberries in pie shell. Pour sugar mixture over top. Bake at 350 degrees for 40 minutes or until set. Yield: 6 to 8 servings.

Wylma Colehour, Illinois

BLACK RASPBERRY PIE

2 c. black raspberries
¾ c. sugar
½ c. cornstarch
¾ c. shortening
2 c. flour
1 tsp. salt

Heat raspberries, sugar and cornstarch in saucepan over medium heat until thickened, stirring constantly. Cool. Cut shortening into mixture of flour and salt in bowl until crumbly. Add ⅓ cup water. Knead lightly to form ball. Roll half the dough on floured surface; fit into pie plate. Spoon in raspberry mixture. Top with remaining pastry; seal edges and trim. Bake at 350 degrees for 25 minutes.
Yield: 6 to 8 servings.

Lisa Coulter, Maryland

RASPBERRY RIBBON PIE

1   3-oz. package raspberry
      gelatin
¼ c. sugar
1 tbsp. lemon juice
1   10-oz. package frozen
      raspberries
⅓ c. sifted confectioners' sugar
3 oz. cream cheese, softened
1 tsp. vanilla extract
¼ tsp. salt
1 c. whipping cream, whipped
1   9-in. graham cracker pie
      shell

Dissolve gelatin and sugar in 1¼ cups boiling water in bowl. Add lemon juice and raspberries; mix until raspberries thaw. Chill until partially set. Cream confectioners' sugar, cream cheese, vanilla and salt in mixer bowl until light and fluffy. Blend in a small amount of whipped cream. Fold in remaining whipped cream gently. Layer cream cheese mixture and raspberry mixture ½ at a time in pie shell. Chill until set. Yield: 6 servings.

June Patrick, Maryland

RASPBERRY TART

1½ c. mashed raspberries
2½ c. sugar
3 tbsp. cornstarch
2 tbsp. lemon juice
1½ c. whole raspberries
1 c. plus 2 tbsp. shortening
3 eggs
3 tsp. vanilla extract
6½ c. flour
4 tsp. baking powder
1 tsp. salt
1 c. plus 2 tbsp. milk
2 c. confectioners' sugar

Bring mashed raspberries and 1½ cups sugar to a boil in saucepan. Add mixture of cornstarch and ½ cup water. Cook until thickened. Stir in lemon juice and whole berries. Cool. Cream 1 cup sugar and 1 cup shortening in bowl until light. Add eggs and 2 teaspoons vanilla. Add mixture of flour, baking powder and salt alternately with 1 cup milk, beating well after each addition. Reserve 1 cup dough. Pat remaining dough in greased 10x15-inch baking pan. Pour raspberry filling over top. Crumble reserved dough over berries. Bake at 350 degrees for 35 minutes. Drizzle warm tart with mixture of confectioners' sugar and remaining 2 tablespoons shortening, 1 teaspoon vanilla and 2 tablespoons milk.
Yield: 12 to 16 servings.

RASPBERRY-ALMOND SQUARES

1 c. butter, softened
1 c. sugar
1 egg
½ tsp. almond extract
2½ c. flour
½ tsp. baking powder
⅛ tsp. salt
⅓ c. raspberry jam

Cream butter and sugar in bowl until light. Blend in egg and flavoring. Add flour, baking powder and salt; beat until smooth. Spread in 9x9-inch baking dish. Make 5 diagonal indentations the width of the pan with moistened finger. Spoon jam into indentations. Bake at 350 degrees for 12 minutes or until edges are golden brown. Cool. Cut into squares. Yield: 16 servings.

RASPBERRY TURNOVER COOKIES

½ c. butter, softened
3 oz. cream cheese, softened
1 c. flour
2 tsp. grated orange rind
⅛ tsp. salt
¼ c. raspberry preserves
1 c. confectioners' sugar
2 tbsp. orange juice

Cream butter and cream cheese in bowl until fluffy. Add mixture of flour, 1 teaspoon orange rind and salt; mix well. Chill, covered, for 1 hour. Roll ⅛ inch thick on lightly floured surface. Cut into 2½-inch circles. Place about ½ teaspoon preserves on each. Fold over to enclose filling; seal edge with fork. Place 1 inch apart on ungreased cookie sheet. Bake in preheated 375-degree oven for 8 to 10 minutes or until light brown on edges. Cool on wire rack. Combine confectioners' sugar, remaining 1 teaspoon orange rind and orange juice in small bowl; mix well. Drizzle over cookies. Yield: 2½ dozen.

Tami Dunn, Oregon

RHUBARB

RHUBARB CRUNCH

1 c. sifted flour
¾ c. oats
1 c. packed brown sugar
½ c. melted margarine
1 tsp. cinnamon
4 c. chopped rhubarb
1 c. sugar
2 tbsp. cornstarch
1 tsp. vanilla extract

Mix first 5 ingredients in bowl. Press half the mixture into 9-inch baking pan. Place rhubarb in prepared pan. Combine sugar, cornstarch, vanilla and 1 cup water in saucepan. Cook until thick and clear. Pour over rhubarb. Top with remaining oats mixture. Bake at 350 degrees for 1 hour. Serve warm with whipped cream. Yield: 8 servings.

Joeann Moyers, Oregon

RHUBARB CRUMBLE

3 c. chopped rhubarb
3 tbsp. orange juice
¾ c. sugar
¼ tsp. cinnamon
1 tbsp. butter, softened
⅔ c. flour
½ c. packed brown sugar
¼ tsp. soda
⅔ c. quick-cooking oats
¼ c. butter, softened

Spread rhubarb in 8x8-inch baking pan. Sprinkle with orange juice, sugar and cinnamon. Dot with 1 tablespoon butter. Mix remaining dry ingredients in bowl. Cut in ¼ cup butter until crumbly. Sprinkle over rhubarb. Bake at 375 degrees for 40 minutes.
Yield: 4 to 6 servings.

Minnie Pike, New York

MICROWAVE RHUBARB DESSERT

2 c. chopped rhubarb
⅓ c. sugar
2 tbsp. butter
¼ c. packed brown sugar
¼ c. whole wheat flour
¼ c. quick-cooking oats
¼ tsp. cinnamon
¼ c. chopped walnuts

Combine rhubarb and sugar in 1-quart glass baking dish; mix well. Microwave on High for 2½ to 3 minutes, stirring once. Combine butter, brown sugar, flour, oats and cinnamon in bowl; mix until crumbly. Add walnuts. Sprinkle evenly over rhubarb. Microwave on Medium for 6 minutes. Let stand for 4 to 6 hours to improve flavor. Serve at room temperature with ice cream. Yield: 4 servings.

B. J. Scheid, California

Avoid using baking dishes with sloping sides in the microwave because food on the edges receives the most energy and may overcook. Stir foods from the outside toward the center to equalize the temperature.

RHUBARB SHORTCAKE

2 c. cut rhubarb
3 tbsp. margarine, softened
1¾ c. sugar
½ c. milk
1 c. flour
1 tsp. baking powder
1 egg
Dash of salt
¾ tsp. cinnamon
1 tbsp. cornstarch

Place rhubarb in greased 8x8-inch baking dish. Cream margarine and ¾ cup sugar in mixer bowl until light and fluffy. Add milk, flour, baking powder, egg and salt; mix well. Pour over rhubarb. Mix remaining 1 cup sugar, cinnamon and cornstarch in bowl. Sprinkle over top. Pour 1 cup boiling water over all. Bake at 350 degrees for 45 minutes. Yield: 9 servings.

Grace Duesterbeck, Wisconsin

RHUBARB CAKE

½ c. margarine, softened
1½ c. packed light brown sugar
1 egg
2 c. flour
1 tsp. soda
¼ tsp. salt
1 c. milk
1 tsp. vanilla extract
2½ c. 1-in. rhubarb pieces
1 tsp. cinnamon
½ c. sugar

Cream margarine and brown sugar in mixer bowl. Beat in egg at low speed. Add combined dry ingredients alternately with milk, mixing well after each addition. Stir in vanilla and rhubarb. Spoon into greased and floured 9x13-inch baking pan. Sprinkle with mixture of cinnamon and sugar. Bake at 350 degrees for 40 minutes or until cake tests done. Yield: 16 servings.

Betty Wingrove, West Virginia

Rhubarb comes in red and pink varieties. The usual season is from January to July. Look for crisp, fairly thick stalks. Trim off leaves and discolored ends and scrub in cold water. Store rhubarb in refrigerator.

RHUBARB-STRAWBERRY CAKE

2 c. strawberries
2 c. chopped rhubarb
1½ tbsp. lemon juice
2⅓ c. sugar
¼ c. cornstarch
3 c. Rice Chex cereal, crushed
2½ c. flour
1 tbsp. baking powder
1 tsp. salt
1¼ c. butter
1¼ c. milk
2 eggs, beaten
½ tsp. almond extract

Cook strawberries and rhubarb in covered saucepan over low heat for 10 minutes. Add lemon juice and mixture of ⅔ cup sugar and cornstarch. Cook for 8 minutes or until thick, stirring constantly. Combine cereal, 1 cup sugar, 2 cups flour, baking powder and salt in bowl; mix well. Cut in 1 cup butter until crumbly. Add milk, eggs and flavoring; mix well. Reserve 1 cup batter. Pour remaining batter into greased and floured 9x13-inch cake pan. Spoon cooked mixture over batter. Top with reserved batter. Combine remaining ½ cup flour and ⅔ cup sugar in bowl. Cut in remaining ¼ cup butter until crumbly. Sprinkle over cake. Bake at 350 degrees for 1 hour. Cool in pan.
Yield: 16 servings.

Genevieve Gowans, Michigan

BLUEBARB PIE

3 c. ½-inch rhubarb slices
2 c. blueberries
¼ c. unbleached flour
1 c. sugar
1 recipe 2-crust pie pastry
1 tbsp. butter
1 egg, beaten

Combine rhubarb, blueberries, flour and sugar in bowl; mix well. Pour into pastry-lined 10-inch pie plate. Dot with butter. Top with remaining pastry; seal edge and cut vents. Brush with egg. Bake at 400 degrees for 20 minutes. Reduce temperature to 350 degrees. Bake for 20 minutes longer. Cool for 30 minutes before serving.
Yield: 6 to 8 servings.

Mary Ellen Dahlgreen, Washington

CUSTARD RHUBARB PIE

3 *eggs, beaten*
1 *c. sugar*
1 *tbsp. flour*
½ *tsp. vanilla extract*
¼ *c. melted margarine*
3 *stalks rhubarb, cut into 1-in.*
   pieces
1 *unbaked 9-in. pie shell*

Combine eggs, sugar, flour, vanilla and margarine in bowl; mix well. Pour over rhubarb in pie shell. Bake at 300 degrees for 30 minutes or until set. Yield: 6 servings.

Shirley Eddy, Arkansas

SPICED RHUBARB PIES

8 *c. chopped rhubarb*
4 *c. sugar*
⅔ *c. flour*
1 *c. raisins*
¼ *c. melted butter*
2 *tbsp. lemon juice*
1 *tsp. pumpkin pie spice*
1 *tsp. cloves*
3 *unbaked 8-inch pie shells*

Cook rhubarb in a small amount of water in saucepan until tender; drain. Add next 7 ingredients; mix well. Spoon into pie shells. Bake at 425 degrees for 20 minutes. Reduce temperature to 350 degrees. Bake for 15 minutes longer or until crust is brown. Yield: 3 pies.

Mary Scherzer, Michigan

RHUBARB BARS

3 *tbsp. cornstarch*
3 *c. chopped rhubarb*
1½ *c. sugar*
1 *tsp. vanilla extract*
1½ *c. oats*
1½ *c. flour*
1 *c. packed brown sugar*
½ *tsp. soda*
1 *c. shortening*
½ *c. chopped nuts*

Dissolve cornstarch in ¼ cup cold water in saucepan. Add rhubarb, sugar and vanilla. Cook over medium heat until thickened, stirring occasionally. Combine remaining ingredients in bowl; mix until crumbly. Pat ¾ of the crumb mixture into greased 9x13-inch baking pan. Top with rhubarb mixture. Sprinkle with remaining crumbs. Bake at 375 degrees for 30 minutes. Cool. Cut into bars. Yield: 2 dozen.

Rita Poncelet, South Dakota

STRAWBERRY

STRAWBERRY ANGEL DESSERT

16 *oz. frozen strawberries,*
   thawed
8 *oz. cream cheese, softened*
1 *c. confectioners' sugar*
2 *c. whipping cream*
1 *angel food cake, cubed*
10 *oz. frozen raspberries,*
   thawed
½ *c. sugar*
2 *tsp. cornstarch*
½ *c. currant jelly*

Drain strawberries, reserving ½ cup juice. Combine strawberry juice, cream cheese and ½ cup confectioners' sugar in mixer bowl. Beat for 3 minutes. Beat whipping cream and ½ cup confectioners' sugar until soft peaks form. Fold half the whipped cream gently into cream cheese mixture. Fold in strawberries and cake. Spoon into glass serving bowl. Chill for 2 hours. Drain raspberries, reserving juice. Add enough water to reserved juice to measure 1 cup. Press raspberries through sieve. Combine raspberry purée, reserved juice, sugar, cornstarch and jelly in saucepan. Cook mixture until thickened, stirring constantly. Cool. Decorate dessert with remaining whipped cream and fresh strawberries. Spoon into dessert dishes. Serve with cooled raspberry sauce. Yield: 8 servings.

Marilyn Senn, Maryland

STRAWBERRY CHEESECAKE

5 *tbsp. butter*
1¼ *c. graham cracker crumbs*
1 *tbsp. plus ½ c. sugar*
12 *oz. cream cheese, softened*
2 *eggs*
2 *tbsp. flour*
⅔ *c. light cream*
¼ *c. lemon juice*
2 *tsp. grated lemon rind*
1 *to 2 c. sour cream*
1 *to 2 pt. whole strawberries*
½ *c. strawberry jelly, melted*

Melt 3 tablespoons butter in saucepan. Add cracker crumbs and 1 tablespoon sugar; mix well. Press over bottom of 8-inch springform pan. Cream 2 tablespoons softened butter, cream cheese and remaining ½ cup sugar in bowl until light. Blend in eggs 1 at a time. Add flour, cream, lemon juice and rind; mix well. Pour into prepared pan. Bake at 325 degrees for 35 minutes or until set. Spread sour cream over top. Bake for 5 minutes longer. Dip strawberries in jelly. Arrange on cooled cheesecake. Chill for 4 hours. Place on serving plate; remove side of pan. Yield: 12 servings.

Dodie Cabernock, Indiana

FROZEN STRAWBERRY DESSERT

1 *c. flour*
½ *c. butter*
¼ *c. packed brown sugar*
½ *c. chopped nuts*
2 *egg whites*
1 *c. sugar*
2 *tsp. lemon juice*
1 *10-oz. package frozen strawberries, thawed*
1 *c. whipping cream, whipped*

Mix first 4 ingredients in bowl until crumbly. Press into 8x8-inch pan. Bake at 350 degrees for 20 to 25 minutes. Cool. Stir until crumbly. Sprinkle half the mixture into greased 9x9-inch pan. Combine egg whites, sugar, lemon juice and strawberries in mixer bowl. Beat for 20 minutes or until mixture triples in bulk. Fold into whipped cream gently. Spread in prepared pan. Top with remaining crumbs. Freeze until firm. Yield: 8 servings.

STRAWBERRY YOGURT AND RICE PARFAITS

½ *c. strawberry yogurt*
¾ *c. cooked rice, chilled*
5 *oz. frozen strawberries, thawed*
Whipped topping

Stir yogurt and rice together in bowl. Chill, covered, in refrigerator. Layer rice and strawberries alternately in parfait glasses. Garnish with whipped topping. Yield: 2 servings.

Lynn Covington, Texas

STRAWBERRY PRETZEL DESSERT

2 *c. crushed pretzels*
3 *tbsp. plus ¾ c. sugar*
¾ *c. melted margarine*
8 *oz. cream cheese, softened*
8 *oz. whipped topping*
1 *6-oz. package strawberry gelatin*
2 *c. boiling pineapple juice*
2 *10-oz. packages frozen strawberries*

Toss pretzels, 3 tablespoons sugar and melted margarine in bowl. Press into 9x13-inch baking dish. Bake at 325 degrees for 10 minutes. Cool. Cream remaining ¾ cup sugar and cream cheese in mixer bowl until light. Blend in whipped topping. Spread over cooled layer. Chill. Dissolve gelatin in boiling pineapple juice in bowl. Stir in strawberries. Chill until partially set. Spoon over cream cheese layer. Chill until set. Yield: 12 servings.

Lisa Bartley, Pennsylvania

STRAWBERRY-CROWNED TORTE

1 *2-layer pkg. white cake mix*
2 *egg yolks*
1½ *tsp. almond extract*
4 *egg whites*
¼ *tsp. cream of tartar*
1 *c. sugar*
½ *tsp. nutmeg*
2 *c. whipping cream, whipped*
4 *c. strawberry halves*

Prepare cake mix according to package directions substituting egg yolks for whites and adding 1 teaspoon almond flavoring. Pour into 3 waxed paper-lined 9-inch layer pans. Chill in refrigerator. Beat egg whites with cream of tartar until soft peaks form. Add sugar and nutmeg gradually, beating constantly until stiff peaks form. Spread over cake batter. Bake at 325 degrees for 40 minutes. Cool in pans for 10 minutes. Remove to wire rack to cool completely. Add remaining ½ teaspoon almond flavoring to whipped cream. Reserve ⅓ of the whipped cream and half the strawberries. Layer cake, remaining whipped cream and strawberries on serving plate ending with cake. Frost side with reserved whipped cream. Top with reserved strawberries. Yield: 9 servings.

VICTORIAN JAM TORTE

1   *2-layer pkg. yellow cake mix*
2   *c. Kraft strawberry preserves*
Sifted confectioners' sugar

Prepare and bake cake mix according to package directions for two 8-inch cake layers. Cool in pans for 10 minutes. Remove to wire rack to cool completely. Split each layer into 2 layers. Spread each of 3 layers with ¼ cup preserves. Stack layers. Place doily on top of cake; sprinkle with confectioners' sugar. Remove doily carefully. Spoon remaining preserves into center. Yield: 12 servings.

Photograph for this recipe on page 35.

FROSTED STRAWBERRY CAKE

1   *2-layer pkg. white cake mix*
3   *tbsp. flour*
1   *3-oz. package strawberry*
    gelatin
1   *c. oil*
4   *eggs, beaten*
½   *10-oz. package frozen*
    strawberries, thawed
2   *tbsp. melted butter*
2 to 3 *tbsp. strawberry juice*
1   *c. confectioners' sugar*

Mix first 3 ingredients in bowl. Add oil, eggs, strawberries and ½ cup cold water; mix well. Pour into greased and floured 9x13-inch baking pan. Bake at 350 degrees for 40 to 50 minutes or until cake tests done. Blend butter and strawberry juice in bowl. Stir in enough confectioners' sugar to make of spreading consistency. Spread over cooled cake. Yield: 16 servings.

Peggy Hicks, West Virginia

STRAWBERRY-NUT POUND CAKE

1   *c. shortening*
3   *c. sugar*
4   *eggs*
⅔   *c. buttermilk*
1½ *tsp. butter flavoring*
1½ *tsp. vanilla extract*
1   *tsp. strawberry extract*
1½ *tsp. red food coloring*
3   *c. sifted flour*
½   *tsp. baking powder*
1   *tsp. soda*
½   *tsp. salt*
½   *c. chopped strawberries*
½   *c. chopped pecans*
½   *c. strawberry juice*

Cream shortening and 2 cups sugar in mixer bowl until light and fluffy. Add eggs 1 at a time, beating well after each addition. Mix buttermilk, 1 teaspoon butter flavoring, 1 teaspoon vanilla, ½ teaspoon strawberry extract and red food coloring. Sift flour, baking powder, soda and salt together. Add to batter alternately with buttermilk mixture, mixing well after each addition. Fold in ¼ cup strawberries and pecans. Pour into greased and floured 10-inch tube pan. Bake at 350 degrees for 1 hour and 20 minutes or until toothpick inserted near center comes out clean. Invert onto serving plate. Combine remaining 1 cup sugar, ¼ cup chopped strawberries, ½ teaspoon vanilla, ½ teaspoon butter flavoring, ½ teaspoon strawberry extract and strawberry juice in small saucepan. Bring to a boil, stirring constantly. Cook for 1 minute. Brush over top and side of hot cake. Yield: 16 servings.

Wilma Hayes, Texas

OLD-FASHIONED STRAWBERRY SHORTCAKE

    2 c. sifted flour
    2 tbsp. sugar
    1 tbsp. baking powder
    ½ tsp. salt
    ½ c. plus 3 tbsp. butter
    1 egg, beaten
    ½ c. light cream
    4 c. sweetened sliced
        strawberries
    1 c. whipping cream, whipped

Sift dry ingredients together into bowl. Cut in butter until crumbly. Add mixture of egg and light cream. Mix just until dough clings together. Knead several times on floured surface. Pat ¾ inch thick. Cut into 2½-inch circles. Place on ungreased baking sheet. Bake at 450 degrees for 8 to 10 minutes or until brown. Split shortcakes. Spread with 3 tablespoons butter. Spoon strawberries between and over tops of shortcake halves. Serve warm with whipped cream. Yield: 8 servings.

Merle Campbell, Kansas

STRAWBERRY SHORTCUT CAKE

    1   2-layer pkg. white cake mix
    3 eggs
    1 c. oil
    3   10-oz. packages frozen
        sweetened strawberries,
        thawed
    1   3-oz. package strawberry
        gelatin
    2 c. miniature marshmallows

Combine cake mix, eggs, oil and ¾ cup water in mixer bowl. Beat at high speed for 2 minutes. Combine strawberries and dry gelatin in bowl; mix well. Sprinkle marshmallows in bottom of greased 9x13-inch cake pan. Pour batter over marshmallows. Spoon strawberry mixture evenly over top. Bake at 350 degrees for 40 minutes or until cake tests done. Marshmallows rise to top and strawberries settle to bottom during baking. Cool completely. Cut into squares. Invert servings on dessert plates. Serve with whipped cream. Yield: 8 servings.

STRAWBERRY TART

    ½ c. butter
    1½ c. flour
    ½ c. sugar
    1 tsp. cinnamon
    5 egg yolks
    ⅓ c. cornstarch
    ¼ tsp. salt
    ¼ tsp. nutmeg
    2 c. milk
    1 tsp. vanilla extract
    2 c. strawberry halves
    ½ c. red currant jelly
    ¼ c. pistachio nuts

Cut butter into mixture of flour, ¼ cup sugar and cinnamon in bowl until crumbly. Add 1 egg yolk; mix with fork until mixture forms ball. Chill for several minutes. Roll into 12-inch circle on lightly floured surface; fit into 9-inch springform tart pan. Prick with fork. Chill for 1 hour. Bake at 400 degrees for 12 minutes. Cool on wire rack. Mix remaining ¼ cup sugar, cornstarch, salt and ⅛ teaspoon nutmeg in saucepan. Stir in milk gradually. Blend in 4 egg yolks. Bring to a boil over medium-low heat, stirring constantly. Boil for 1 minute, stirring constantly. Stir in vanilla. Chill, covered, in refrigerator. Spread in tart shell. Arrange strawberries over top, leaving ½-inch border. Blend jelly and remaining ⅛ teaspoon nutmeg in small saucepan. Heat until bubbly. Drizzle over strawberries. Sprinkle nuts around edge. Chill until serving time. Place on serving plate; remove side of pan. Yield: 10 to 12 servings.

FRESH STRAWBERRY PIE

    1 c. sugar
    3 tbsp. cornstarch
    3 tbsp. strawberry gelatin
    ¾ to 1 qt. strawberries
    1 baked pie shell

Mix sugar, cornstarch and 1 cup water in saucepan. Cook until mixture thickens, stirring constantly; remove from heat. Add gelatin, stirring until dissolved. Stir in strawberries. Pour into pie shell; cool. Serve with whipped cream. Yield: 6 servings.

Mrs. Noah Blosser, Ohio

STRAWBERRY BARS

1 c. butter, softened
1 c. sugar
2 egg yolks
2 c. flour
1 c. chopped walnuts
½ c. strawberry jam

Cream butter in bowl until smooth. Add sugar gradually, creaming until light and fluffy. Beat in egg yolks. Mix in flour gradually. Fold in walnuts. Spread half the batter in greased 8-inch square baking pan. Top with jam. Cover with remaining batter. Bake at 325 degrees for 1 hour or until light brown. Cool. Cut into bars. Yield: 1½ dozen.

Peggy Cutlip, Iowa

STRAWBERRY COOKIES

1 2-layer pkg. strawberry cake mix
2 c. whipped topping
2 eggs
Confectioners' sugar

Combine cake mix, whipped topping and eggs in bowl; mix well. Shape by teaspoonfuls into balls. Roll in confectioners' sugar. Place on greased cookie sheet. Bake at 350 degrees for 10 minutes. Cool on wire rack. Yield: 3½ dozen.

Gloria Carrier, Texas

ICE CREAM KOLACHES

4 c. flour
1 lb. butter, softened
1 pt. vanilla ice cream, softened
Strawberry preserves
Confectioners' sugar

Combine flour, butter and ice cream in bowl; mix well. Roll ⅛ inch thick on floured surface. Cut into small circles. Place on cookie sheet. Spoon ½ teaspoon preserves onto each cookie. Bake at 350 degrees for 20 minutes or until golden on bottom. Sprinkle with confectioners' sugar. Cool on wire rack. Yield: 2 dozen.

Carla Warnock, Oklahoma

SWEET POTATO

SOUTHERN YAM DESSERT SQUARES

2 c. quick-cooking oats
1½ c. flour
½ tsp. soda
½ tsp. salt
1 c. margarine, softened
1 c. packed light brown sugar
1 tsp. vanilla extract
1 lb. yams, cooked, peeled, mashed
1 14-oz. can sweetened condensed milk
2 eggs, beaten
1½ tsp. allspice
1 tsp. grated orange rind
½ c. chopped nuts

Combine oats, flour, soda and salt in bowl; set aside. Cream margarine, brown sugar and vanilla in mixer bowl until fluffy. Add dry ingredients; mix until crumbly. Reserve 1 cup crumb mixture. Press remaining mixture on bottom of 9x13-inch baking dish. Bake at 350 degrees for 10 minutes. Combine yams, sweetened condensed milk, eggs, allspice and orange rind in bowl; mix well. Pour over prepared crust. Combine nuts with reserved crumb mixture; crumble evenly over top. Bake for 25 to 30 minutes or until golden brown. Cool. Serve warm or chilled. Yield: 10 to 12 servings.

SWEET POTATO PUDDING

4 c. grated uncooked sweet potatoes
2 c. corn syrup
1 c. packed brown sugar
1 tsp. cinnamon
Grated rind of 1 orange
Grated rind of 1 lemon
1 tsp. ginger

Combine all ingredients in bowl in order listed; mix well. Pour into buttered 9x13-inch baking dish. Bake at 350 degrees for 45 minutes or until crisp crust forms on top and around edges. Serve warm with sweet cream or whipped cream. Yield: 4 to 6 servings.

Mrs. Robert L. Scofield, Ohio

HARVEST BUNDT CAKE

2 c. sugar
1½ c. oil
½ c. grated carrots
½ c. grated apple
3 c. grated sweet potato
1 c. chopped walnuts
3 c. flour
2 tsp. cinnamon
1 tsp. salt
3 tbsp. baking powder
1 tsp. soda
4 eggs

Mix sugar and oil in bowl. Add carrots, apple, sweet potato and walnuts. Add sifted dry ingredients to sweet potato mixture; mix well. Blend in eggs 1 at a time. Pour into greased 10-inch bundt pan. Bake at 350 degrees for 1 hour or until cake tests done. Cool on wire rack. Yield: 12 servings.

SWEET POTATO-RAISIN PIES

2 c. mashed cooked sweet
    potatoes
½ c. margarine, softened
4 eggs
2 c. sugar
1½ c. raisins
2½ tsp. cinnamon
½ tsp. ginger
½ tsp. nutmeg
2 unbaked pie shells

Combine sweet potatoes, margarine, eggs, sugar, raisins and spices in bowl; mix well. Pour into pie shells. Bake at 350 degrees for 35 to 40 minutes or until set. Yield: 12 servings.

Michael L. Brodie, Texas

SPICY SWEET POTATO PIE

2 tbsp. butter, melted
1½ c. mashed cooked sweet
    potatoes
½ c. packed brown sugar
1 tsp. cinnamon
½ tsp. ginger
¼ tsp. mace
¼ tsp. salt
2 eggs, beaten
1½ c. milk, scalded
1 unbaked 10-in. pie shell

Blend butter into sweet potatoes in bowl. Add mixture of brown sugar, spices, salt and eggs; mix well. Beat in milk. Pour into pie shell. Bake at 450 degrees for 10 minutes. Reduce temperature to 350 degrees. Bake for 30 to 35 minutes or until knife inserted between center and edge comes out clean. Cool. Garnish with sweetened whipped cream and slivered almonds.
Yield: 6 to 8 servings.

Nora Westman, Oregon

TANGERINE

TANGERINE CHEESECAKE

1 graham cracker pie shell
½ tsp. cinnamon
16 oz. cream cheese, softened
2 eggs
1 tsp. vanilla extract
1 c. sugar
16 oz. sour cream
Sections of 3 tangerines
1 kiwifruit, sliced
Fresh strawberries
1 tbsp. cornstarch
⅓ c. orange juice

Sprinkle pie shell with cinnamon. Bake at 350 degrees for 5 minutes. Combine cream cheese, eggs, vanilla and ½ cup sugar in bowl; mix well. Pour into prepared pie shell. Bake at 350 degrees for 30 minutes. Mix sour cream and ¼ cup sugar in small bowl. Spread over cheesecake. Bake for 15 minutes or until set. Cool. Arrange fruit on top. Mix cornstarch and remaining ¼ cup sugar in small saucepan. Stir in orange juice. Cook over medium heat until thickened and clear. Cool. Spoon over cheesecake. Chill. Yield: 8 servings.

Dereth Haag, Saskatchewan, Canada

TANGERINE PARFAITS

1 c. fresh tangerine juice
2 tbsp. grated tangerine rind
3 tbsp. flour
2 tbsp. fresh lemon juice
½ tsp. grated orange rind
½ c. sugar
3 eggs, separated

Blend first 6 ingredients with beaten egg yolks in double boiler. Cook over hot water until thickened, stirring constantly; cool. Fold in stiffly beaten egg whites. Spoon into parfait glasses. Chill. Yield: 6 servings.

Prue Bryson, Georgia

TANGERINE TRIFLE

1 *sm. pound cake, cut into*
 ½-in. slices
4 *to 6 tbsp. orange juice*
1 *lg. package French vanilla*
 instant pudding, prepared
Sections of 6 tangerines
4 *c. sweetened whipped cream*
Toasted almonds

Place half the cake slices in bottom of glass bowl. Sprinkle with 2 to 3 tablespoons orange juice. Layer with half the pudding, half the tangerine sections and half the whipped cream. Layer remaining cake, orange juice, pudding and whipped cream over top. Top with remaining tangerine sections and almonds. Chill. Yield: 10 servings.

F. Jewell Patton, Florida

TANGERINE SUNSHINE CAKE

1   *2-layer pkg. yellow cake mix*
1 *sm. package vanilla instant*
 pudding mix
4 *tsp. grated tangerine rind*
3 *tbsp. fresh tangerine juice*
4 *eggs*
⅓ *c. oil*
¼ *c. confectioners' sugar*

Combine cake mix, pudding mix, tangerine rind, tangerine juice, eggs, oil and 1 cup water in mixer bowl. Beat at medium speed for 4 minutes. Pour into greased 10-inch bundt pan. Bake at 350 degrees for 50 minutes or until cake tests done. Cool in pan for 5 minutes. Invert onto serving plate. Sprinkle with confectioners' sugar. Garnish with whipped topping and tangerine sections. Yield: 12 servings.

TANGERINE CHIFFON PIE

1 *env. unflavored gelatin*
½ *c. plus ⅓ c. sugar*
Dash of salt
4 *eggs, separated*
¼ *c. fresh lemon juice*
1 *c. tangerine juice*
1 *tbsp. grated tangerine rind*
1 *baked 9-in. pie shell*
3 *tbsp. orange juice*
1 *c. heavy cream, whipped*
2 *tangerines, peeled, sectioned*

Combine gelatin, ½ cup sugar and salt in double boiler. Beat in egg yolks and juices. Cook over boiling water until sugar and gelatin are dissolved and mixture thickens, stirring constantly. Stir in tangerine rind. Chill until partially set. Beat egg whites with remaining ⅓ cup sugar until stiff. Fold into custard. Spoon into pie shell. Chill for 3 hours or longer. Blend orange juice into whipped cream. Spread over pie. Top with tangerine sections. Yield: 6 to 8 servings.

Doreen Kirk, Missouri

TOFFEE

TOFFEE ICE CREAM

7 *eggs, separated*
1 *tbsp. almond extract*
½ *tsp. salt*
1½ *c. sugar*
2 *c. whipping cream*
6 *Heath bars, crushed*
Milk

Beat egg whites until stiff peaks form. Beat egg yolks until frothy. Fold gently into egg whites. Add flavoring, salt, sugar, cream and crushed candy. Pour into freezer container. Put dasher in place. Add milk to fill line. Freeze according to manufacturer's instructions. Yield: 10 servings.

Marvis T. Hogen, South Dakota

TOFFEE BAR CAKE

2 c. packed brown sugar
2 c. flour
½ c. butter
1 tsp. soda
½ tsp. salt
1 egg
1 c. milk
1 tsp. vanilla extract
6 chocolate-covered toffee bars,
   chopped
½ c. chopped pecans

Mix brown sugar and flour in bowl. Cut in butter until crumbly. Reserve 1 cup mixture. Add soda and salt to remaining mixture. Blend in egg, milk and vanilla; beat until smooth. Pour into greased and floured 9x13-inch cake pan. Sprinkle with toffee bars, pecans and reserved crumb mixture. Bake at 350 degrees for 35 minutes. Cool. Yield: 18 servings.

TOFFEE BARS

½ c. margarine
1 c. oats
½ c. packed brown sugar
½ c. flour
½ c. finely chopped walnuts
¼ tsp. soda
1 can sweetened condensed
   milk
2 tsp. vanilla extract
6 oz. semisweet chocolate chips

Melt 6 tablespoons margarine in medium saucepan. Stir in oats, brown sugar, flour, nuts and soda. Press into greased 9x13-inch baking pan. Bake at 350 degrees for 10 to 15 minutes or until lightly browned. Combine remaining 2 tablespoons margarine and sweetened condensed milk in medium saucepan. Cook over medium heat for 15 minutes or until thickened, stirring constantly; remove from heat. Stir in vanilla. Pour over crust. Bake for 10 to 15 minutes longer or until golden brown. Sprinkle chocolate chips on top. Let stand for 1 minute; spread evenly. Cool to room temperature. Chill well. Cut into bars. Yield: 3 dozen.

TOFFEE SQUARES

½ c. butter
1 c. packed brown sugar
¼ tsp. salt
1 c. flour
1 egg yolk
1 tsp. vanilla extract
6 chocolate candy bars
½ c. chopped pecans

Cream butter and sugar in bowl until fluffy. Add salt and flour; mix well. Add egg yolk and vanilla; mix well. Spread in 10x15-inch baking pan. Bake at 350 degrees for 30 to 35 minutes or until toothpick inserted in center comes out clean. Arrange candy bars over top; let melt. Spread over top; sprinkle with pecans. Cut into squares. Yield: 5 dozen.

Linda R. Swales, Oklahoma

TOFFEE

½ c. butter
½ c. margarine
1 c. sugar
1 tbsp. light corn syrup
1 c. chopped nuts
12 oz. chocolate chips
2 tbsp. melted paraffin

Melt butter and margarine in heavy 3-quart saucepan over medium heat. Add sugar, 3 tablespoons water and corn syrup. Cook, covered, over medium heat for 2 to 3 minutes or until steam washes sugar crystals from side of pan. Cook, uncovered, to 270 to 290 degrees on candy thermometer, soft-crack stage; do not stir. Add nuts. Cook for 3 minutes longer. Pour into buttered 10x15-inch dish. Spread into thin layer. Let stand until firm. Place on waxed paper; blot with paper towel. Melt chocolate chips in double boiler. Blend in paraffin. Spread chocolate over toffee. Let stand until firm. Break into pieces. Yield: 2 pounds.

Mary Louise Hedrick, West Virginia

WALNUT

GREEK WALNUT BAKLAVA

8 c. chopped walnuts
1 tsp. cinnamon
¼ tsp. nutmeg
7¼ c. sugar
2 lb. phyllo
1½ lb. melted butter
Juice of ½ lemon
1 stick cinnamon

Combine walnuts, cinnamon, nutmeg and ¼ cup sugar in bowl. Keep phyllo covered with damp towel to prevent breaking. Brush each sheet of phyllo with melted butter. Layer 6 sheets into buttered 12x17-inch baking pan. Add a layer of walnut mixture. Repeat layers, ending with 9 sheets buttered phyllo on top. Cut through phyllo with sharp knife to make 1½ to 2-inch diamonds or squares. Bake at 325 degrees for 1½ to 2 hours. Combine remaining ingredients and 5 cups water in saucepan. Boil for about 30 minutes or until syrupy. Pour over warm Baklava. Yield: 48 to 60 pieces.

Ethel B. Focas, Maryland

WALNUT CHIFFON CAKE

2 c. flour
1½ c. sugar
1 tbsp. baking powder
½ tsp. salt
9 egg yolks
½ c. oil
1 tsp. vanilla extract
1 c. chopped black walnuts
1 c. egg whites
½ tsp. cream of tartar

Sift first 4 ingredients into mixer bowl; make well in center. Add egg yolks, oil, ¾ cup cold water and vanilla; beat well. Add walnuts. Beat egg whites and cream of tartar until stiff peaks form. Fold in walnut mixture gently. Pour into ungreased tube pan. Bake at 350 degrees for 1 hour. Invert on funnel to cool completely. Invert onto cake plate. Yield: 16 servings.

Susan Uhler, Pennsylvania

FROZEN WALNUT MOUSSE

2 eggs, separated
½ c. sugar
1 pt. heavy cream
1 tsp. vanilla extract
1 c. ground walnuts

Beat egg whites until stiff peaks form. Add ¼ cup sugar gradually, beating until glossy. Beat egg yolks with remaining ¼ cup sugar until thick and lemony. Whip cream in bowl until soft peaks form. Add vanilla. Combine egg yolks with whipped cream and walnuts; mix well. Fold gently into egg whites. Spoon into mold. Freeze, covered, until serving time. Unmold onto serving plate. Serve with rum sauce, if desired. Yield: 8 servings.

Jackie Westfield, New York

RICH WALNUT TORTE

16 eggs, separated
2 c. sugar
1½ c. ground walnuts
1 tbsp. baking powder
3 tbsp. cracker meal
1 tbsp. whiskey
⅓ c. flour
1 c. coffee
½ c. butter
1 tsp. vanilla extract

Beat egg yolks in mixer bowl for 10 minutes. Add 1 cup sugar, walnuts, baking powder, cracker meal and whiskey; mix well. Beat egg whites until stiff peaks form. Fold gently into egg yolk mixture. Spread into 4 greased, floured and waxed paper-lined 8-inch cake pans. Bake at 350 degrees for 30 minutes. Cool for 5 minutes in pans. Remove to wire rack to cool completely. Blend flour with small amount of coffee. Bring remaining coffee to a boil in saucepan; reduce heat. Stir in flour mixture. Cook until thickened, stirring constantly. Cool. Cream butter and remaining 1 cup sugar in bowl gradually until light and fluffy. Beat in coffee mixture gradually. Add vanilla. Spread between torte layers. Refrigerate until serving time. Yield: 12 servings.

WALNUT TASSIES

1 c. margarine, softened
8 oz. cream cheese, softened
2½ c. flour
1 c. chopped walnuts
4 eggs
1 16-oz. package brown sugar
2 tbsp. melted margarine
½ tsp. vanilla extract

Combine first 3 ingredients in bowl; mix well. Chill for 1 hour. Shape into balls. Press into tart pans. Place 1 teaspoon chopped walnuts in each shell. Add eggs to brown sugar, 1 at a time, in bowl, mixing well after each addition. Add margarine and vanilla; mix well. Spoon into tart shells. Bake at 350 degrees for 15 to 20 minutes or until set. Yield: 3 to 4 dozen.

Maryann Reibsome, Maryland

ZUCCHINI

ZUCCHINI CRISP

4 c. flour
3 c. sugar
½ tsp. salt
1½ c. margarine
8 c. chopped zucchini
⅔ c. lemon juice
¼ tsp. nutmeg
1½ tsp. cinnamon

Mix flour, 2 cups sugar and salt in bowl. Cut in margarine until crumbly. Press half the mixture over bottom of greased 9x13-inch baking pan. Bake at 375 degrees for 10 minutes. Mix zucchini with lemon juice in saucepan. Cook until tender. Add remaining 1 cup sugar, nutmeg and 1 teaspoon cinnamon. Simmer for 1 minute. Stir in ½ cup crumb mixture. Cook for 1 minute, stirring constantly. Cool. Pour into greased pan. Sprinkle mixture of remaining ½ teaspoon cinnamon and crumb mixture over zucchini. Bake at 375 degrees for 35 minutes or until light brown. Yield: 10 servings.

Doris Burns, Michigan

ZUCCHINI FRUITCAKES

3 eggs
1 c. oil
2 c. packed brown sugar
1 tbsp. vanilla extract
3 c. flour
1 tsp. soda
1 tsp. cinnamon
1 tsp. allspice
1 tsp. cloves
1 tsp. nutmeg
½ tsp. baking powder
1 tsp. salt
2 c. coarsely shredded zucchini
2 c. coarsely chopped walnuts
2 c. raisins
1 c. currants
2 c. mixed candied fruit

Beat eggs, oil, brown sugar and vanilla in mixer bowl. Stir in combined dry ingredients. Fold in zucchini, walnuts and fruits. Pour into 2 greased 5x9-inch loaf pans. Bake at 325 degrees for 1 to 1½ hours or until cake tests done. Yield: 2 cakes.

ZUCCHINI BARS

1½ c. packed brown sugar
½ c. butter, softened
¼ c. oil
2 eggs
1 tsp. vanilla extract
¼ tsp. nutmeg
1½ c. wheat bran cereal
1½ c. flour
½ c. whole wheat flour
1 tsp. soda
½ tsp. salt
2½ c. grated zucchini
1 c. raisins
1 c. flaked coconut

Combine sugar, butter and oil in mixer bowl; beat until light and fluffy. Add eggs, 2 tablespoons water, vanilla and nutmeg; mix well. Combine cereal, flour, whole wheat flour, soda and salt. Add to creamed mixture alternately with zucchini, mixing well after each addition. Stir in raisins and coconut. Spoon into greased 9x13-inch baking pan. Bake at 360 degrees for 40 minutes. Cool. Cut into bars. Yield: 2 dozen.

CELEBRATION DESSERTS

CREATIVE TOUCHES

Holidays are, by definition, very special occasions marked with festivities and celebrations. They are times filled with tradition and the anticipation of good fun and good food shared with family and friends.

The foods associated most pleasurably with holidays always include our favorite desserts. Some are so traditional that it would be hard to imagine the holidays without them. What would Thanksgiving be without cranberry and pumpkin desserts, or Christmas without mincemeat and fruitcakes? We always expect cherry desserts in February, strawberries at Easter and fresh fruit and ice cream on the fourth of July. All of these time-honored favorites are included in this holiday section.

These special occasions also offer us a chance to try something new. Each holiday section contains recipes which celebrate the holiday in a different and special way. What could be more festive than the heart-shaped Valentine Mold, Easter Egg Cake and Easter Bonnets, Plum Fireworks, Jack-O'-Lantern Cake, Autumn Shortcake or Holly Wreaths?

The real secret to success, however, is the imagination to adapt dessert recipes to any special occasion. Basic cookie recipes can be cut or shaped into bunnies, hearts, turkeys, owls, pumpkins or bells and decorated to carry out the motif. Cake batter can be poured into a mold to fit the occasion. A plain cake can be decorated with red candy hearts or red and green candied cherries. Gumdrops can be cut out to form spring flowers or jack-o'-lantern faces. The Easter Bonnets could double easily as Pilgrims' Hats. In short, anything is possible with imagination and a few versatile garnishes.

The following garnishes can be adapted to celebrate any special occasion. Start with these and add your own creative touches.

Brazil Nut Flowers: Place Brazil nuts in boiling water; remove from heat. Let stand for 5 minutes. Slice each nut quickly lengthwise with vegetable peeler. Arrange slices which will curl slightly as petals around cherry half centers.

Crushed Candy: Crush peppermint, hard candies or toffee bars. Sprinkle over desserts. Divide top of cake into wedges with tautly held string pressed into frosting. Sprinkle different color candy in each wedge, using colors appropriate to the holiday.

Cherry Flowers: Snip well-drained red maraschino cherries into 6 sections, cutting ¾ of the way through. Spread sections apart gently to resemble flower petals. Cut leaves from green maraschino cherries.

Chocolate Curls: Warm a square or bar of chocolate in hands. Draw blade of vegetable peeler along smooth surface, shaving as thin as possible to form curls. Transfer curls to dessert with toothpick.

Chocolate Shapes: Melt 4 ounces sweet or semisweet chocolate in double boiler over hot water, stirring constantly. Spread to ⅛-inch thickness on waxed paper-lined tray. Chill for 15 minutes or until firm. Invert onto waxed paper. Peel bottom sheet of waxed paper carefully from chocolate. Cut around paper patterns with sharp knife for desired shapes or cut with cookie cutters. Chill cut-outs until serving time.

Citrus Cartwheels and Twists: Slice lemons, limes or oranges cross-wise very thinly. Cut v-shaped notches in rind from edge toward pulp for cartwheels. Make 1 cut from edge into center of slice and turn cut sides in opposite directions for twists.

Tinted Coconut: Dilute several drops of food coloring with ½ tea-spoon milk or water; toss with 1 to 1⅓ cups coconut until evenly tinted. Sprinkle over ice cream or fruit. Sprinkle green coconut around edge of pie, cake or cheesecake and dot with cherries for wreath. Sprinkle red coconut in heart design.

Cookie Butterflies: Place 2 cookies at an angle to resemble butterfly in ice cream, parfaits or puddings.

Frosted Grapes: Cut grapes into small clusters of 3 to 5 grapes. Brush with egg white slightly beaten with a small amount of water. Sprinkle with sugar; place on wire rack to dry. Mix different kinds of grapes for color. Tint sugar with food coloring if desired.

Gumdrop Roses: Roll 4 gumdrops for each rose into ovals ⅛ inch thick on sugared board. Sprinkle with additional sugar. Cut ovals into halves crosswise. Roll 1 half-oval tightly to form center of rose. Spiral remaining half-ovals around center, overlapping slightly. Press together at base; trim base. Cut leaves from flat-tened green gumdrops.

Mint Balloons: Arrange pastel mint wafers on top of dessert. Place shoestring licorice to serve as balloon strings.

Dipped Strawberries: Dip strawberries in melted chocolate or white chocolate and let stand until set.

Whipped Cream: Sweeten whipped cream to taste. Add cocoa or food coloring if desired. Pipe directly onto dessert or pipe rosettes onto waxed paper and freeze until needed.

CUPID'S BAKED ALASKA

4 *egg whites*
Pinch of salt
½ *c. sugar*
4 *slices pound cake*
4 *scoops ice cream*
1 *c. sweetened raspberries*

Beat egg whites and salt in medium bowl until soft peaks form. Add sugar gradually, beating until stiff. Place cake slices on cookie sheet. Place 1 scoop ice cream on each slice. Spread meringue over ice cream and cake, covering each completely. Bake at 450 degrees for 4 minutes or until lightly browned. Remove to serving plates with spatula. Top with raspberries. Serve immediately. Yield: 4 servings.

Sherry Pattison, New Hampshire

FROZEN CHOCOLATE BOMBE

1 *c. butter, softened*
2 *c. confectioners' sugar*
4 *oz. baking chocolate, melted*
4 *eggs*
1½ *tsp. vanilla extract*
½ *tsp. peppermint extract*
1½ *c. crushed chocolate wafers*

Cream butter and confectioners' sugar in mixer bowl until light. Blend in chocolate. Add eggs 1 at a time, mixing well after each addition. Stir in flavorings. Spread half the crumbs, chocolate mixture and remaining crumbs in 9x13-inch dish. Freeze for 4 hours or longer. Garnish with whipped cream and marschino cherries. Yield: 16 servings.

CHERRY CREAM PUFF RING

½ *c. butter*
1 *c. flour*
4 *eggs*
1 *c. milk*
¾ *c. sour cream*
1 *sm. package vanilla instant pudding mix*
¼ *tsp. almond extract*
1 *can cherry pie filling*

Bring butter and 1 cup water to a boil in saucepan. Stir in flour. Beat vigorously for 1 minute; remove from heat. Add eggs 1 at a time, beating well after each addition. Drop by tablespoonfuls into 8-inch circle on greased baking sheet; smooth with spatula. Bake at 400 degrees for 50 to 60 minutes or until puffed and golden. Cool. Cut off top; remove soft center. Combine milk, sour cream, pudding mix and flavoring in mixer bowl. Beat at low speed for 1 minute. Spoon into ring. Top with half the pie filling. Replace top of ring. Drizzle remaining pie filling over top. Yield: 8 servings.

Tisha Nunley, Ohio

RASPBERRIES AND CREAM

1 *10-oz. package frozen raspberries, thawed*
½ *c. champagne*
1 *pt. Häagen-Daz raspberry and cream sorbet*

Drain raspberries, reserving ¼ cup juice. Mix reserved juice with champagne in cup. Place large scoop ice cream in each dessert glass. Pour raspberry juice mixture around ice cream. Top with raspberries. Garnish with mint leaves. Yield: 4 servings.

Photograph for this recipe on Cover.

STRAWBERRY MERINGUES

4 *egg whites*
½ *tsp. cream of tartar*
Pinch of salt
1 *c. sugar*
1 *tsp. vanilla extract*
1 *qt. ice cream*
8 *to 10 oz. fresh strawberries*

Beat egg whites, cream of tartar and salt until soft peaks form. Add sugar gradually, beating until stiff. Stir in vanilla. Shape into 4-inch hearts on brown paper, forming edges higher than the center. Bake at 250 degrees for 50 to 60 minutes; cool. Place on serving plates. Spoon ice cream and sweetened strawberries into cooled hearts. Yield: 12 servings.

Helen Moor, Indiana

A TRIFLE ROMANTIC

1 pkg. angel food cake mix
1 lg. package vanilla instant
  pudding mix, prepared
1 16-oz. package frozen
   strawberries
8 lg. bananas, sliced
1 lg. carton whipped topping
¼ c. slivered almonds

Prepare and bake cake mix according to package directions; cool. Tear into bite-sized pieces. Layer half the cake, pudding, fruit and whipped topping in large bowl. Repeat layers with remaining ingredients. Top with almonds. Chill until serving time.
Yield: 25 servings.

Barbara Richter, Texas

VALENTINE MOLD

1 8-oz. jar red maraschino
   cherries
1 env. unflavored gelatin
⅛ tsp. salt
1 c. milk
½ tsp. grated lemon rind
2 tbsp. lemon juice
Red food coloring (opt.)
3 egg whites
¼ c. sugar

Drain cherries, reserving ⅓ cup syrup. Chop enough cherries to equal ¼ cup; reserve remaining whole cherries for garnish. Soften gelatin in reserved cherry syrup in saucepan. Cook over low heat until gelatin dissolves. Remove from heat. Stir in salt and milk. Chill until mixture mounds from spoon. Stir in lemon rind, lemon juice, chopped cherries and several drops of red food coloring. Beat egg whites until soft peaks form. Add sugar gradually, beating until stiff. Fold in cherry mixture. Spoon into 5-cup heart-shaped mold. Chill for 4 hours to overnight. Unmold onto serving plate. Garnish with reserved whole cherries and whipped cream. Yield: 6 servings.

Kate Mabry, Illinois

RASPBERRY CAKE ROLL

4 eggs, at room temperature
¾ c. sugar
¾ c. sifted cake flour
1 tsp. baking powder
½ tsp. salt
Confectioners' sugar
1 c. raspberry preserves

Beat eggs in small mixer bowl until thick and lemon-colored. Beat in sugar 2 tablespoons at a time. Fold in flour combined with baking powder and salt just until mixed. Grease bottom of 10x15-inch baking pan and line with waxed paper. Spread batter in prepared pan. Bake at 400 degrees for 9 minutes or until cake tests done. Invert on towel sprinkled with confectioners' sugar; remove waxed paper. Roll with towel as for jelly roll from narrow end. Cool seam side down on wire rack for 20 minutes. Unroll cake; remove towel. Spread with preserves; reroll. Place on serving plate. Let stand, covered, for 1 hour. Sift confectioners' sugar over top. Slice diagonally and serve with whipped cream. Yield: 12 servings.

Rhonda Davis, Ohio

SWEETHEART
CHOCOLATE TRUFFLES

1½ lb. milk chocolate
⅓ c. heavy cream
⅓ c. half and half
1½ tsp. vanilla extract

Melt milk chocolate in double boiler over hot water; beat until smooth. Bring cream and half and half just to the simmering point in saucepan. Cool to 130 degrees. Add to melted chocolate; beat until smooth. Stir in vanilla. Cool. Beat until light and fluffy. Chill until firm. Shape into small balls. Dip into melted dipping chocolate or roll in cocoa or chocolate dragées. Yield: 2 pounds.

Polly McGee, Arkansas

CHOCOLATE LOVER'S PIE

1 c. chocolate chips
6 oz. cream cheese, softened
⅛ tsp. salt
¾ c. packed brown sugar
2 egg yolks
1 tsp. vanilla extract
2 egg whites
1 c. whipping cream, whipped
1   9-in. graham cracker pie
  shell

Melt chocolate chips in double boiler over hot water. Cool for 10 minutes. Beat cream cheese with salt in bowl until fluffy. Add ½ cup brown sugar. Beat well. Add egg yolks 1 at a time, beating well after each addition. Blend in chocolate and vanilla. Beat egg whites until stiff peaks form. Add remaining ¼ cup brown sugar, beating until very stiff peaks form. Fold chocolate mixture gently into egg whites. Fold in whipped cream gently. Spoon into pie shell. Chill until firm.
Yield: 6 to 8 servings.

Deborah J. Dewart, California

CHERRY TART

1 c. shortening
1 c. sugar
2 eggs
3 c. flour
2 tsp. baking powder
1 tsp. soda
1 tsp. vanilla extract
½ c. milk
1 can cherry pie filling

Beat shortening, sugar and eggs in mixer bowl until smooth. Add dry ingredients, vanilla and milk; mix well. Reserve 1 cup dough. Press remaining dough onto 11x18-inch baking sheet. Turn up edges. Spoon pie filling over dough. Roll reserved dough into rectangle on floured surface. Cut into strips. Place over cherries. Bake at 350 degrees until light brown. Yield: 12 servings.

Jennifer and Lisa Rensel, Pennsylvania

GEORGE WASHINGTON BARS

1¼ c. sifted flour
½ c. butter
3 tbsp. confectioners' sugar
2 eggs, lightly beaten
1 c. sugar
1 tsp. vanilla extract
½ tsp. baking powder
¼ tsp. salt
¾ c. chopped nuts
½ c. coconut
½ c. chopped maraschino
  cherries

Mix 1 cup flour, butter and confectioners' sugar in bowl. Pat into 8x10-inch baking pan. Bake at 350 degrees for 25 minutes. Beat eggs, sugar and vanilla in bowl. Add mixture of remaining flour, baking powder and salt; mix well. Stir in nuts, coconut and cherries. Pour over hot baked layer. Bake for 25 minutes. Cool. Cut into bars.
Yield: 1½ dozen.

Lucinda Hollander, Wisconsin

CHOCOLATE-COVERED CHERRY COOKIES

½ c. butter, softened
1 c. sugar
1 egg
1½ tsp. vanilla extract
1½ c. flour
½ c. baking cocoa
¼ tsp. salt
¼ tsp. soda
¼ tsp. baking powder
36 maraschino cherries, drained
6 oz. semisweet chocolate
  chips, melted
½ c. sweetened condensed milk
2 tsp. maraschino cherry juice

Cream butter, sugar, egg and vanilla in mixer bowl until light. Add mixture of flour, cocoa, salt, soda and baking powder. Shape into 1-inch balls. Place on greased cookie sheet. Press cherry firmly into each ball. Blend melted chocolate, condensed milk and cherry juice in bowl. Top each cookie with ½ teaspoon chocolate mixture. Bake at 350 degrees for 8 minutes or until firm. Cool on wire rack.
Yield: 3 dozen.

Daniel Williams, Texas

EASTER

LACY DESSERT BASKETS

¾ c. quick-cooking oats
⅓ c. flour
¼ tsp. baking powder
2 tbsp. milk
2 tbsp. light corn syrup
1¼ c. sugar
6 tbsp. plus ½ cup butter
2 eggs
1 tsp. vanilla extract
⅓ c. currant jelly
1   12-oz. package frozen
    raspberries, thawed, drained
2½ tbsp. red wine

Mix first 5 ingredients, ½ cup sugar and 6 tablespoons melted butter. Drop 4 well-spaced tablespoonfuls onto 4 well-greased baking sheets. Spread batter into 3-inch circles. Bake at 375 degrees for 6 minutes. Cool for 30 seconds. Shape quickly around inverted 6-ounce custard cups to form baskets. Remove when cool. Cream remaining ½ cup softened butter and ¾ cup sugar in mixer bowl. Add eggs 1 at a time, beating for 5 minutes after each addition. Stir in vanilla. Spoon ⅓ cup into each basket. Melt jelly in saucepan. Stir in raspberries and wine. Chill, covered, in refrigerator. Spoon over filling. May add 1 ounce melted unsweetened chocolate to filling and top with whipped cream and chocolate sprinkles if desired. Yield: 16 servings.

Marilyn K. Price, Maryland

COTTONTAILS

½ can sweetened condensed
    milk
1   14-oz. package caramels
¾ c. margarine
50 lg. marshmallows
Crisp rice cereal

Melt first 3 ingredients in double boiler; mix well. Dip marshmallows in mixture; roll in cereal. Let stand on waxed paper until set. Yield: 50 servings.

Harriett Laws, Iowa

STRAWBERRY CHARLOTTE

3 pts. fresh strawberries
1 tbsp. lemon juice
2 env. unflavored gelatin
½ c. sugar
4 eggs, separated
1¼ c. milk
4 oz. semisweet chocolate,
    melted
12 ladyfingers, split
1 c. sliced almonds, toasted
1 c. whipping cream, whipped

Slice enough strawberries to measure 5 cups; reserve remaining strawberries. Process 3 cups sliced strawberries in blender until smooth. Add lemon juice; set aside. Soften gelatin with ¼ cup sugar, egg yolks and milk in saucepan. Heat until gelatin is dissolved, stirring constantly. Mix with puréed strawberries. Chill until partially set. Spread melted chocolate over rounded sides of ladyfingers. Sprinkle with almonds. Line side of 9-inch springform pan with ladyfingers, turning cut side in. Beat egg whites until soft peaks form. Add ¼ cup sugar, beating until stiff. Fold egg whites, whipped cream and remaining 2 cups sliced strawberries into partially congealed mixture. Spoon into prepared pan. Chill until firm. Place on serving plate. Remove side of pan. Garnish with reserved strawberries and additional whipped cream. Yield: 12 servings.

PASSOVER SPONGE CAKE

8 eggs, separated
1¼ c. sugar
¾ c. matzo cake meal
Juice of ½ orange
Juice and grated rind
    of ½ lemon
¾ c. finely chopped walnuts

Beat egg yolks with half the sugar until thick. Beat egg whites until soft peaks form. Add remaining sugar gradually, beating until stiff. Fold egg yolks gently into egg whites alternately with remaining ingredients. Spoon into tube pan. Bake at 325 degrees for 1 hour or until cake tests done. Cool in inverted pan for 1 hour. Loosen cake from pan. Remove to serving plate.

EASTER EGG CAKE AND EASTER BONNETS

> 1   2-layer pkg. yellow cake mix
> Florida orange juice
> 2 tsp. grated orange rind
> Assorted candies
> 9 strips orange peel
> 9 candied violets

Prepare cake mix according to package directions, substituting orange juice for water and adding orange rind. Pour 2 cups of cake batter into waxed paper-lined 9x9-inch cake pan. Spoon ½ cup batter into each of 9 paper-lined muffin cups. Pour remaining batter into a greased and floured 1-quart muffin mold. Bake at 350 degrees until cakes test done. Cool on wire rack. Frost with 1 cup Orange Buttercream Frosting. Tint ⅓ cup Frosting dark orange with yellow and red food coloring. Spoon Frosting into decorating bag fitted with number 48 serrated ribbon tip. Pipe the lattice-design basket and ribbon around base of cake. Use star tip to pipe the basket handle. Arrange candies and dragées in floral arrangement in the basket. Invert 9x9-inch cake onto tray. Cut out 9 circles with 2½-inch cutter. Remove the paper liners from muffins. Invert muffins onto circles to form hats. Tint remaining ⅔ cup Frosting orange with red and yellow food coloring. Frost Easter Bonnets. Decorate with strip of orange peel for hat band and candied violets. Yield: One 4-serving Easter Egg Cake and 9 Easter Bonnets.

Orange Buttercream Frosting

> ½ c. butter, softened
> 1   16-oz. package
>   confectioners' sugar
> 1 egg
> 1 tsp. grated orange rind
> Pinch of salt
> 3 to 4 tbsp. Florida orange juice

Beat butter and confectioners' sugar in mixer bowl until light and fluffy. Add egg, orange rind and salt; beat until smooth. Add enough orange juice to make of desired consistency.

Photograph for this recipe on Page 1.

EASTER SHORTCAKE

> 1 loaf angel food cake, sliced
> 1 lg. package vanilla instant
>   pudding mix
> ½ c. milk
> 1 pt. vanilla ice cream,
>   softened
> 1 lg. package strawberry gelatin
> 4 c. sliced strawberries

Place cake slices in 9x13-inch dish. Combine pudding mix and milk in large bowl; mix well. Add ice cream. Beat until blended. Pour into prepared dish. Dissolve gelatin in ½ cup boiling water. Stir in strawberries. Chill until partially set. Spoon over pudding mixture. Chill until firm. Yield: 12 servings.

SHAVUOTH NOODLE PUDDING

> 1½ c. medium noodles, cooked
> 2 c. canned apple slices
> 1 c. cottage cheese
> ½ c. sour cream
> 1 egg
> ½ c. sugar
> ¾ c. packed brown sugar
> 1 c. raisins
> ¼ c. dry bread crumbs
> 2 tbsp. butter
> ½ tsp. cinnamon

Combine noodles, apples, cottage cheese, sour cream, egg, sugar, ½ cup brown sugar and raisins in bowl; mix well. Spoon into buttered 2-quart baking dish. Mix remaining ¼ cup brown sugar, bread crumbs, butter and cinnamon in small bowl until crumbly. Sprinkle over pudding. Bake at 350 degrees for 20 minutes or until bubbly. Yield: 10 servings.

Mrs. Chaim Seiger, Tennessee

EASTER BUNNY'S RICE PUDDING

> 2 eggs
> ⅓ c. sugar
> ¼ tsp. salt
> 2 c. milk
> 1 tsp. vanilla extract
> 2 c. cooked rice
> ¾ c. raisins
> Nutmeg to taste

Combine eggs, sugar and salt in bowl; beat lightly to blend. Scald milk in saucepan. Stir a small amount of hot milk into eggs; stir eggs into hot milk. Stir in vanilla, rice and raisins. Pour into greased 1-quart casserole. Sprinkle with nutmeg. Set in pan with 1 inch water. Bake at 350 degrees for 1¼ hours. Spoon into dessert dishes. Serve warm with cream. Yield: 6 servings.

Traci Green, New Mexico

EASTER EGG COOKIES

3½ *c. flour*
¾ *c. sugar*
2 *tsp. grated orange rind*
¼ *tsp. salt*
1¼ *c. butter*
¼ *c. Florida orange juice*

Mix flour, sugar, orange rind and salt in bowl. Cut in butter until crumbly. Add orange juice; mix well. Form into ball. Chill, wrapped, for 30 minutes. Roll ⅛ inch thick on lightly floured board. Cut with egg cookie cutter. Place on ungreased cookie sheet. Bake at 400 degrees for 8 minutes or until light brown. Cool on wire rack. Spread with Chocolate Glaze. Let stand for 1 hour or until set. Decorate as desired with Decorator's Frosting. Yield: 7 dozen.

Chocolate Glaze

2 *oz. semisweet chocolate*
2 *c. confectioners' sugar*
6 *tbsp. Florida orange juice*

Melt chocolate in double boiler over hot water. Add confectioners' sugar and orange juice. Beat until smooth.

Decorator's Frosting

½ *c. butter, softened*
1 *c. confectioners' sugar*

Cream butter in mixer bowl until light. Add confectioners' sugar, beating until fluffy. Divide into 3 portions. Tint 1 portion blue with blue food coloring. Tint 1 portion pink with red food coloring. Place each portion in decorating bag fitted with plain or star tip.

Photograph for this recipe on page 1.

BUTTERCREAM EASTER EGGS

1 *c. plus 1 tbsp. butter,*
  softened
8 *oz. cream cheese, softened*
3 *lb. confectioners' sugar*
8 *oz. semisweet chocolate*
2 *tbsp. melted paraffin*
¼ *tsp. vanilla extract*

Beat 1 cup butter and cream cheese in mixer bowl until light. Add confectioners' sugar gradually, beating until light and fluffy. Shape into eggs. Combine remaining 1 tablespoon butter and remaining ingredients in double boiler. Heat over hot water until melted; blend well. Dip eggs into chocolate mixture to coat; place on waxed paper. Let stand until set. Yield: 8 dozen.

Nancy Sykes, Georgia

ANGEL FOOD CAKE

1¾ *c. egg whites*
1¼ *c. sifted cake flour*
1¾ *c. sugar*
½ *tsp. salt*
1½ *tsp. cream of tartar*
1 *tsp. vanilla extract*
½ *tsp. almond extract*

Place egg whites in large mixer bowl. Let stand for 1 hour. Sift flour and ¾ cup sugar together 4 times. Beat egg whites with salt and cream of tartar at high speed until soft peaks form. Add remaining 1 cup sugar, ¼ cup at a time, beating well after each addition. Beat until stiff peaks form. Fold in vanilla and almond extracts. Sift ¼ cup flour mixture over egg whites, gently folding into egg whites. Fold in remaining flour mixture, ¼ cup at a time, blending well. Push gently with rubber scraper into 10-inch tube pan. Cut through batter twice with knife; spread evenly to edges of pan. Bake at 375 degrees for 35 to 40 minutes. Invert pan over neck of bottle. Cool completely before removing from pan. Yield: 12 to 16 servings.

Lisa Gaither, Alabama

INDEPENDENCE DAY

SUMMERTIME AMBROSIA

1 *c. strawberries*
1 *c. blueberries*
1½ *c. chopped pineapple*
1 *c. applesauce*
2 *c. chopped apples*
⅔ *c. grape halves*
1 *c. shredded coconut*
4 *bananas, chopped*
2 *c. white grape juice*
2 *c. pineapple juice*
1 *c. chopped pecans*

Mix all ingredients in bowl. Chill until serving time. Spoon into dessert dishes. Garnish with additional coconut and fresh cherry.
Yield: 6 servings.

FESTIVE FRUIT CUPS

2 *lg. ripe bananas, sliced*
1 *red Delicious apple, chopped*
1 *pear, peeled, chopped*
Lemon juice
2 *navel oranges, sectioned*
1⅓ *c. flaked coconut*
1 *c. pineapple yogurt*

Dip bananas, apple and pear in lemon juice; drain. Combine with orange sections in glass bowl. Chill for 1 hour. Fold in coconut and yogurt. Spoon into dessert dishes. Yield: 6 to 8 servings.

OLD-FASHIONED CHOCOLATE ICE CREAM

2 *c. sugar*
¼ *c. flour*
¼ *tsp. salt*
4 *c. milk*
4 *oz. baking chocolate, melted*
4 *eggs, beaten*
1 *qt. half and half*
2 *tsp. rum flavoring*

Mix dry ingredients in 3-quart saucepan. Add milk gradually. Cook over medium heat until thickened, stirring constantly. Cook for 2 minutes longer. Remove from heat. Stir in melted chocolate. Blend a small amount of hot mixture into eggs; stir eggs into hot mixture. Cook for 1 minute; do not boil. Remove from heat. Cool. Add cream and rum flavoring. Chill thoroughly. Place in 4-quart freezer container. Freeze according to manufacturer's instructions. Yield: 3 quarts.

Variations:
Chocolate Cookie: Stir in 2 cups coarsely crumbled chocolate cookies.
Rocky Road: Stir in 2 cups miniature marshmallows and 1 cup chopped pecans with half and half.
Marshmallow Swirl: Blend 1 cup marshmallow creme with small amount of water. Arrange alternate layers of just-frozen ice cream and marshmallow creme in plastic freezer container, swirling each layer with spatula for marbled effect. Place mixture in freezer to ripen.

Donna Tignor, Alabama

PICNIC PEACH ICE CREAM

3½ *c. sugar*
5 *eggs*
1 *13-oz. can evaporated milk*
1 *tsp. vanilla extract*
4 *c. sliced peeled peaches*
Milk

Combine sugar, eggs, evaporated milk, vanilla and peaches in blender container. Process until smooth. Pour into 1-gallon ice cream freezer container. Add milk to fill line. Freeze using manufacturer's instructions.
Yield: 12 servings.

Ginger Maxwell, Texas

PLUM FIREWORKS

⅔ *c. sugar*
½ *tsp. ginger*
1½ *lb. plums*
2 *tbsp. vodka*
1 *tsp. vanilla extract*
1 *tsp. almond extract*

Bring sugar, ginger and ⅓ cup water to a boil in saucepan; reduce heat. Simmer for 10 minutes, stirring frequently. Cut plums into halves lengthwise; discard pits. Place in sugar syrup. Cook for 6 to 12 minutes or until tender but still firm. Remove plums to flameproof dish with slotted spoon. Boil syrup until reduced by ⅓. Pour over plums. Cool to room temperature; do not chill. Heat vodka and flavorings almost to the boiling point in small saucepan. Pour over plums. Ignite. Spoon plums into dessert dishes when flames subside. Spoon sauce over plums. Yield: 6 servings.

Harriet Glasscock, Oklahoma

OLD GLORY DESSERT PIZZA

    2 *c. buttermilk baking mix*
    ½ *c. sugar*
    ¼ *c. margarine, softened*
    3 *oz. cream cheese, softened*
    1 *tsp. vanilla extract*
    1 *c. whipping cream*
    2 *c. raspberries*
    14 *apricot halves*
    1 *c. blueberries*
    ½ *c. apple jelly, melted*

Mix baking mix and ¼ cup sugar in bowl. Cut in margarine until crumbly. Press over bottom and side of 12-inch pizza pan. Bake at 350 degrees for 12 minutes or until light brown. Cool. Beat cream cheese, remaining ¼ cup sugar and vanilla in small mixer bowl until light and fluffy. Add whipping cream. Beat at medium speed until soft peaks form. Spread over crust, leaving ¼-inch border. Arrange fruit in circular pattern over top. Brush jelly over fruit. Chill for 2 hours or longer. Cut into wedges. Yield: 8 servings.

Shawn Coffey, Texas

CELEBRATION SHORTCAKE

    1 *2-layer pkg. angel food cake mix*
    1½ *c. orange juice*
    ¾ *c. sugar*
    2 *tbsp. cornstarch*
    ¼ *tsp. salt*
    1 *tsp. grated orange rind*
    1 *tsp. grated lemon rind*
    3 *peaches, peeled, sliced*
    1 *c. blueberries*
    1 *c. pitted cherries*

Prepare cake mix according to package directions. Spread in 10x15-inch baking pan lined with greased waxed paper. Bake at 375 degrees for 20 minutes. Loosen from pan sides; invert onto waxed paper-lined wire rack. Peel off waxed paper. Cool completely. Combine orange juice, sugar, cornstarch, salt and fruit rinds in glass bowl; mix well. Microwave, covered, on High for 6 minutes or until thickened, stirring every 2 minutes. Chill for 1 hour. Invert cake onto serving tray. Brush with half the sauce. Arrange fruit in decorative pattern. Brush with remaining sauce. Yield: 12 to 15 servings.

Adeline Hoffman, New Jersey

BROWNIE SUNDAE
IN STRAWBERRY SAUCE

    1 *10-oz. package frozen strawberries in syrup, thawed*
    4 *2½-inch brownies*
    1 *pt. Häagen-Daz vanilla ice cream*

Place strawberries with syrup in blender container. Process until smooth. Spoon purée into dessert plates. Place brownie in sauce. Top with scoop of ice cream. Garnish with whole strawberries and whipped cream piped into rosettes. Yield: 4 servings.

Photograph for this recipe on Cover.

PATRIOT'S FLAG CAKE

1½ c. butter, softened
2 c. sugar
6 eggs, separated
2½ c. flour
2 tsp. baking powder
¼ tsp. salt
2 tbsp. vanilla extract
2 tbsp. lemon juice
Fresh blueberries
Fresh strawberries

Cream butter and 1 cup sugar in mixer bowl until light and fluffy. Add egg yolks, 2 at a time, beating well after each addition. Blend in dry ingredients. Stir in vanilla and lemon juice. Beat egg whites in bowl until soft peaks form. Add remaining 1 cup sugar gradually, beating until stiff peaks form. Fold gently into batter. Pour into greased, waxed paper-lined 9x13-inch cake pan. Bake at 325 degrees for 1 hour or until cake tests done. Cool in pan on wire rack for 10 minutes. Invert onto rack to cool completely. Place cake on serving tray. Frost top and side of cake with Vanilla Cream Cheese Frosting. Decorate cake with blueberries and strawberry slices to resemble the American flag.
Yield: 16 servings.

Vanilla Cream Cheese Frosting

8 oz. cream cheese, softened
1 tbsp. vanilla extract
1 tbsp. milk
1   16-oz. package
    confectioners' sugar

Beat cream cheese, vanilla and milk in bowl until smooth. Add confectioners' sugar gradually, beating until mixture is creamy.

Francis Summers, South Carolina

RED, WHITE AND BLUEBERRY PIE

2 c. fresh blueberries
1 baked 9-in. pie shell
9 tbsp. sugar
5 tsp. cornstarch
¼ tsp. salt
¼ tsp. cinnamon
¼ c. grenadine syrup
2 tsp. lemon juice
½ c. whipping cream, chilled

Spread 1½ cups blueberries in baked pie shell. Combine ½ cup sugar, cornstarch, salt and cinnamon in saucepan. Blend in ¾ cup water. Bring to a boil, stirring constantly. Boil for 1 minute, stirring constantly. Stir in grenadine and lemon juice. Pour over blueberries. Arrange remaining blueberries around edge of pie. Chill in refrigerator. Beat whipping cream with remaining 1 tablespoon sugar in chilled small mixer bowl until soft peaks form. Serve pie with sweetened whipped cream.
Yield: 8 servings.

Marlene Abney, Georgia

ALL-AMERICAN CHOCOLATE CHIP COOKIES

1 c. shortening
1 c. sugar
½ c. packed brown sugar
2 eggs
2 tsp. vanilla extract
2 c. flour
1 tsp. soda
1½ tsp. salt
12 oz. chocolate chips

Cream shortening and sugars in large bowl. Add eggs and vanilla; mix well. Sift in dry ingredients. Stir in chocolate chips. Drop by teaspoonfuls onto greased cookie sheet. Bake at 350 degrees for 10 to 12 minutes or until lightly browned. Remove to wire rack to cool.
Yield: 6 dozen.

Cheryl Lafferty, Virginia

Always leave 1 to 2 inches between cookies dropped on baking sheet to allow room to spread. Thin dough will spread more than thicker dough. Cool cookies completely in a single layer on a wire rack before storing. Store soft and chewy cookies in an airtight container and crisp cookies in a jar with a loose-fitting lid.

HALLOWEEN

CARAMEL APPLES

1 *can sweetened condensed*
  milk
1 *c. sugar*
½ *c. light corn syrup*
⅛ *tsp. salt*
1 *tsp. vanilla extract*
6 *med. apples*
6 *wooden skewers*

Mix milk, sugar, corn syrup and salt in heavy 2-quart saucepan. Cook over low heat, stirring constantly, until mixture comes to a boil and sugar is dissolved. Continue cooking over low heat, stirring constantly, for about 30 to 40 minutes or to 230 degrees on candy thermometer, spun-thread stage. Remove from heat. Stir in vanilla. Cool for 5 minutes. Insert wooden skewers in apples; dip in caramel until well covered, tilting pan as needed. Cool on lightly greased baking sheet. Yield: 6 servings.

Evelyn Bratton, Missouri

MINIATURE
BLACK BOTTOM CHEESECAKES

1⅓ *c. sugar*
8 *oz. cream cheese, softened*
¼ *tsp. salt*
1 *egg, beaten*
6 *oz. chocolate chips*
⅓ *c. baking cocoa*
1½ *c. flour*
1 *tsp. soda*
⅓ *c. oil*
1 *tbsp. white vinegar*
1 *tsp. vanilla extract*

Cream ⅓ cup sugar, cream cheese and salt in mixer bowl until light and fluffy. Blend in egg. Stir in chocolate chips; set aside. Combine cocoa, remaining 1 cup sugar, flour and soda in mixer bowl. Add oil, vinegar, vanilla and 1 cup water; mix well. Spoon into 48 miniature muffin cups. Place 1 teaspoon chocolate chip mixture in each muffin cup. Bake at 350 degrees for 20 minutes. Cool on wire rack.
Yield: 4 dozen.

Joan Scales, Oklahoma

ICE CREAM MINI CUPS

Häagen-Daz Ice Cream
Miniature chocolate cups

Scoop ice cream with melon baller. Place 2 small scoops ice cream in each chocolate cup. Garnish with chopped nuts, chocolate drizzles or curls, cocoa, whipped cream rosettes or choice of sauces.

Photograph for this recipe on Cover.

MYSTERY CRESCENTS

½ *c. margarine, softened*
3 *oz. cream cheese, softened*
1 *c. sifted flour*
⅛ *tsp. salt*
1 *can apple pie filling*
1 *egg white*
1 *tbsp. cinnamon*
½ *c. sugar*

Beat margarine and cream cheese in bowl. Blend in flour and salt. Chill for 2 hours to overnight. Roll dough on floured surface. Cut with biscuit cutter. Spoon apple pie filling onto each circle. Fold to enclose filling; seal edge with fork. Place on baking sheet. Mix egg white and 1 tablespoon water. Brush over crescents. Sprinkle with mixture of cinnamon and sugar. Bake at 350 degrees for 15 minutes. Yield: 3 dozen.

Annabelle Hall, Texas

SPOOKY PUMPKIN CRUNCH

4 *oz. marshmallows, chopped*
1 *c. pumpkin*
¼ *tsp. cinnamon*
⅛ *tsp. ginger*
1 *pt. vanilla ice cream, softened*
1 *c. ginger cookie crumbs*

Combine marshmallows, pumpkin and spices in double boiler. Cook over hot water until marshmallows are melted, stirring occasionally. Cool slightly. Stir in ice cream. Sprinkle ¾ of the crumbs in 9x9-inch pan. Spoon pumpkin mixture into prepared pan. Sprinkle with remaining cookie crumbs. Freeze. Let stand at room temperature for 10 minutes before serving. Cut into squares. Yield: 9 servings.

JACK-O'-LANTERN CAKE

3¼ c. sifted flour
2½ c. sugar
2 tsp. soda
1½ tsp. salt
¼ tsp. baking powder
1 tsp. cinnamon
½ tsp. cloves
¾ tsp. nutmeg
¾ c. shortening
6 tbsp. orange juice
1   15-oz. can applesauce
3 eggs
1½ c. raisins
1 c. chopped nuts
Green and orange food coloring
½ unpeeled banana

Sift flour, sugar and next 6 ingredients into large mixer bowl. Add shortening, orange juice, 6 tablespoons water and applesauce. Beat at medium speed for 2 minutes. Add eggs. Beat for 2 minutes longer. Stir in raisins and nuts. Pour into greased and floured 10-inch tube pan. Bake at 350 degrees for 1¼ hours or until cake tests done. Cool in pan for 15 to 20 minutes. Invert onto cake plate to cool completely. Tint ½ cup Orange Seven-Minute Frosting with green food coloring. Tint remaining frosting orange. Trim cake to resemble pumpkin. Place on serving plate. Stand banana in center for stem. Frost cake with orange frosting and banana stem with green frosting. Yield: 16 servings.

Orange Seven-Minute Frosting

2 egg whites
1½ c. sugar
½ tsp. cream of tartar
½ c. orange juice
1 tsp. vanilla extract

Combine egg whites, sugar, cream of tartar, orange juice and vanilla in double boiler over boiling water. Beat with electric mixer at high speed for 5 to 7 minutes or until stiff peaks form.

Mavis Michaels, Colorado

Every time the oven door is opened during baking, the temperature drops from 25 to 30 degrees.

PUMPKIN CAKE ROLL

3 eggs
1 c. sugar
⅔ c. pumpkin
1 tsp. lemon juice
¾ c. flour
1 tsp. baking powder
2 tsp. cinnamon
1 tsp. ginger
½ tsp. nutmeg
½ tsp. salt
1 c. finely chopped walnuts
Confectioners' sugar
6 oz. cream cheese, softened
¼ c. margarine, softened
½ tsp. vanilla extract

Beat eggs and sugar in mixer bowl for 5 minutes. Stir in pumpkin and lemon juice. Sift flour, baking powder, spices and salt together. Fold into batter. Spread in greased and floured 10x15-inch pan. Top with walnuts. Bake at 375 degrees for 15 minutes. Invert onto towel sprinkled with confectioners' sugar. Roll cake in towel. Cool on wire rack. Combine 1 cup confectioners' sugar, cream cheese, margarine and vanilla in bowl; beat until smooth. Unroll cake; spread with filling. Reroll cake as for jelly roll. Store in refrigerator. Yield: 12 to 16 servings.

Beverley Clear Goodman, Virginia

CUPCAKE CONES

1   2-layer pkg. chocolate cake mix
24   2 to 3-in. high flat-bottom ice cream cones
2   16½-oz. cans prepared chocolate frosting
M and M's chocolate candies, sprinkles, gumdrops, toasted coconut, chopped nuts

Prepare cake mix batter according to package directions. Spoon 3 tablespoons into each cone. Place 3 inches apart on ungreased baking sheet. Bake at 350 degrees for 30 to 35 minutes or until toothpick inserted in center comes out clean. Cool on wire rack. Frost and decorate with candies, coconut or nuts. Yield: 2 dozen.

GOBBLIN' CUPCAKES

1 2-layer pkg. orange cake mix
1 c. whipping cream
1 tsp. grated orange rind
1 tsp. grated lemon rind
6 tbsp. honey

Prepare cake mix according to package directions. Fill greased and floured miniature muffin cups half full. Bake at 375 degrees for 15 minutes. Cool in pans. Cover cupcakes with towel to keep moist. Whip cream in bowl until soft peaks form. Stir in rinds and honey. Cut out centers of each cupcake. Fill with honey-cream, mounding slightly. Replace tops. Garnish as desired.
Yield: 4 dozen.

DEVIL'S FOOD PIE

¾ c. sugar
½ c. flour
2 eggs, beaten
½ c. melted margarine
⅓ c. light corn syrup
½ c. chopped pecans
6 oz. chocolate chips
½ tsp. vanilla extract
1 unbaked 9-in. pie shell

Mix sugar and flour in bowl. Add eggs, margarine, corn syrup, pecans, chocolate chips and vanilla; mix well. Pour into pie shell. Bake at 325 degrees for 1 hour. Serve warm.
Yield: 8 servings.

Pat Koeppen, Indiana

CHESS TARTS

1 c. butter
2½ c. sugar
3 eggs, beaten
1 tbsp. cider vinegar
1 tbsp. vanilla extract
¼ tsp. salt
8 unbaked tart shells
Raisins

Combine butter and sugar in saucepan. Cook over medium heat until very smooth, stirring constantly. Remove from heat. Add eggs; mix well. Stir in vinegar, vanilla and salt. Pour into tart shells. Bake at 300 degrees for 30 minutes or until set. Decorate with raisins to resemble Jack-O'-Lanterns.
Yield: 6 servings.

Opal Wingate, North Carolina

CRUNCHY CRITTERS

6 oz. semisweet chocolate chips
⅔ c. sweetened condensed milk
1 tsp. vanilla extract
1½ c. salted Spanish peanuts

Melt chocolate chips in top of double boiler over hot water; remove from heat. Add condensed milk, vanilla and peanuts; mix well. Drop by teaspoonfuls onto waxed paper. Cool.
Yield: 1½ dozen.

Megan Martin, Illinois

TRICKIN' TREATS

1 c. packed brown sugar
1 c. light corn syrup
2 c. peanut butter
Oats
Soy nuts
Peanuts
Raisins
Granola
Sesame seed
Sunflower seed

Mix brown sugar and corn syrup in large saucepan. Boil for several minutes. Blend in peanut butter. Combine enough of the remaining ingredients to measure 6 cups in bowl; mix well. Mix into peanut butter mixture. Shape into small balls. Store in plastic bags. May use half cup honey for sugar and half the corn syrup.

Jeanette Laxton, Washington

COOKIE OWLS

⅔ c. shortening, softened
1 c. packed brown sugar
1 egg
1 tsp. vanilla extract
1 c. crunchy peanut butter
1⅓ c. sifted flour
1 tsp. baking powder
½ tsp. salt
1 c. oats
1   1-oz. package pre-melted
   chocolate
Semisweet chocolate chips
Whole cashews

Beat shortening and sugar in bowl until fluffy. Add egg, vanilla and peanut butter; blend well. Add sifted flour, baking powder and salt; mix well. Stir in oats. Divide dough into 2 portions. Shape 1 portion into 8-inch roll. Add chocolate to remaining dough. Roll chocolate dough to 8-inch square on waxed paper. Place plain roll on chocolate dough. Wrap the chocolate dough around roll; seal edge. Chill, wrapped in waxed paper for 1 hour or longer. Let stand at room temperature for 10 minutes. Cut into ¼-inch slices. Pinch chocolate dough to form 2 ears for each owl face. Use 2 chocolate chips for eyes and 1 cashew for beak. Place on ungreased cookie sheet. Bake at 350 degrees for 12 to 15 minutes. Cool on wire rack. Yield: 2½ dozen.

FROSTED PUMPKIN COOKIES

¾ c. shortening
1 c. sugar
1 c. plus 6 tbsp. packed brown
   sugar
½ tsp. salt
3 c. flour
2 tsp. soda
½ tsp. nutmeg
1 tsp. cinnamon
¼ tsp. ginger
1 tsp. baking powder
2 c. pumpkin
¼ c. butter
¼ c. milk
1 tsp. vanilla extract
Confectioners' sugar

Cream shortening, sugar and 1 cup packed brown sugar in large bowl. Sift next 7 ingredients together. Add to creamed mixture alternately with pumpkin, beating well after each addition. Drop by spoonfuls onto cookie sheet. Bake at 350 degrees for 12 minutes. Cool on wire rack. Mix butter, milk and 6 tablespoons brown sugar in saucepan. Bring to a boil; remove from heat. Stir in vanilla. Cool. Add enough confectioners' sugar to make of desired consistency; mix well. Frost cooled cookies. Decorate as desired. Yield: 5 dozen.

Zelda Sikes, Indiana

MERRY JACK-O'-LANTERNS

6 c. puffed rice cereal
¼ c. butter
4 c. miniature marshmallows
1 tsp. orange extract
¼ tsp. red food coloring
¼ tsp. yellow food coloring
8 green gumdrops
Confectioners' sugar frosting
8 black gumdrops
8   2-in. pieces black string
   licorice

Place puffed rice in shallow baking pan. Bake at 350 degrees for 10 minutes. Pour into large greased bowl. Melt butter and marshmallows in double boiler over boiling water, stirring until smooth. Stir in orange extract and food colorings. Stir mixture into puffed rice until evenly coated. Shape into 8 balls with greased hands. Let stand for several hours or until firm. Fasten green gumdrops on top of each ball with frosting for stem. Cut each black gumdrop into 3 triangles; arrange triangles on each ball for nose and eyes. Add black string licorice for mouth. Let stand until frosting is set. Yield: 8 servings.

Be careful not to use too much flour when rolling cookies; excessive flour will make cookies dry and tough. Make cookies a uniform size to assure even baking.

HOT CHOCOLATE WITH CAPPUCCINO

4 c. hot chocolate
1 pt. Häagen-Daz cappucchino
   ice cream
½ tsp. cinnamon
4 cinnamon sticks

Pour hot chocolate into serving mugs. Place scoop of ice cream in each mug. Sprinkle with cinnamon. Place cinnamon stick in each mug. Serve immediately. Yield: 4 servings.

Photograph for this recipe on Cover.

THANKSGIVING

THANKSGIVING AMBROSIA

2 grapefruit, sectioned
3 oranges, sectioned
2 tangerines, sectioned
⅓ to ½ c. sugar
½ c. shredded coconut

Place half the fruits in serving dish; sprinkle with half the sugar and coconut. Add remaining fruits, sugar and coconut. Chill for 1 hour or longer. Yield: 8 servings.

GRANNY SMITH CHEESECAKE

1¼ c. graham cracker crumbs
¼ c. melted butter
2 tbsp. plus ¾ c. sugar
¼ tsp. cinnamon
2 env. unflavored gelatin
1 c. milk
2 eggs, separated
1 tbsp. lemon juice
½ tsp. grated lemon rind
¼ tsp. salt
2 c. cottage cheese
2 c. shredded Granny Smith
   apples

Combine cracker crumbs, butter, 2 tablespoons sugar and cinnamon in bowl; mix well. Press over bottom and 1¼ inches up side of 9-inch springform pan. Chill for 1 hour. Soften gelatin in milk in saucepan. Add ½ cup sugar, egg yolks, lemon juice, lemon rind and salt; mix well. Cook over low heat until gelatin is dissolved, stirring constantly; remove from heat. Process cottage cheese in blender container until smooth. Add cottage cheese and apples to gelatin mixture. Chill until partially set. Beat egg whites until soft peaks form. Add remaining ¼ cup sugar gradually, beating until stiff peaks form. Fold gently into apple mixture. Spoon into prepared pan. Chill overnight. Place on serving plate; remove side of pan. Yield: 12 servings.

CRANBERRY CRUNCH

3 c. chopped unpeeled apples
1 can whole cranberry sauce
1½ c. quick-cooking oats
½ c. packed brown sugar
⅓ c. flour
⅓ c. chopped pecans
½ c. melted margarine

Combine apples and cranberry sauce in 2-quart casserole. Combine remaining ingredients in bowl; mix well. Spread over fruit. Bake at 350 degrees for 1 hour. Yield: 8 servings.

Frances H. Campbell, North Carolina

FROZEN FRUIT CUPS

1 17-oz. can apricots
1 17-oz. can crushed
   pineapple
½ c. sugar
1 6-oz. can frozen orange
   juice concentrate
2 tbsp. lemon juice
3 10-oz. packages frozen
   strawberries, thawed
3 bananas, chopped

Drain apricots and crushed pineapple, reserving liquid; chop apricots. Add enough water to reserved liquid to measure 1 cup. Heat liquid and sugar in saucepan, stirring to dissolve sugar. Stir in orange juice concentrate, lemon juice and fruit, mixing well. Spoon into paper-lined muffin cups. Freeze until firm. Remove from freezer 10 to 20 minutes before serving. Yield: 30 servings.

Dorothy Eckert, Ohio

SPICED FRUIT COMPOTE

1 *16-oz. can sliced peaches*
1 *16-oz. can sliced pears*
1 *16-oz. can apricot halves*
½ *c. whole cranberry sauce*
2 *tbsp. sugar*
¼ *tsp. cinnamon*
⅛ *tsp. cloves*
⅛ *tsp. nutmeg*

Drain fruits. Place cranberry sauce in 1½-quart glass casserole. Microwave on High for 1½ minutes. Add fruits. Sprinkle with sugar and spices. Microwave for 2 minutes; mix gently. Microwave, covered, for 1 minute. Spoon into dessert dishes. Garnish with nuts and whipped cream.
Yield: 8 servings.

FILLED WALNUT MERINGUE

3 *egg whites*
¼ *tsp. cream of tartar*
⅛ *tsp. salt*
1 *c. sugar*
½ *tsp. cinnamon*
½ *c. finely chopped walnuts*

Beat egg whites with cream of tartar and salt in deep bowl until soft peaks form. Beat in sugar gradually until stiff peaks form. Fold in cinnamon and walnuts. Spoon into greased 10-inch pie plate. Spread over bottom and up side to form crust. Bottom of shell should be ¼ inch thick, side about 1 inch. Bake at 275 degrees for 50 minutes or until very light brown. Turn off oven. Let cool in closed oven. Meringue will crack and fall in center; press center lightly to level. Fill with Chiffon Cranberry Filling or Chiffon Pumpkin Filling. Chill until serving time. Garnish with additional walnuts. Yield: 8 servings.

Chiffon Cranberry Filling

1 *c. whole cranberry sauce*
1½ *env. unflavored gelatin*
1 *c. sugar*
2 *egg whites*
¼ *tsp. cream of tartar*
1 *c. whipping cream, whipped*

Press cranberry sauce through sieve. Soften gelatin in 2 tablespoons water in saucepan. Add ⅔ cup sugar and cranberry sauce. Bring to a boil, stirring constantly. Remove from heat; cool. Chill until mixture begins to thicken. Beat egg whites and cream of tartar until soft peaks form. Beat in remaining ⅓ cup sugar until stiff. Fold in egg whites and whipped cream.

Chiffon Pumpkin Filling

1 *env. unflavored gelatin*
¼ *c. orange juice*
⅔ *c. packed brown sugar*
½ *tsp. salt*
1 *tsp. cinnamon*
½ *tsp. nutmeg*
½ *tsp. ginger*
3 *eggs, separated*
¾ *c. milk*
1 *c. canned pumpkin*
⅓ *c. sugar*
1 *c. finely chopped walnuts*

Soften gelatin in orange juice. Combine with brown sugar, salt, spices, beaten egg yolks and milk in saucepan. Cook until mixture thickens, stirring constantly. Remove from heat. Add pumpkin. Chill until thickened. Beat egg whites until soft peaks form. Add sugar, beating until stiff. Fold egg whites and walnuts into pumpkin mixture.

AUTUMN SHORTCAKE

2 *c. chopped cranberries*
2 *c. chopped tart apples*
1 *c. pineapple tidbits*
2 *c. sugar*
¼ *tsp. salt*
3 *c. buttermilk baking mix*
1 *egg yolk, slightly beaten*
2 *tbsp. butter, softened*
1 *c. whipping cream, whipped*

Mix cranberries, apples, pineapple, sugar and salt in bowl. Chill for 2 hours. Prepare baking mix shortcake using package directions. Spread in greased 8-inch cake pan. Brush with egg yolk; sprinkle with additional sugar. Bake at 450 degrees for 18 to 20 minutes; remove from pan. Slice in half horizontally. Spread butter on cut surfaces. Spread cranberry mixture between layers and over top of shortcake. Serve with whipped cream. Yield: 8 servings.

Kathy Woodard, Kansas

BREAD PUDDING
WITH BUTTERSCOTCH SAUCE

3 c. bread crumbs
1 c. sugar
2 eggs
1 tsp. vanilla extract
½ tsp. cinnamon
½ tsp. nutmeg
1 c. cream
½ c. raisins

Mix all ingredients in bowl. Place in buttered baking dish. Bake at 350 degrees for 40 minutes. Spoon into dessert dishes. Spoon Butterscotch Sauce over top. Yield: 6 servings.

Butterscotch Sauce

¾ c. sugar
½ c. light corn syrup
¼ tsp. salt
¼ c. butter
1 c. cream
½ tsp. vanilla extract

Combine sugar, syrup, salt, butter and ½ cup cream in saucepan. Mix well. Cook over low heat to 234 to 240 degrees on candy thermometer, soft-ball stage. Stir in remaining ½ cup cream. Cook until of desired consistency. Remove from heat. Add vanilla extract. Cool.

Alice Bell, Texas

BUTTERNUT
SQUASH-ALMOND TORTE

1   1¼-lb. butternut squash
4 eggs, separated
⅓ c. oil
¼ tsp. cream of tartar
¾ c. sugar
1½ c. flour
2 tsp. baking powder
½ tsp. salt
½ tsp. almond extract
½ c. sliced almonds
1   12-oz. jar apricot preserves
1 c. whipping cream
½ tsp. vanilla extract

Cut squash in half lengthwise; remove seed. Steam in saucepan until tender; drain and cool. Scoop out pulp and mash. Mix with egg yolks, oil and ⅓ cup water in bowl. Beat egg whites with cream of tartar in mixer bowl until soft peaks form. Beat in sugar, 2 tablespoons at a time, until stiff peaks form. Combine flour, baking powder, salt, 1 cup beaten egg whites and almond extract with squash mixture in mixer bowl. Beat at low speed until blended. Fold in remaining egg whites. Spoon into 9-inch springform pan. Bake at 325 degrees for 1 hour and 10 minutes. Invert on wire rack to cool. Place almonds on foil-lined baking sheet. Bake at 350 degrees for 10 minutes. Cool. Slice cake horizontally into 4 layers. Spread apricot preserves between layers, beginning with cake layer cut side up and ending with cake layer cut side down. Beat whipping cream with vanilla in bowl until soft peaks form. Spread over top and side of torte. Decorate top with half the almond slices. Mince remaining almonds; press into side. Chill until serving time. Yield: 12 servings.

Therese Caron, New Hampshire

CRANBERRY CAKE

2½ c. flour
1 tsp. salt
1 tsp. baking powder
1 tsp. soda
1½ c. sugar
1 c. chopped dates
1 c. whole cranberries
1 c. chopped pecans
2 eggs
1 c. buttermilk
¾ c. oil
½ c. orange juice

Sift first 4 ingredients and 1 cup sugar into bowl. Stir in dates, cranberries and pecans; make well in mixture. Place eggs, buttermilk and oil in well; mix well. Pour into ungreased tube pan. Bake at 325 degrees for 1 hour. Mix remaining ½ cup sugar with orange juice. Pour over hot cake in pan. Cool completely. Remove to serving plate. Yield: 16 servings.

Gay Trabher, Pennsylvania

141

PINEAPPLE-CARROT CAKE

1   20-oz. can crushed
    pineapple
3 eggs
1½ c. oil
2 tsp. vanilla extract
2 c. sugar
2 c. flour
2 tsp. cinnamon
1 tsp. baking powder
1½ tsp. soda
1½ tsp. salt
2 c. grated carrots
1½ c. pecans

Drain pineapple; reserve half the pineapple and all the juice. Use remaining pineapple for another purpose. Mix eggs, oil, vanilla and reserved juice in bowl. Beat in sugar until creamy. Sift in flour, cinnamon, baking powder, soda and salt. Beat for 3 minutes. Stir in pineapple, carrots and pecans. Pour into greased and floured bundt pan. Bake at 350 degrees for 1½ hours or until cake tests done. Remove to wire rack to cool. Frost with Raisin-Nut Cream Cheese Frosting. Yield: 15 servings.

Raisin-Nut Cream Cheese Frosting

½ c. raisins
½ c. butter, softened
8 oz. cream cheese, softened
2 tbsp. milk
2 tbsp. vanilla extract
1   16-oz. package
    confectioners' sugar
¼ c. pecans

Soak raisins in water to cover in bowl until plump; drain. Cream butter and cream cheese in bowl. Beat in milk and vanilla. Add confectioners' sugar; mix well. Stir in raisins and nuts.

James Eckard, Indiana

PUMPKIN PIE CAKE

1   2-layer pkg. yellow cake mix
4 eggs
¾ c. butter, softened
1 can pumpkin
½ c. packed brown sugar
½ c. sugar
⅔ c. milk
1 tsp. cinnamon
½ c. chopped pecans

Reserve 1 cup cake mix. Mix remaining cake mix with 1 beaten egg and ½ cup butter. Press into 9x13-inch baking pan. Mix pumpkin, brown sugar, ¼ cup sugar, milk, cinnamon and remaining 3 eggs in bowl. Pour over cake mixture. Combine reserved cake mix, pecans, remaining ¼ cup butter and remaining ¼ cup sugar in bowl, mixing until crumbly. Sprinkle over pumpkin mixture. Bake at 350 degrees for 55 to 60 minutes or until filling is set.
Yield: 16 servings.

Lola D. Ammons, Tennessee

CRANBERRY-APPLE PIE

½ c. shortening
1½ c. flour
Pinch of salt
1½ c. shredded Cheddar cheese
1½ c. sugar
3 tbsp. quick-cooking tapioca
½ tsp. cinnamon
2 c. cranberries
6 c. sliced peeled apples
1 tbsp. margarine

Cut shortening into flour and salt in bowl until crumbly. Mix in cheese. Add 4 to 6 tablespoons cold water, mixing lightly with fork to form dough. Divide into 2 portions. Roll 1 portion into 11-inch circle on floured surface. Fit into 9-inch pie plate. Mix sugar, tapioca and cinnamon in saucepan. Stir in cranberries and ⅓ cup water. Bring to a boil, stirring constantly; remove from heat. Add apples. Cool slightly. Spoon into pastry-lined pie plate. Dot with margarine. Top with remaining pastry. Trim and seal edges; cut vents. Bake at 400 degrees for 45 to 50 minutes or until apples are tender and crust is golden.
Yield: 6 servings.

MINCEMEAT CRUNCH PIE

1   28-oz. jar mincemeat
3 apples, peeled, chopped
1 unbaked 9-in. pie shell
1 tbsp. grated orange rind
¼ c. margarine
½ c. flour
½ c. packed brown sugar
½ c. chopped nuts

Mix mincemeat and apples in bowl. Spoon into pie shell. Sprinkle with orange rind. Cut margarine into flour and sugar in bowl until crumbly. Mix in nuts. Sprinkle over pie. Bake at 350 degrees for 30 minutes. Yield: 6 servings.

PUMPKIN ICE CREAM PIES

2 pt. vanilla ice cream, softened
2 9-in. graham cracker pie
    shells
1 16-oz. can pumpkin
1½ c. sugar
1 tsp. cinnamon
½ tsp. ginger
¼ tsp. cloves
½ tsp. salt
1 tsp. vanilla extract
1 c. whipping cream, whipped

Spread ice cream in pie shells. Freeze until firm. Combine pumpkin, sugar, spices, salt and vanilla in bowl; mix well. Fold in whipped cream gently. Spoon over ice cream layers. Freeze for 4 hours or longer. Let stand at room temperature for 15 minutes before serving. Garnish with additional whipped cream and slivered almonds. Yield: 2 pies.

SWEET POTATO PIE

2 eggs, beaten
2 tsp. allspice
¾ c. melted butter
6 oz. cream cheese, softened
2 c. sugar
1 tsp. vanilla extract
1 tbsp. cornstarch
1½ c. mashed cooked sweet
    potato
1 c. chopped nuts
1 unbaked 9-in. pie shell

Combine eggs, allspice, butter, cream cheese, sugar and vanilla in bowl; mix well. Mix cornstarch with ¼ cup cold water. Stir cornstarch mixture into egg mixture. Add sweet potato and nuts; mix well. Pour into pie shell. Bake at 425 degrees for 10 minutes. Reduce temperature to 325 degrees. Bake for 35 to 45 minutes longer. Yield: 6 servings.

HARVEST BARS

¼ c. melted shortening
1 c. packed brown sugar
2 eggs
⅔ c. pumpkin
¾ c. self-rising flour
½ tsp. cinnamon
½ tsp. nutmeg
½ tsp. ginger
½ tsp. vanilla extract
1 c. chopped dates
½ c. chopped nuts
Confectioners' sugar

Combine melted shortening, brown sugar, eggs and pumpkin in mixer bowl. Add flour, spices and vanilla; mix well. Stir in dates and nuts. Spoon into greased 9x13-inch baking pan. Bake at 350 degrees for 25 to 30 minutes or until brown. Sprinkle confectioners' sugar over top. Cool. Cut into bars.
Yield: 2 dozen.

Gayle Manson, Kansas

ROCKY ROAD BARS

½ c. flour
½ tsp. baking powder
¼ tsp. salt
⅔ c. packed brown sugar
2 eggs
2 tbsp. butter, softened
1 tsp. vanilla extract
1 c. chopped walnuts
1 c. miniature marshmallows
1 c. semisweet chocolate chips

Sift flour, baking powder and salt into mixer bowl. Add brown sugar, eggs, butter and vanilla; beat until smooth. Stir in ½ cup walnuts. Pour into greased 9-inch square pan. Bake at 350 degrees for 15 minutes or until top is lightly browned and cake tests done. Sprinkle marshmallows, remaining ½ cup walnuts and chocolate chips over top of hot cake. Bake for 2 minutes or until chocolate has softened. Swirl chocolate over marshmallows and walnuts. Cool until chocolate is set. Cut into bars.
Yield: 15 servings.

Laura Murphy, Maryland

SOUR CREAM SUGAR COOKIES

2 *c. sugar*
1 *c. shortening*
1 *tsp. salt*
1 *tsp. vanilla extract*
1 *c. sour cream*
¼ *c. buttermilk*
3 *eggs*
1 *tsp. grated orange rind*
3 *c. (about) flour*
2 *tsp. baking powder*
1 *tsp. soda*
Juice of 1 orange

Cream sugar, shortening, salt and vanilla in bowl until fluffy. Combine sour cream, buttermilk, eggs and orange rind in mixer bowl; mix well. Add to sugar mixture; mix well. Sift flour, baking powder and soda together. Add to sugar mixture alternately with orange juice, mixing well after each addition. Add additional flour if necessary to make a stiff batter. Drop by teaspoonfuls onto greased cookie sheet. Flatten with bottom of glass dipped in additional flour. Sprinkle with additional sugar. Bake at 375 degrees for 7 to 8 minutes or just until cookies begin to brown. Yield: 4 dozen.

Paula J. Thomas, Washington

CHRISTMAS

CHRISTMAS BOMBE

1½ *qt. French vanilla ice cream*
1 *tsp. rum flavoring*
6 *maraschino cherries*
1½ *c. pistachio ice cream*
1¼ *c. whipping cream*
⅓ *c. semisweet chocolate chips,*
  melted
10 *oz. frozen red raspberries,*
  thawed, drained
¼ *c. confectioners' sugar*

Mix vanilla ice cream and rum flavoring in chilled 2-quart metal bowl. Spread over bottom and side of bowl. Arrange cherries in circle on bottom; press into ice cream. Freeze until firm. Spread layer of pistachio ice cream over vanilla. Freeze until firm. Whip ¾ cup whipping cream in bowl. Fold in melted chocolate gently. Spread over pistachio layer. Freeze until firm. Press raspberries through sieve. Whip ½ cup whipping cream with confectioners' sugar until stiff peaks form. Fold in raspberries. Spoon into center of bowl. Freeze, covered with foil, for 24 hours. Unmold onto serving plate. Yield: 12 servings.

Iris Hart, Minnesota

ROCKY ROAD CHEESECAKE

2 *c. chocolate wafer crumbs*
½ *c. confectioners' sugar*
½ *c. melted butter*
2 *env. unflavored gelatin*
⅓ *c. flour*
¾ *c. sugar*
1½ *c. milk*
4 *eggs, separated*
6 *oz. semisweet chocolate chips*
1 *c. whipping cream*
2 *c. cottage cheese*
1 *tsp. vanilla extract*
½ *tsp. almond extract*

Combine first 3 ingredients in bowl; mix well. Press over bottom and halfway up side of 9-inch springform pan. Chill until firm. Soften gelatin in ½ cup cold water. Combine flour and ¼ cup sugar in saucepan. Stir in milk. Cook over medium heat until thickened, stirring constantly. Stir a small amount of hot mixture into beaten egg yolks; stir egg yolks into hot mixture. Cook for 1 minute. Add gelatin. Stir until gelatin dissolves. Cool to lukewarm. Melt chocolate chips in ⅓ cup cream in saucepan over low heat, stirring constantly. Cool. Beat cottage cheese in mixer bowl for 5 minutes. Add flavorings and gelatin mixture. Beat egg whites until foamy. Add remaining ½ cup sugar gradually, beating until stiff. Fold gently into cottage cheese mixture. Whip remaining ⅔ cup whipping cream in chilled bowl. Fold into cottage cheese mixture. Layer cottage cheese mixture and chocolate ⅓ at a time in prepared pan, cutting through each layer gently to marbleize. Chill for 6 hours or longer. Place on serving plate; remove side of pan. Yield: 10 servings.

Photograph for this recipe on page 9.

FROZEN TUTTI-FRUTTI DELIGHT

20 *ladyfingers, split*
2 *qt. vanilla ice cream*
1 *6-oz. can frozen orange
    juice concentrate, thawed*
2 *10-oz. packages frozen
    raspberries, thawed*
2 *c. drained crushed pineapple*
1 *tbsp. frozen lemonade
    concentrate*
1 *tsp. rum extract*
1 *tsp. almond extract*
⅓ *c. chopped maraschino
    cherries*
¼ *c. chopped pistachio nuts*
½ *c. whipped cream*
8 *whole maraschino cherries*

Cover bottom of 9-inch springform pan with ladyfingers. Arrange ladyfingers vertically around side of pan. Cut any remaining ladyfingers to fill in spaces on bottom. Soften 1 quart ice cream in mixer bowl for several minutes. Add orange juice concentrate; mix well. Spoon into prepared springform pan. Freeze for several hours or until firm. Combine raspberries, pineapple and lemonade concentrate in blender container. Purée until smooth; strain. Pour into shallow pan. Freeze for 1 hour or until partially frozen. Beat slightly. Pour over ice cream layer. Freeze for several hours or until firm. Soften remaining 1 quart ice cream in mixer bowl for several minutes. Add flavorings, chopped cherries and pistachio nuts; mix well. Spoon over raspberry layer. Freeze, covered, for 8 hours or longer. Place on serving plate; remove side of pan. Thaw in refrigerator for several minutes. Garnish with whipped cream and whole cherries. Yield: 16 servings.

SNOW ICE CREAM

½ *c. cream*
1 *bowl clean fresh snow*
½ *c. sugar*
1 *tsp. vanilla extract*
Pinch of salt

Combine cream and snow in bowl; mix well. Add remaining ingredients; mix well. Serve immediately. Yield: 4 servings.

Missy Prater, Virginia

HOLIDAY FRUIT FREEZE

1 *20-oz. can pineapple tidbits*
1 *c. chopped green and red
    maraschino cherries*
1 *16-oz. can white cherries*
1 *c. chopped almonds*
1 *lg. package miniature
    marshmallows*
¼ *c. sugar*
4 *eggs, separated*
2 *c. whipping cream, whipped*

Drain pineapple, reserving ¼ cup juice. Drain and chop maraschino cherries and white cherries. Mix with almonds, pineapple and marshmallows in bowl. Blend reserved juice, sugar and egg yolks in saucepan. Cook over medium heat until thickened, stirring constantly. Stir into fruit mixture. Fold in stiffly beaten egg whites and whipped cream gently. Spoon into mold. Freeze until firm. Unmold on serving plate. Garnish with additional cherries. Yield: 24 servings.

Mary Jane Smith, Indiana

LEMON CURD

Juice of 3 lemons
5 *eggs*
1 *c. sugar*
½ *c. unsalted butter*
Grated rind of 3 lemons

Combine lemon juice, eggs, sugar and butter in blender container. Process until smooth. Combine with lemon rind in double boiler. Cook over hot water until thickened, stirring frequently. Chill in refrigerator. Serve with muffins, crumpets or pound cake. Yield: 1⅓ cups.

Dovie Simpkins, Florida

Read recipes all the way through before you start to be sure you have all the required ingredients and plenty of time to complete it.

CHRISTMAS MOUSSE

1   6-oz. package fresh
      cranberries
1 orange, unpeeled, sliced,
      seeded
1½ c. sugar
2 sm. packages raspberry
      gelatin
2 lg. bananas, chopped
2 tbsp. lemon juice
1 pt. sour cream

Combine cranberries, orange and sugar in food processor container. Process until finely chopped. Dissolve gelatin in 1 cup boiling water in bowl. Add chopped mixture. Chill until mixture begins to thicken. Toss bananas with lemon juice. Fold bananas and sour cream into partially congealed mixture. Spoon into 2-quart ring mold. Chill until firm. Unmold onto serving plate. Garnish with fresh fruit.
Yield: 10 servings.

Helen Malone, Idaho

CHOCOLATE RUM MOUSSE

1 oz. baking chocolate
¾ c. dark rum
6 egg yolks
1 c. (scant) sugar
1 tbsp. unflavored gelatin
1 pt. whipping cream, whipped

Melt chocolate with rum in double boiler over hot water; mix well. Beat egg yolks and sugar in bowl until thick and lemon-colored. Soften gelatin in ½ cup water in saucepan. Bring to a simmer, stirring to dissolve gelatin. Stir a small amount of hot mixture into egg yolks; stir egg yolks into hot mixture. Cook until thickened, stirring constantly. Cool slightly. Blend in chocolate mixture. Fold in whipped cream gently. Spoon into dessert dishes. Chill until set. Garnish with grated chocolate.
Yield: 12 servings.

Inez Johnson, Texas

To chop sticky foods such as figs, dates or candied fruit, cut them with kitchen shears dipped in cold water.

CHRISTMAS PUDDING

2¾ c. day-old bread crumbs
1 c. chopped figs
1½ c. seedless raisins
¾ c. mixed candied fruit
½ c. dried currants
½ c. toasted filberts, chopped
2 c. ground suet
1½ tsp. salt
¾ tsp. cinnamon
½ tsp. mace
¼ tsp. cloves
1 c. scalded milk
½ c. packed dark brown sugar
4 eggs
2 tsp. brandy flavoring
2 tbsp. orange juice

Sprinkle greased 2-quart mold with 3 to 4 tablespoons bread crumbs, coating well. Combine fruits, filberts and suet in large bowl. Mix remaining bread crumbs, salt, spices, milk and brown sugar together in bowl; stir until sugar dissolves. Add eggs, brandy flavoring and orange juice; beat until well blended. Stir into fruit mixture. Pour into prepared mold; cover tightly. Place mold on rack in large saucepan. Add enough boiling water to cover ⅔ of the mold. Steam for 5 hours, adding water as needed. Pour off any excess fat from top of steamed pudding. Cool in mold for 1 hour. Unmold on serving plate. Serve warm with Hard or Lemon Sauce.
Yield: 12 servings.

Hard Sauce

½ c. butter
½ tsp. vanilla extract
1 c. confectioners' sugar

Beat butter and vanilla in bowl until smooth. Add confectioners' sugar gradually, beating until fluffy. Chill.

Lemon Sauce

1 tbsp. cornstarch
½ c. sugar
1 tsp. grated lemon rind
¼ c. lemon juice
2 tbsp. butter

Mix cornstarch and sugar in saucepan. Stir in 1 cup water. Bring to a boil. Cook mixture for 1 minute, stirring constantly. Stir in lemon rind, lemon juice and butter. Serve hot.

CRANBERRY PUDDING

½ c. molasses
2 tsp. soda
1 c. cranberries
1⅓ c. flour
1 tsp. baking powder
1 c. sugar
1 c. cream
2 tbsp. brown sugar
⅓ c. butter

Blend molasses, soda and ½ cup boiling water in bowl. Toss cranberries with a small amount of flour in bowl. Sift remaining flour and baking powder together. Add to molasses mixture; mix well. Stir in cranberries. Pour into greased 1-pound can with tight fitting lid. Place, covered, in saucepan with water to half the depth of can. Steam, covered, for 1½ hours. Invert onto serving plate. Combine remaining ingredients in saucepan. Cook until well blended and heated through. Serve over pudding. Yield: 8 servings.

Kent Jones, North Dakota

SNOWFLAKE PUDDING
WITH RASPBERRY SAUCE

1 env. unflavored gelatin
1 c. sugar
½ tsp. salt
1¼ c. milk
1 tsp. vanilla extract
2 c. whipping cream, whipped
1⅓ c. flaked coconut
1   10-oz. package frozen
     raspberries, crushed
1½ tsp. cornstarch
½ c. currant jelly

Mix gelatin, sugar, salt and milk in saucepan. Cook over medium heat until gelatin and sugar dissolve, stirring constantly. Chill until partially set. Fold in vanilla, whipped cream and coconut. Spoon into 9x13-inch dish. Chill until firm. Combine remaining ingredients in saucepan. Cook over medium heat until thickened, stirring constantly; strain. Chill in refrigerator. Serve over pudding. Yield: 12 to 15 servings.

Janet A. Jensen, South Dakota

SNOWBALLS

2½ c. crushed pineapple,
    drained
1½ c. finely chopped nuts
½ c. butter, softened
1 tsp. vanilla extract
Confectioners' sugar
6 doz. vanilla wafers
1 c. whipping cream, whipped
Flaked coconut
Maraschino cherry halves
1 recipe confectioners' sugar
    frosting, tinted green

Mix first 4 ingredients with 2 cups confectioners' sugar in medium bowl. Spread between 3 vanilla wafers. Repeat with remaining vanilla wafers. Frost with whipped cream sweetened with confectioners' sugar. Sprinkle with coconut. Top with cherry half. Decorate with green frosting holly. Freeze until serving time. Yield: 2 dozen.

Jo Ann Smith, California

LINZER TORTES

1 c. butter, softened
2 c. sugar
3 eggs, beaten
1 tbsp. coffee Brandy
1 tsp. almond extract
½ tsp. lemon juice
4 c. flour
2 tsp. baking powder
½ tsp. salt
4 tsp. cinnamon
¼ tsp. nutmeg
⅓ c. ground almonds
⅔ c. ground pecans
Black raspberry jam

Cream butter and sugar in mixer bowl until fluffy. Mix in eggs, Brandy, flavoring and lemon juice. Add sifted dry ingredients; mix well. Stir in almonds and pecans. Chill overnight. Divide into 4 portions. Pat 3 portions over bottom and sides of three 8-inch pie plates. Spread lightly with jam. Cut remaining portion into strips; arrange lattice-fashion over tops. Bake at 350 degrees for 30 minutes. Fill spaces in lattice with jam. Garnish with confectioners' sugar. Yield: 18 servings.

Paula C. Dalton, Florida

BÛCHE DE NOËL

4 eggs, separated
¾ c. plus 1 tbsp. sugar
½ c. flour
⅓ c. baking cocoa
½ tsp. soda
¼ tsp. salt
1 tsp. vanilla extract

Beat egg yolks at medium speed for 2 minutes. Add ½ cup sugar gradually, beating constantly for 2 minutes. Combine flour, cocoa, ¼ cup sugar, soda and salt in bowl. Add to eggs alternately with ⅓ cup water, beating just until smooth. Stir in vanilla. Beat egg whites until foamy. Add remaining 1 tablespoon sugar, beating until stiff. Fold into chocolate batter. Spread in 10x15-inch baking pan lined with greased foil. Bake at 375 degrees for 15 minutes or until cake tests done. Invert onto towel sprinkled with confectioners' sugar; remove foil. Roll in towel from narrow end. Cool on wire rack. Unroll cake. Spread with Rum Cream Filling. Roll from narrow end. Place on serving plate. Frost with Chocolate Frosting. Mark with spatula to resemble bark. Garnish with candied cherries.
Yield: 10 servings.

Rum Cream Filling

1 tsp. unflavored gelatin
1 c. whipping cream
¼ c. confectioners' sugar
½ tsp. rum extract

Soften gelatin in 1 tablespoon cold water in cup. Add 2 tablespoons boiling water; stir until gelatin is dissolved. Whip cream with confectioners' sugar in bowl until soft peaks form. Blend in rum flavoring. Add gelatin gradually. Chill for 10 to 15 minutes or just until mixture begins to set.

Chocolate Frosting

6 tbsp. butter, softened
½ c. baking cocoa
2⅔ c. confectioners' sugar
4 to 5 tbsp. milk
1 tsp. vanilla extract

Cream butter and cocoa in mixer bowl until light. Add confectioners' sugar alternately with milk and vanilla, beating until of spreading consistency.

Photograph for this recipe on page 2.

CHOCOLATE ALMOND BUNDT CAKE

¾ c. butter, softened
1⅔ c. sugar
2 eggs
¾ c. sour cream
1 tsp. vanilla extract
1 tsp. almond extract
2 tsp. soda
1 c. buttermilk
2 c. flour
⅔ c. baking cocoa
½ tsp. salt
1 c. toasted sliced almonds

Cream butter and sugar in mixer bowl until light and fluffy. Blend in eggs, sour cream and flavorings. Blend soda and buttermilk in measuring cup. Add mixture of flour, cocoa and salt alternately with buttermilk, mixing well after each addition. Beat at medium speed for 2 minutes. Pour into greased and floured bundt pan. Bake at 350 degrees for 55 minutes or until cake tests done. Cool in pan for 10 minutes. Remove to wire rack to cool completely. Place on serving plate. Frost with Almond Buttercream Frosting. Press toasted almonds lightly onto frosting. Garnish with cherries. Yield: 16 servings.

Almond Buttercream Frosting

5 tbsp. butter, softened
2½ c. confectioners' sugar
3 tbsp. (about) milk
1 tsp. vanilla extract
½ tsp. almond extract

Cream butter in mixer bowl until light. Add confectioners' sugar alternately with milk, mixing well after each addition. Blend in flavorings. Beat until of spreading consistency, adding a few drops of additional milk if necessary.

Photograph for this recipe on page 2.

CHOCOLATE ANGEL FOOD CAKE

¾ c. sifted flour
1 c. (scant) sugar
¼ c. cocoa
1½ c. egg whites
1½ tsp. cream of tartar
¼ tsp. salt
1 tsp. vanilla extract

Sift flour, sugar and cocoa together 3 times. Beat egg whites with cream of tartar and salt in mixer bowl until stiff peaks form. Fold in sifted mixture 2 tablespoons at a time; do not overmix. Fold in vanilla. Pour into ungreased tube pan. Bake at 300 degrees for 1 hour and 5 minutes. Cool upright in pan. Loosen sides with knife. Remove to serving plate. Yield: 16 servings.

CRANBERRY SPICE CAKE

½ c. shortening
1 c. sugar
1 egg, beaten
1 c. raisins
½ c. chopped pecans
1¾ c. flour
¼ tsp. salt
1 tsp. soda
1 tsp. baking powder
1 tsp. cinnamon
½ tsp. cloves
1 c. cranberry sauce

Cream shortening and sugar in bowl until light and fluffy. Add egg; mix well. Stir in raisins and pecans. Add combined flour, salt, soda, baking powder, cinnamon and cloves to creamed mixture; mix well. Stir in cranberry sauce. Spoon into 2 greased and floured 8-inch cake pans. Bake at 350 degrees for 25 minutes. Remove to wire rack to cool. Frost with Creamy Cranberry Frosting. Yield: 16 servings.

Creamy Cranberry Frosting

3 oz. cream cheese, softened
¼ c. cranberry sauce
¼ tsp. salt
1 16-oz. package
  confectioners' sugar

Combine cream cheese, cranberry sauce and salt in mixer bowl; beat until smooth. Beat in confectioners' sugar.

Carole Nash, Michigan

CHERRY CHOCOLATE CAKE

½ c. butter, softened
1 c. sugar
6 eggs, separated
4 oz. semisweet chocolate,
  melted
Kirsch
1½ c. grated toasted filberts
¼ c. unsifted all-purpose flour
1 16-oz. jar red maraschino
  cherries
1½ tbsp. cornstarch
1 tbsp. lemon juice
3 c. whipping cream
⅓ c. sifted confectioners' sugar
¼ c. cherry juice
Chocolate curls

Cream butter and sugar in mixer bowl until light. Beat in egg yolks, 1 at a time. Blend in chocolate and 2 tablespoons Kirsch. Stir in filberts and flour. Beat egg whites until stiff but not dry. Fold gently into batter. Pour into greased and floured 8-inch springform pan. Bake at 375 degrees for 1 hour or until cake tests done; cake may have slight crack. Cool in pan for 10 minutes. Remove to cake rack to cool completely. Drain maraschino cherries, reserving syrup and 13 cherries. Slice remaining cherries. Combine reserved cherry syrup and enough Kirsch to make ¾ cup liquid. Blend into cornstarch in saucepan. Add lemon juice. Cook over medium heat for 30 seconds or just until mixture comes to a boil, stirring constantly. Add sliced cherries; cool. Slice cake horizontally into 3 layers. Invert top layer on cake platter. Spread with half of the cherry filling. Whip cream in bowl until soft peaks form. Add confectioners' sugar and cherry juice gradually. Spread over cherry filling. Add middle layer of cake; spread with remaining cherry filling and layer of whipped cream. Add remaining cake layer; frost with remaining whipped cream. Decorate with reserved whole cherries and chocolate curls.

Photograph for this recipe on page 123.

The top layer of a layer cake won't slip as you ice it if you hold it in place with a wire cake-tester or thin skewers inserted through all layers. Remove the tester just before completing the job.

SOUTHERN LANE CAKE

3 c. flour
2¼ c. sugar
5¼ tsp. baking powder
1½ tsp. salt
¾ c. shortening
1½ tsp. vanilla extract
1½ c. milk
6 egg whites

Combine first 6 ingredients and 1 cup milk in large mixer bowl. Beat at low speed until blended. Beat at high speed for 2 minutes. Add remaining ½ cup milk and egg whites. Beat at high speed for 2 minutes. Spoon batter into 3 greased and floured 9-inch cake pans. Bake at 350 degrees for 35 to 40 minutes or until cake tests done. Cool on wire rack. Spread Filling between layers and on top of cake. Frost side of cake with Lane Frosting. Yield: 16 servings.

Lane Filling

6 egg yolks
¾ c. sugar
⅓ c. butter
⅓ c. Bourbon
1 c. chopped pecans
1 c. chopped raisins
1 c. grated coconut

Beat egg yolks until thick and lemon-colored. Add sugar gradually, beating constantly. Melt butter in saucepan. Stir in egg mixture and Bourbon. Cook until thickened, stirring constantly. Stir in remaining ingredients. Cool.

Lane Frosting

½ c. sugar
¼ c. white corn syrup
2 egg whites, stiffly beaten
2 tsp. lemon juice
1 tsp. vanilla extract

Combine sugar, syrup and 2 tablespoons water in saucepan. Cook until sugar is dissolved, stirring constantly. Cook, covered, over medium heat until steam washes sugar crystals from side of pan. Cook, uncovered, to 240 degrees on candy thermometer. Pour hot syrup slowly into stiffly beaten egg whites, beating constantly until stiff peaks form. Beat in lemon juice and vanilla.

Phyllis Baker, Michigan

OLD-FASHIONED DARK FRUITCAKES

1 lb. butter, softened
1½ c. sugar
1 lb. brown sugar
12 eggs
1 c. dark molasses
1 c. buttermilk
9 c. sifted flour
2 tsp. soda
1 tsp. salt
2 tsp. cinnamon
2 tsp. ginger
1 tsp. allspice
1 c. grape juice
3 lb. dried figs, chopped
1 lb. dates, chopped
8 oz. candied pineapple, chopped
3 lb. raisins
1 lb. currants
8 oz. candied orange peel
8 oz. almonds, chopped
8 oz. walnuts, chopped
8 oz. Brazil nuts, chopped
4 oz. unsweetened chocolate, melted
2 tbsp. rum extract

Cream butter, sugar and brown sugar in large mixer bowl until light and fluffy. Blend in eggs. Add molasses and buttermilk; beat until smooth. Add sifted mixture of 8 cups flour, soda, salt and spices. Mix in remaining 1 cup flour and grape juice. Stir in fruits and nuts. Mix melted chocolate with rum flavoring in small bowl. Add to batter; mix well. Spoon into 6 to 8 greased and floured loaf pans. Bake at 275 degrees for 2½ hours or until cakes test done. Remove to wire rack to cool. Wrap in cloth moistened with fruit juice, wine or Brandy. Store in airtight containers. Yield: 6 to 8 fruitcakes.

Ida Malone, Arkansas

To prevent a soggy or heavy cake, be sure that the layers, filling and frosting are completely cool before assembling the cake.

TRADITIONAL CAKE

2 c. flour
1½ c. sugar
2 tsp. soda
1 tsp. cinnamon
½ tsp. nutmeg
½ tsp. cloves
1 tbsp. cornstarch
3 tbsp. baking cocoa
1 c. raisins
½ c. candied fruit mix, chopped
1 c. chopped almonds
2 c. unsweetened applesauce
½ c. melted butter

Sift flour, sugar, soda, spices, cornstarch and cocoa into bowl. Add raisins, fruit and almonds; mix well. Add applesauce and butter; mix well. Pour into greased 5x9-inch loaf pan. Bake at 350 degrees for 1 hour. Cool on wire rack. Wrap in foil. Let stand for 2 days before slicing.

Priscilla Morrow, California

TWELFTH NIGHT CAKE

2½ c. flour
1 tsp. soda
1 tsp. salt
½ tsp. cinnamon
¾ c. butter, softened
1¾ c. sugar
¾ c. orange juice
½ c. milk
2 eggs
1 tbsp. grated orange rind
1 tsp. vanilla extract
½ c. chopped walnuts
½ c. golden raisins
¼ c. currants
1 c. chopped almonds
1 whole almond

Sift first 4 ingredients together; set aside. Cream butter and 1½ cups sugar in bowl until light and fluffy. Add ½ cup orange juice, milk, eggs, orange rind and vanilla; mix well. Add sifted ingredients ¼ at a time, beating well after each addition. Fold in walnuts, raisins, currants, chopped almonds and whole almond. Pour into well greased 8-inch bundt pan. Bake at 350 degrees for 55 minutes or until cake tests done. Cool in pan on wire rack for 15 minutes. Combine remaining ¼ cup sugar and ¼ cup orange juice in saucepan. Bring to a boil. Cool for several minutes. Prick top of cake with fork. Spoon orange juice mixture over cake until liquid is completely absorbed. Cool cake completely. Wrap in plastic wrap. Let stand for 12 hours before slicing. Yield: 16 servings.
Note: Whoever has the whole almond in his serving is king or queen for the night and will have good luck for the new year.

CHRISTMAS DATE CUPS

1 pkg. dates
1 c. chopped pecans
1½ tsp. soda
¾ c. butter
2 c. sugar
1 egg
1½ c. flour
¼ tsp. salt
1 c. whipping cream
1 tsp. vanilla extract

Mix dates, pecans, 1 teaspoon soda and 1 cup boiling water in bowl. Let stand for 10 to 15 minutes. Cream ¼ cup butter and 1 cup sugar in mixer bowl until fluffy. Mix in egg. Sift in flour, salt and remaining ½ teaspoon soda; mix well. Stir in date mixture. Fill 18 muffin cups ⅔ full. Bake at 350 degrees for 35 minutes. Cook remaining ½ cup butter, 1 cup sugar, cream and vanilla in saucepan for 10 minutes, stirring constantly. Serve over warm date cups. Yield: 1½ dozen.

Margie Wills, Florida

CUPCAKE TREATS

⅓ c. sugar
8 oz. cream cheese, softened
1 egg
6 oz. semisweet chocolate chips
1 2-layer pkg. chocolate cake mix

Cream sugar and cream cheese in mixer bowl. Beat in egg. Stir in chocolate chips. Prepare cake mix using package directions. Fill paper-lined muffin cups ⅔ full. Add rounded teaspoonful cheese mixture to each. Bake using package directions. Yield: 30 cupcakes.

Carol Harding, Texas

SPIRITED EGGNOG CUSTARD PIE

1 unbaked 9-in. pie shell
1 can sweetened condensed
   milk
2 tbsp. light rum
1 tbsp. Brandy
1 tsp. vanilla extract
½ tsp. nutmeg
3 eggs, well beaten

Bake pastry shell at 425 degrees for 8 minutes. Combine sweetened condensed milk, rum, Brandy, vanilla, nutmeg and 1⅓ cups warm water in bowl; mix well. Stir in eggs. Pour into prepared pie shell. Bake for 10 minutes. Reduce temperature to 325 degrees. Bake for 25 to 30 minutes or until knife inserted near center comes out clean. Cool. Yield: 6 to 8 servings.

MINCEMEAT-SOUR CREAM PIE

1   9-oz. package condensed
    mincemeat
1   unbaked 9-in. pie pastry
    shell
2 eggs, beaten
16 oz. sour cream
2 tbsp. sugar
1 tsp. vanilla extract
2 tbsp. chopped nuts

Crumble mincemeat into saucepan. Add 1 cup water. Bring to a boil. Cook for 1 minute. Pour into pie shell. Bake at 425 degrees for 20 minutes. Combine eggs, sour cream, sugar and vanilla in bowl; mix well. Pour over pie. Sprinkle with nuts. Bake for 8 to 10 minutes longer or until topping is set. Chill until serving time. Yield: 6 servings.

WHITE CHRISTMAS PIE

1 c. sugar
¼ c. flour
1 env. unflavored gelatin
½ tsp. salt
1¾ c. milk
¾ tsp. vanilla extract
¼ tsp. almond flavoring
3 egg whites
¼ tsp. cream of tartar
½ c. whipping cream, whipped
1 c. shredded coconut
1 baked 9-in. pie shell

Combine ½ cup sugar, flour, gelatin and salt in saucepan. Stir in milk gradually. Boil for 1 minute, stirring constantly. Cool in pan of cold water until thickened. Stir in flavorings. Beat egg whites and cream of tartar until soft peaks form. Add remaining ½ cup sugar gradually, beating until stiff. Fold the cooked mixture into egg whites. Fold in whipped cream and coconut. Spoon into pie shell. Chill until serving time. Garnish with coconut tinted green and red marschino cherries.

Kay Spikes, Kansas

GERMAN CHOCOLATE TARTLETS

1 oz. German's sweet chocolate,
   grated
1 c. flour
¼ c. packed brown sugar
¼ tsp. salt
6 tbsp. plus ¼ c. butter
2 tsp. vanilla extract
3 oz. German's sweet chocolate
1   13-oz. can evaporated milk
3 eggs, beaten
1 c. sugar
¾ c. flaked coconut, toasted
½ c. chopped pecans

Mix grated chocolate, flour, brown sugar and ⅛ teaspoon salt in bowl. Cut in 6 tablespoons butter until crumbly. Add 4 teaspoons water and 1 teaspoon vanilla; mix until mixture forms ball. Divide into 48 portions. Press each over bottom and side of 2-inch muffin cup with flour-dusted fingers. Bake at 375 degrees for 12 minutes. Melt remaining ¼ cup butter and 3 squares chocolate in saucepan over low heat, stirring constantly; remove from heat. Blend in evaporated milk. Mix with eggs in bowl. Add sugar, remaining 1 teaspoon vanilla and ⅛ teaspoon salt; mix well. Pour into tart shells. Bake for 9 minutes or until almost set. Top with coconut and pecans. Bake for 6 minutes longer or until set. Cool in pans for 10 to 15 minutes. Loosen edges of tart shells with spatula. Remove carefully to wire rack to cool completely. Yield: 4 dozen.

Mildred Pickerell, Kentucky

CANDY CANE COOKIES

3 *c. sifted flour*
1 *tsp. baking powder*
¾ *tsp. salt*
½ *c. shortening*
1½ *c. sugar*
2 *eggs*
1½ *tsp. vanilla extract*
1 *tbsp. milk*
½ *tsp. red food coloring*

Sift flour, baking powder and salt together. Cream shortening and sugar in mixer bowl until light and fluffy. Beat in eggs, 1 at a time. Stir in vanilla and milk. Add flour mixture; mix well. Divide dough into 2 portions. Tint 1 portion dough with food coloring. Wrap each portion in waxed paper. Chill for 2 hours. Shape dough into ¼x6-inch rolls on lightly floured surface. Place plain roll and tinted roll together and twist to form cane. Place on cookie sheet. Repeat with remaining rolls. Bake at 375 degrees for 8 to 10 minutes. Remove to rack to cool. Yield: 2 dozen.

Sally Broccoli, Connecticut

CHRISTMAS FRUIT COOKIES

2 *lb. dates*
3 *slices candied pineapple*
1½ *lb. candied cherries*
1 *lb. raisins*
1 *lb. Brazil nuts*
½ *lb. cashews*
½ *lb. almonds*
5 *c. flour*
2 *tsp. soda*
2 *tsp. cinnamon*
2 *tsp. salt*
1 *lb. walnuts*
1 *lb. pecans*
1 *lb. butter, softened*
3 *c. packed brown sugar*
4 *eggs*
½ *c. cream*

Chop fruit, Brazil nuts, cashews and almonds. Sift flour, soda, cinnamon and salt into bowl. Coat mixture of all nuts and fruit with 1 cup flour mixture in bowl. Cream butter and brown sugar in large mixer bowl until light and fluffy. Blend in eggs 1 at a time. Add remaining flour mixture alternately with ½ cup cream, mixing well after each addition.

Fold in fruit and nuts. Drop by spoonfuls onto greased cookie sheet. Bake at 275 degrees for 25 to 30 minutes or until brown. Cool on wire rack.
Yield: 12 dozen.

Helen Williams, California

HOLLY WREATHS

1 *c. shortening*
3 *oz. cream cheese, softened*
½ *c. sugar*
1 *tsp. vanilla extract*
1 *c. sifted flour*
2 *drops of green food coloring*

Cream shortening, cream cheese and sugar in mixer bowl until light and fluffy. Blend in vanilla. Add flour gradually, mixing well after each addition. Tint with food coloring. Fill cookie press fitted with number 2 star plate. Hold press at 45-degree angle. Pipe dough into circles on ungreased cookie sheet. Bake at 375 degrees for 8 to 10 minutes or until set. Cool on wire rack. Decorate with frosting leaves and red cinnamon candies if desired. Yield: 4 dozen.

HOLIDAY MACAROONS

2 *eggs*
¾ *c. sugar*
⅓ *c. flour*
¼ *tsp. baking powder*
⅛ *tsp. salt*
1 *tbsp. melted butter*
1 *tsp. vanilla extract*
1 *tsp. grated lemon rind*
2⅔ *c. flaked coconut*
24 *candied cherry halves*

Beat eggs in bowl until light. Add sugar gradually, beating for 5 minutes or until thickened. Add sifted dry ingredients; mix well. Stir in butter, vanilla, lemon rind and coconut. Drop by teaspoonfuls onto greased and floured cookie sheet. Decorate with candied cherries. Bake at 325 degrees for 15 minutes. Cool completely. Store in tightly covered container. Yield: 2 dozen.

Pauline Cuykendall, New York

MADELEINES

2 eggs
1/8 tsp. salt
1/3 c. sugar
1/2 c. flour
1 tsp. grated lemon rind
1/2 c. melted butter, cooled
Sifted confectioners' sugar

Beat eggs and salt in mixer bowl. Add 1/3 cup sugar gradually, beating for 15 minutes or until thick and lemon-colored. Fold in flour and lemon rind. Fold in butter 1 tablespoon at a time. Spoon by tablespoonfuls into greased and floured madeleine molds. Bake at 400 degrees for 8 to 10 minutes or until light brown. Remove from molds; cool flat side down on wire racks. Sprinkle with confectioners' sugar. Store in airtight container. Yield: 1 dozen.

MANDELBRATT HANUKKAH COOKIES

1 c. sugar
1/2 c. oil
3 eggs
1 tsp. vanilla extract
1/2 tsp. orange extract
3 1/2 c. flour
1 1/2 tsp. baking powder
1/4 tsp. salt
1 1/2 c. chopped nuts

Beat sugar, oil and eggs in bowl until thick and lemon-colored. Add flavorings; mix well. Stir in dry ingredients and nuts. Shape into 4 long rolls on lightly floured surface. Place on greased and floured baking sheets. Bake at 350 degrees for 20 minutes or until browned. Slice warm rolls into 1-inch slices. Place slices on baking sheet. Bake for 2 minutes longer or until crisp. Yield: 6 dozen.

Annette Lawson, Tennessee

MOON CRESCENTS

1 c. butter, softened
5 tbsp. confectioners' sugar, sifted
1 tsp. vanilla extract
2 1/2 c. flour
1 1/2 c. chopped pecans

Cream butter in mixer bowl. Add confectioners' sugar gradually, beating until light and fluffy. Stir in vanilla. Add flour and chopped pecans, mixing just until well blended. Shape into small crescents. Place 2 inches apart on ungreased cookie sheet. Bake at 250 degrees for 40 to 50 minutes or until light brown. Remove to wire rack to cool. Roll in additional confectioners' sugar. Yield: 2 dozen.

Alice Jefferson, Wisconsin

MINCEMEAT DROP COOKIES

3/4 c. shortening
3/4 c. sugar
2 eggs, well beaten
1 c. mincemeat
2 1/4 c. flour
3/4 tsp. soda
1/2 tsp. cinnamon
1/4 tsp. nutmeg
1/4 tsp. allspice
1/2 tsp. salt
3/4 c. chopped walnuts

Cream shortening and sugar in mixer bowl until fluffy. Add eggs and mincemeat. Sift dry ingredients 3 times. Add dry ingredients to creamed mixture gradually, mixing well after each addition. Add walnuts. Drop by teaspoonfuls onto greased cookie sheet. Bake at 350 degrees for 15 to 20 minutes or until light brown. Cool on wire rack.
Yield: 4 dozen.

Dorothy Shumaker, Vermont

CHRISTMAS SPRINGERLE

4 eggs
1 16-oz. package confectioners' sugar
1/2 c. butter, softened
1 tsp. powdered hartshorn
1 tbsp. milk
6 drops of anise oil
5 c. flour

Beat eggs in mixer bowl for 10 minutes or until thickened and lemon-colored. Add confectioners' sugar; beat well. Add butter, hartshorn, milk and anise oil; mix well. Stir in flour gradually. Dough will be very stiff. Roll 1/2 inch thick on floured surface. Mark with springerle rolling pin. Place on greased cookie sheet. Cut apart. Let stand for 2 to 3 hours. Bake at 350 degrees for 10 minutes or until golden. Cool on wire rack. Yield: 6 dozen.

JoBerta Hein, Indiana

SPECIAL MARZIPAN COOKIES

4 *egg white*
2 *c. sugar*
1 *lb. almond paste, chopped*
1 *tsp. almond flavoring*

Beat 2 egg whites in mixer bowl until foamy. Add sugar gradually, beating constantly. Add almond paste gradually, beating well after each addition. Add remaining 2 egg whites and almond flavoring; beat until stiff. Drop by teaspoonfuls 2 inches apart onto waxed paper-lined cookie sheet. Place in 325-degree oven; leave door ajar. Bake for 5 minutes. Close oven door. Bake for 15 minutes longer. Yield: 6 dozen.

Irene Oliekan, Utah

CREAM CHEESE SPRITZ

1 *c. butter, softened*
3 *oz. cream cheese, softened*
1 *c. sugar*
1 *egg yolk*
1 *tsp. vanilla extract*
2½ *c. sifted flour*
¼ *tsp. cinnamon*
½ *tsp. salt*
Red and green tinted sugar

Cream butter, cream cheese and sugar in mixer bowl until light and fluffy. Blend in egg yolk and vanilla. Add sifted flour, cinnamon and salt gradually, beating well after each addition. Chill until firm. Spoon dough into cookie press. Press onto chilled cookie sheet. Sprinkle with tinted sugar. Bake at 350 degrees for 15 minutes or until edges are brown. Cool on wire rack. Yield: 3 dozen.

Edwina Theresa Grier, Georgia

CHOCOLATE BONBONS

8 *oz. baking chocolate*
3 *tbsp. butter*
¾ *c. confectioners' sugar*
1 *tbsp. light corn syrup*
1 *tbsp. milk*
⅓ *c. chopped candied fruit*
1 *tsp. rum extract*

Melt 2½ squares chocolate and 1½ tablespoons butter in saucepan over very low heat; blend well. Spread in bottom of 5x9-inch loaf pan lined on bottom and sides with waxed paper. Chill until firm. Heat 3 squares chocolate in saucepan over very low heat until partially melted. Remove from heat. Stir vigorously until completely melted. Add confectioners' sugar, corn syrup and milk; blend well. Stir in candied fruit and flavoring. Spread over chocolate layer. Chill until firm. Melt remaining butter and chocolate in saucepan over very low heat; spread over top. Chill until firm. Cut into squares. Store in tightly covered container in refrigerator. Yield: 1 pound.

Annie Mason, Alabama

CHRISTMAS TREES

3 *tbsp. margarine*
32 *lg. marshmallows*
½ *tsp. vanilla extract*
½ *tsp. green food coloring*
4 *c. Cheerios*
Small gumdrops, sliced

Melt margarine and marshmallows in saucepan over low heat, stirring constantly. Remove from heat. Stir in vanilla and food coloring. Pour over cereal in large bowl; mix to coat. Shape warm mixture ⅔ cup at a time into Christmas trees on waxed paper with buttered hands. Decorate with gumdrops to represent tree ornaments; add paper stars for tops. Let stand until cool. Yield: 6 trees.

Amy Boyles, Pennsylvania

Bonbons can be dipped in melted chocolate or rolled in cocoa, confectioners' sugar, ground nuts, chocolate sprinkles, coconut, grated fruit rind or candy sprinkles.

CHRISTMAS WREATH

½ c. margarine
30 marshmallows
1 tsp. vanilla extract
1½ tsp. green food coloring
4 c. cornflakes
Red cinnamon candies

Melt margarine and marshmallows in saucepan, stirring frequently; remove from heat. Add vanilla and food coloring. Stir in cornflakes. Shape into wreath with buttered fingers. Place on plate. Decorate with clusters of red candies. May shape into miniature wreaths if desired. Yield: 8 servings.

Brenda Hall Ferguson, Virginia

HOLIDAY DIVINITY

2 c. sugar
1 tsp. vanilla extract
¼ tsp. salt
1   7-oz. jar marshmallow
    creme
36 red and green candied cherry
    halves

Bring ½ cup water to the boiling point in saucepan. Remove from heat. Add sugar, vanilla and salt; stir until sugar is completely dissolved. Cook, covered, over high heat for 2 to 3 minutes or until steam washes sugar crystals from side of pan. Cook, uncovered, to 234 to 240 degrees on candy thermometer, soft-ball stage; do not stir. Place marshmallow creme in bowl. Add hot syrup gradually, beating until candy loses its luster. Drop by spoonfuls onto buttered surface. Top each piece with cherry. Cool until firm. Store in airtight container. Yield: 1 pound.

Bobbie Nix, Texas

STAINED GLASS FUDGE

2 c. sugar
½ c. sour cream
⅓ c. light corn syrup
2 tbsp. margarine
¼ tsp. salt
2 tsp. vanilla extract
½ c. chopped red and green
    candied cherries
½ c. chopped walnuts

Combine first 5 ingredients in saucepan. Bring to a boil over medium heat, stirring to dissolve sugar. Cook, covered, over medium heat until steam washes sugar crystals from side of pan. Cook, uncovered, to 234 to 240 degrees on candy thermometer, soft-ball stage. Do not stir. Let stand for 15 minutes. Do not stir. Add vanilla. Beat for 8 minutes or until mixture begins to lose its luster. Stir in cherries and walnuts. Pour into greased pan. Let stand until cool. Cut into squares. Yield: 1½ pounds.

Juanita Dabbs, Tennessee

ALMOND CRUNCH TOFFEE

1 c. melted butter
1⅓ c. sugar
1 tbsp. light corn syrup
1 c. coarsely chopped blanched
    almonds, toasted
18 oz. milk chocolate, melted
1 c. finely chopped blanched
    almonds, toasted

Mix butter, sugar, corn syrup and 3 tablespoons water in saucepan. Stir over low heat until sugar is dissolved. Do not boil. Cook, covered, over medium heat for 2 or 3 minutes or until steam washes sugar crystals from side of pan. Cook, uncovered, to 300 to 310 degrees on candy thermometer, hard-crack stage, stirring occasionally. Stir in coarsely chopped almonds. Spread in buttered 9x13-inch dish. Cool. Invert onto waxed paper. Spread with half the chocolate; sprinkle with half the finely chopped almonds. Turn candy over. Spread evenly with remaining chocolate; sprinkle with remaining almonds. Chill until firm. Break into pieces. Yield: 2 pounds.

Mary Utley, Tennessee

If fudge crystallizes, add a small amount of hot water or cream and bring to a boil again. Cool to lukewarm and beat.

INDEX

Add To Your Cookbook Collection
or
Give As A Gift

FOR ORDERING INFORMATION

Favorite Recipes Press
a division of Great American Opportunities Inc.
P.O. Box 305142, Nashville, TN   37230
or
Call Toll-free
1-800-251-1542